# Truth Without Objectivity

'This is the most interesting, carefully constructed, and challenging exposition and defence of the – initially repugnant – view that truth is relative which I have read. Whilst written with admirable simplicity and clarity, its argumentation has both philosophical depth and great subtlety.'

*Bob Hale, University of Glasgow*

According to the mainstream view in the philosophy of language, to know the meaning of a sentence is to know the conditions under which the sentence would be true. The view, however, is challenged by non-objective sentences such as sentences on matters of taste or value: these do not appear to be either true or false, but are generally taken to be meaningful. How can this conflict be resolved?

*Truth Without Objectivity* examines different ways of resolving this fundamental problem, before developing and defending a relativist theory of truth. Standard solutions maintain either that in uttering non-objective sentences speakers make implicit reference to their own preferences and thus have unproblematic truth conditions, or that they have no truth conditions at all. Max Kölbel argues that both of these proposed solutions are inadequate, and that the third well-known position, minimalism, can only solve the problem if it is developed in the direction of relativism about truth.

Kölbel defends the idea that truth (as invoked in semantics) is a neutral notion: a sentence's possessing a truth condition does not yet entail that it concerns an objective subject matter, because truth and objectivity are independent of one another. He argues that this notion of 'truth without objectivity' leads directly to a relativist theory of truth, and goes on to defend his form of relativism against the usual objections to such theories.

*Truth Without Objectivity* is a valuable and clear discussion of one of the most interesting questions in philosophy. It will be of particular interest to all students of the philosophy of language, metaphysics and metaethics.

**Max Kölbel** is Lecturer in Philosophy at the University of Birmingham.

# International Library of Philosophy

Edited by José Luis Bermúdez, Tim Crane and Peter Sullivan

*Advisory Board: Jonathan Barnes, Fred Dretske, Frances Kamm, Brian Leiter, Huw Price and Sydney Shoemaker*

# Truth Without Objectivity

Max Kölbel

London and New York

First published 2002
by Routledge
11 New Fetter Lane, London, EC4P 4EE

Simultaneously published in the USA and Canada
by Routledge
29 West 35th Street, New York, NY 10001

*Routledge is an imprint of the Taylor & Francis Group*

Typset in Times by Max Kölbel
Printed and bound in Malta by Gutenberg Press Ltd

*British Library Cataloguing in Publication Data*
A catalogue record for this book is available from the British
Library

*Library of Congress Cataloguing in Publication Data*
has been applied for

ISBN 0–415–27244–0 (hbk)
ISBN 0–415–27245–9 (pbk)

# Contents

# Preface

This book has taken a long time to mature. I first started thinking about the metaphysical consequences of truth-conditional semantics in 1993, when I was a postgraduate student at King's College London (KCL). Originally I thought truth-conditional semantics was misguided because of these consequences, and in my MPhil thesis I therefore defended a form of expressivism that leads away from truth-conditional semantics. Later on, however, I realized that truth-conditional semantics is a kind of Kuhnian paradigm. Most theorists who work in semantics (in philosophy, artificial intelligence, computer science, linguistics, cognitive science, psychology) work within this framework. In fact, for many theorists 'semantics' just means truth-conditional semantics. So I started exploring the advantages of truth-conditional semantics, and enquiring whether these advantages couldn't be had without the unwanted metaphysical consequences.

This book is the outcome of that enquiry. An intermediate step was my PhD thesis, which I submitted in September 1996, and which defended the same thesis as this book, under the same title. Because of the kind encouragement of Peter Sullivan and José Bermúdez, I started rethinking and rearranging my material with a book in mind. For various reasons, however, it took five years to complete. First, there were many difficult questions about which I felt I needed more time to think. I no doubt felt this way partly because of the formidable objections made by colleagues whenever I presented my work. Another reason for it taking so long was my (mostly involuntary) nomadic lifestyle: during those five years I lived and worked in five different places and moved house even more often. It is hard to say what overall effect the instability of location had on my frame of mind and on the book. One effect, however, was without doubt desirable: my work got exposed to the criticism of a wider variety of people than it would otherwise have been.

For the same reason, the list of people I would like to thank for their input to this book is very long. It includes my exceptionally generous PhD supervisors, teachers, fellow students and friends from my days as a KCL graduate student. It also includes colleagues and friends from the fabulous Instituto de Investigaciones Filosóficas at the Universidad Nacional Autónoma de México (UNAM) in Mexico City, where I spent two unforgettable years. It further includes colleagues from Christopher Habel's Graduiertenkolleg Kognitionswissenschaft at Hamburg University, where I spent most of 1999. Then there are those of my colleagues, students and friends at Swansea University, who made it possible for me to survive a turbulent year there, and to remember occasionally that I was meant to be working on this book. The list also includes students, colleagues and friends from Cambridge, where I spent the last year in comparative peace and in a stimulating intellectual atmosphere. There are also the many colleagues who have commented on my work in conferences, workshops, talks and the like, especially the two Hamburg–Barcelona Workshops in October 1999 and February 2000, and the Workshop on Belief and Meaning at Regensburg in May 2000. Finally, the list includes my long-standing friends, companions and family, in particular my brother and his family, who allowed me to prepare the penultimate version in their happy company in the summer of 2000.

I warmly thank all the people described above for whatever help they extended to me. What follows is an inadequate attempt to compile the names of most of them:

Arif Ahmed, Brom Anderson, Helen Baldwin, Stephen Barker, José Bermúdez, Simon Blackburn, Johannes Brandl, the British Academy, Krister Bykvist, Marta Campdelacreu, Mat Carmody, Donald Davidson, Peter Dunstan, Rebecca Dunstan-Harvey, Dorothy Edgington, Anne Edwards, Maite Ezcurdia, Miguel-Angel Fernández, Michalis Filippou, Lorena García, Manuel García-Carpintero, Laurence Goldstein, Mario Gómez-Torrente, Aruna Handa, Wolfram Hinzen, Shirin Homann, James Hopkins, Keith Hossack, Guillermo Hurtado, Carrie Jenkins, Peter Kail, Hans Kamp, Ariel Kernberg, Jonathan Knowles, Friederike Kölbel, Johannes Kölbel, Reinhard Kölbel, Sebastian Kölbel, Tilo Kölbel, Martin Kretschmer, Sharon Kretschmer, Wolfgang Künne, Hallvard Lillehammer, Ieuan Lloyd, Dan López de Sa, Fraser McBride, M.M. McCabe, Greg McCulloch, John McDowell, Josep Maciá, Hugh Mellor, the Mind Association, Raymundo Morado, Howard Mounce, the Fellows of New Hall, Cambridge, Samir Okasha, Alex Oliver, Eric Olson, Cathy Osborne, Karla Otero, Martin Otto, David Papineau, Michael Potter, José Antonio Robles, Alexandro Rojas, Rikardo Rojas, Hans Rott, Mark Sainsbury, Ricardo Salles, Katja Sengelmann, Linda Sengelmann, Ruben Sengelmann, Mark Siebel, Wolfgang Spohn, Christian Stein, Pedro Stepanenko, Peter Sullivan, Rupert Summerton, Mark Textor, Alan Thomas, Ian Tipton, Mario von der Ruhr, Neal Wagstaff, Denis Walsh, Ginny Watkins, Ruth Weintraub, Bernhard Weiss and Ieuan Williams.

I would like to thank the editor of *Theoria* for permission to use, in Chapter 2, material originally published as 'A Criterion of Objectivity', in *Theoria: Revista de Teoría, Historia y Fundamentos de la Ciencia* 15 (May 2000), pp. 209–28.

I would like to thank the editors of *Crítica: Revista Hispanoamericana de Filosofía* for permission to use, in Chapter 4, material first published as

'Expressivism and the Syntactic Uniformity of Declarative Sentences' in *Crítica* 29, no. 87 (December 1997), pp. 3–51.

Finally, I would like to thank the editor of *The Journal of Philosophy* for permission to use, in Chapter 5, material originally published as 'Two Dogmas of Davidsonian Semantics' in *The Journal of Philosophy* 97 (December 2001), pp. 613–35.

MK                                                 August 2001

# Introduction

There is a certain approach to theorizing about language that is called 'truth-conditional semantics'. The underlying idea of truth-conditional semantics is often summarized as the idea that the meaning of a sentence can be specified by giving the condition under which it would be true. This is then condensed into the slogan that the meaning of a sentence is its truth condition. The slogan has intuitive appeal, because the meaning of a sentence is what one knows when one understands it, and it is plausible to suppose that knowing the conditions under which a sentence is true is to understand it.[1]

If this characterization is correct, then truth-conditional semantics faces a huge problem. It seems to presuppose that all sentences are evaluable as true or false, but there are many reasons to think that not all sentences are candidates for truth or falsehood. This book is about one kind of reason for doubting that all sentences have truth conditions: non-objectivity.[2] Many philosophers believe that, for example, values and probabilities aren't objective. On this view, if a (declarative) sentence concerns a matter of taste, a moral question or the probability of an event, then it concerns something non-objective. But how can such a sentence then be evaluated as true or false? It seems that truth-conditional semantics rests on a highly dubious presupposition.

This book's aim is to examine possible solutions to this problem. Should truth-conditional semanticists insist that all sentences nevertheless have truth conditions, and if so, does this entail that all sentences describe objective reality? Or should non-objective sentences be exempted from the truth-conditional treatment? These questions have received some attention from metaphysicians and meta-ethicists and they continue to be debated. By contrast, they have been largely neglected by natural language semanticists who work within the truth-conditional paradigm, i.e. by those who attempt to make the truth-conditional approach work for particular natural language constructions. This is surprising. According to the truth-conditional slogan, the meaning of a sentence is its truth condition. So isn't the question whether, say, evaluative sentences are truth evaluable an obvious and urgent preliminary question each truth-conditional semanticist has to settle?

The neglect can be explained. Behind the truth-conditional slogan is a very complex view which has little, if anything, to do with the profound metaphysical significance the slogan suggests. Truth-conditional semantics is a view concerning the *form* a theory of meaning (semantic theory) for a particular natural language should take, namely the view that it should take the form of an axiomatic theory whose recursive axioms generate theorems of the form '*s* is true iff *p*' for every sentence *s* of the language in question. This view has guided the work of many philosophers of language and linguists. But its primary motivation is not the idea that a theory of meaning for a language ought to tell us something about how that language's expressions relate to extra-linguistic reality. Rather, it is motivated by the need to describe in a precise way, how the meanings of complex expressions depend on the meanings of their parts. Most theorists who work within the truth-conditional paradigm do so because it allows them to account for the compositionality of languages, be this because they want to explain learnability, because they are interested in the logical properties of a language or for some other reason. The attraction of truth-conditional semantics lies not in the fact that it connects the notion of meaning with the notion of truth, but rather that in so doing it can map out the semantic structure of particular languages.

My stance on the issue of the truth evaluability of non-objective sentences is driven by the view of truth-conditional semantics I just outlined. Semantic theory is primarily concerned with the phenomena of language, not with metaphysics. Thus, if certain metaphysical intuitions about the objectivity of truth threaten the otherwise healthy project of constructing semantic theories that employ a notion of truth, then the semanticist should, if possible, deny that the notion employed in semantics is identical with the notion whose metaphysical features create the problems. This book defends the view that the notion of truth employed in semantic theories is a metaphysically neutral notion, according to which a sentence's possessing a truth condition does not yet entail that it concerns an objective subject matter. Truth in semantics is truth without objectivity.

Nevertheless, it would be misleading to describe this book as metaphysics-free. I argue that the notion of truth invoked in semantics can be identified with the notion of truth we actually employ — or rather with one of the two notions we employ. I also argue that a notion of truth without objectivity must be a notion of relative truth. Finally, I defend relativism about truth (and other forms of relativism) against the charge of incoherence. Thus, while the semanticist should be allowed to operate with his or her own semantic notion of truth without interference from metaphysics, I believe that there is a coherent metaphysical theory of truth that serves the purposes of semantics. Readers who are not prepared to agree with me on these metaphysical points can still agree with me in the philosophy of language concerning the notion of truth used in semantics. The metaphysics in this book can be separated from the semantics.

My argument for these conclusions is not as quick as the previous two paragraphs suggest. I start by explaining in Chapter 1 what truth-conditional semantics is, or rather how I view it. In Chapter 2, I set up the problem: truth-conditional semantics seems to presuppose that all sentences are truth evaluable and this conflicts with the common view that some sentences aren't truth evaluable because they concern non-objective matters. I distinguish three ways of dealing with this problem: revising the contents assigned to sentences (revisionism), exempting some sentences from truth-conditional treatment (expressivism), and employing a notion of truth that does not entail objectivity (soft truth). I then devise a criterion for objectivity which is inspired by, but in crucial respects different from, Crispin Wright's criterion of 'cognitive command'. According to this criterion, a proposition is objective if a mere disagreement on that proposition shows that a mistake has been made. I argue that the only way in which a proposition could be truth evaluable yet non-objective is that truth is relative. Relativism about truth is therefore a consequence of the soft-truth strategy.

Radical solutions are only palatable if no less radical alternative is available. That's why in Chapters 3 and 4 I examine revisionism and expressivism in some detail. Revisionism is the claim that sentences on non-objective matters are generally elliptical, and involve an implicit indexical element. For example, 'laver bread is tasty' might be claimed to be elliptical for 'I find laver bread tasty'. I argue that any such claim is false, because there are demonstrable differences in meaning between the original sentences and the one s that they are said to be elliptical for.

Expressivism requires a much more detailed examination. Expressivists want to exempt problematic sentences from truth-conditional semantic treatment and account for the meaning of these sentences in some other way, usually claiming that they exhibit some special kind of illocutionary force. They face the problem that the objectivity or non-objectivity of a sentence's subject matter has usually little influence on that sentence's syntactic properties. That is, the sentences the expressivist wants to exempt from truth-conditional treatment can be combined with, and embedded in, other sentences—even those that have been approved for the truth-conditional treatment. In short, the expressivist is up against the syntactic uniformity of sentences that aren't uniform in respect of their objectivity status. I argue that even though sophisticated expressivists might overcome these difficulties, they will end up with a uniform *non*-truth-conditional semantics. Thus, even though expressivism can be a coherent position, it is then no longer a solution to the problem I posed, i.e. not a solution for a fundamental problem *within* truth-conditional semantics.

With revisionism and expressivism discarded as solutions to the problem, I move on to defend my own view in Chapters 5, 6 and 7. First, I show in Chapter 5 how truth-conditional semantics took a wrong turn in the early 1970s, when Davidson started claiming that the notion of truth plays a crucial explanatory role in semantics. I argue, inspired by McDowell's writings from the 1970s, that within the semantics of natural language, truth should be regarded as a theoretical notion that can be fully understood by its role in a semantic theory. I also argue that another Davidsonian dogma, the view that a theory of meaning can only generate extensional theorems, is unjustified.

The path is then clear for my positive account of relative truth in chapter 6. I expound a theory according to which (1) truth is relative to *perspectives*, (2) each thinker *possesses* a perspective and (3) a thinker ought not to believe anything that isn't true in his or her own perspective. A perspective, on this theory, is just a function that evaluates all propositions consistently; thus there is nothing philosophically substantial in the postulation of perspectives. The substantial element of the theory is rather the claim that the relation of perspective possession is constrained in a certain way by certain a priori norms of communication. These norms specify that in some areas of discourse disagreements indicate that a mistake has been made and that therefore reasoned discussion would be worth while. These are areas one might call objective. Thus objectivity, on this view, is the result of certain rules of communication. I also show how this theory of perspective possession can be further refined to make finer distinctions between more or less objective topic areas.

The final chapter examines relativism in general. This is necessary because discussions of relativism are often hampered by a lack of clarity concerning the nature of relativism. Often one form of relativism is dismissed because of problems that arise only for other forms of relativism. I therefore begin the chapter by developing a scheme of classification for different forms of relativism. After that, I use the classificatory scheme to examine how well-known objections to relativism fare against the various forms of relativism. The result of this examination is that the impact of these objections is surprisingly small.

The main conclusions I shall reach thus are: (1) the best response to the problem of non-objective sentences in truth-conditional semantics is the adoption of a truth notion on which mere truth evaluability does not yet entail objectivity; (2) any truth notion to fit that bill must be relative; (3) an independently fruitful theory of perspectives and perspective possession can be devised; and (4) this form of relativism, even though it is a global form, does not fall to any of the usual objections.

# Chapter 1

# Truth-Conditional Semantics

Humans use language to communicate. They utter certain sounds and respond to others uttering sounds in ways that constitute communication. What exactly is going on? How is this possible? We all know that it is because the expressions of a language are *meaningful* that we can use them for communication. Philosophers of language try to expand on this tautological and uninformative answer by constructing a more detailed theory of meaning. Such a theory may answer questions such as 'What is it for an utterance to be meaningful?', 'Why does a particular sound have the meaning it has?', 'How do people know what an utterance means?' and so on. By answering such questions, and by introducing new concepts and principles governing these concepts as well as linking them with other, familiar concepts, a theory of meaning will provide a more detailed explanation of what is going on when humans use language to communicate.

Evidently this description of the task of the philosophy of language leaves room for a very wide variety of theoretical activity, according to the different aspects of language use a theorist might be interested in. Nevertheless, one broad style of theorizing about linguistic meaning currently dominates the philosophy of language (and other disciplines that theorize about linguistic meaning, such as theoretical linguistics and artificial intelligence). I would like to call this common approach 'truth-conditional semantics'. Theorists working within the truth-conditional paradigm are united by the role their theories assign to a notion of truth or truth condition. Very roughly, these theorists believe that it is advantageous to characterize the meaning of a sentence (or at least the central element of its meaning) by giving the condition under which the sentence would be true. The meaning of a subsentential expression then consists just in the contribution it makes to the meaning of sentences in which it occurs. As I shall explain in more detail below, one great advantage and original motivation for this approach is that it provides a way of describing systematically how the meaning of complex expressions depends on the meanings of their simpler constituents.

Any theory of meaning within the truth-conditional paradigm faces a problem: it makes the contentious assumption that every meaningful sentence (or its content) is a candidate for truth or falsehood. There is, of course, an obvious reason why not every sentence is truth-evaluable: some sentences are there to enable us to ask questions or to issue commands, such as 'Is he in?' or 'Leave me alone!'. One would not normally describe such sentences (or utterances of them) as true or false. This is not the problem I have in mind, nor is it an irresolvable problem for a truth-conditional theorist. Typically the theorist will restrict his or her thesis that sentences have truth conditions to declarative sentences only and characterize the meaning of non-declaratives indirectly, e.g. by recourse to corresponding declaratives. Alternatively, the theorist can reformulate the thesis as one about sentence *contents*, so that declaratives and interrogatives alike have truth-evaluable contents. Declarative and interrogative sentences (as opposed to their contents) are then viewed as truth-evaluable only in a derivative sense, if at all. I shall discuss one way of doing this shortly.

But once interrogatives, imperatives etc. are taken care of there is another, more difficult problem with the assumption that all sentences (or their contents) are truth-evaluable. I have in mind declarative sentences that concern matters that are not objective, or for which it is at least debatable whether they are objective. One example are sentences about matters of taste such as 'Johnny Depp is more handsome than Brad Pitt.'.[1] Assuming that such a sentence, or what it says, can be true or false arguably amounts to saying that it is an objective matter whether Depp is more handsome or not. Can the truth-conditional theorist avoid this metaphysical consequence of his or her theory?

This book is an extended attempt to answer the question of how these and similarly problematic sentences should be treated in a truth-conditional theory of meaning. Competently answering it requires a theoretically more sophisticated formulation of the problem. Thus I shall begin my investigation by expounding a truth-conditional account of meaning in this chapter, and continue in the next chapter by setting up the problem in a theoretically tractable manner.

## I  One version of truth-conditional semantics

Accounts of meaning within the truth-conditional paradigm vary considerably. Some differences reflect substantial disagreements, others reflect merely a difference in emphasis—after all, different theories often address different problems. Yet other differences are merely terminological. Consequently, the account I shall expound is just one truth-conditional account among many, and not all truth-conditional theorists will agree with every detail. However, one particular elaboration of a truth-conditional theory of meaning is needed as a concrete theoretical and terminological framework within which to address the problem of sentences about non-objective matters. My elaboration will be sufficiently broadminded to allow most truth-conditionalists to follow the discussion without excessive interpretative charity. More importantly, I believe that my considerations on the problem of non-objective contents apply to my own account of meaning as much as to any other account within the truth-conditional paradigm.

My account will integrate a truth-conditional theory of content within an overall theory of use. A theory of linguistic meaning ought to explain how it is possible to use expressions of a language to communicate. In order to arrive at such a very general explanation, it is useful to consider what would be required to describe the meaning properties of all the expressions of just one particular language, i.e. to construct a theory of meaning for a particular language. Such a theory would explain how it is possible for the users of the language in question to use their language for communication, because such a theory would provide a formal model of the knowledge of language users that enables them to use language (whether or not that model is psychologically accurate). But, more importantly, if we knew how in principle such a theory of meaning for a particular language can be constructed, then we would be in a position to explain generally how it is possible to communicate through language (whichever particular language). Later on in this chapter, I shall formulate a theory of meaning for one particular simple language, and this theory shall serve as a simplified model for theories of meaning for natural languages in general.

## 2 Compositionality

One feature of language is a key motivation for the truth-conditional paradigm: compositionality. Natural languages are compositional in the sense that they allow the composition of compound expressions out of simpler ones in such a way that the meaning of the compound is determined by the meanings of the simpler expressions and their manner of composition. Compositionality seems to be one of the most obvious features of language and can be illustrated by countless examples. What 'wooden box' means obviously depends on what 'wooden' means, on what 'box' means and on how the two words are combined. If 'box' didn't mean what it does, 'wooden box' wouldn't mean what it does. To deny this would be crazy. Could the meaning of any complex expression depend on anything apart from its components and the way they are compounded? Strictly speaking, there could be syntactically complex expressions that are nevertheless not semantically complex. There could be a syntax that provides numerous ways of constructing new expressions without it yet being settled what these new expressions are to mean. Then the meaning of the (syntactic) components (if they have any) would not determine the meaning of the (syntactic) compound.[2] All this shows is that there may in some cases be syntactic complexity that is semantically inert. But this cannot hide the fact that in countless cases the meaning of compounds is compositionally determined.

Considerations about language understanding and language learning also confirm that compositionality is a pervasive feature of natural languages. Language users can understand and construct expressions they have never used or even heard before. For example, the vast majority of the readers of this book will never before have encountered the following sentence: 'My niece collects snails in a wooden box.'. Nevertheless, all moderately competent users of English (including, presumably, all my readers) know the meaning of this sentence. It doesn't take much ingenuity to explain this. The sentence is constructed from words, and in ways, with which competent speakers are familiar. The meaning of the sentence is determined by the meaning of its constituent words and the way in which these constituents are put together. Competent users know (at least implicitly) what the the words mean and how they influence the meaning of the whole sentence, given that they are put together in that particular way.[3]

This observation puts a constraint on theories of meaning for natural languages. Any such theory should explain how exactly the meaning of complex expressions is determined by the meanings of their simpler constituents and the manner of composition. In one word, a theory of meaning for such a language should be *compositional* in order to do justice to the fact of linguistic productivity.

Given the compositionality constraint, we know that a theory of meaning for a natural language cannot just list all the expressions of the language and specify their meaning one by one. Rather, it must first systematically outline all the ways in which expressions can be compounded from a number of primitive elements in a number of admissible ways (syntax). Then it must show how the meaning of compound expressions depends on their compositional make-up by specifying for each mode of composition, and for each primitive element, how they determine the meaning of the expression compounded. As a result, the theory should allow one to derive for every expression of the language what it means. In other words, the theory should have axiomatic structure.

## 3 Force indicators and content indicators

But what sort of information is it that we should expect to be derivable about each expression? How does one state what an expression means? At this point it is useful to introduce the notion of a *communicative act* (or traditionally 'illocutionary act'). By uttering certain expressions or, more accurately, by uttering sentences, language users perform linguistic acts, such as acts of assertion and question. I can assert that Sam smokes by uttering the sentence 'Sam smokes.', or I can ask whether Sam smokes by uttering the sentence 'Does Sam smoke?'. This is not a coincidence. Rather, it is the proper function of these sentences to allow one to do just this. One way, then, of specifying what an expression means is to state what its *proper communicative function* is. For example, one way of saying what the sentence 'Sam smokes.' means is to say that it can be properly used to assert that Sam smokes. The theory of meaning I am going to outline for a sample language will aim to generate meaning specifications of roughly this form. (I shall say more about communicative acts, my notion of proper use, and about the possibility of improper uses in §6 and §7.)

Not every expression, not even every complex expression, of a natural language can be properly used to perform a communicative act. The expression 'does not smoke', for instance, is not a complete sentence, and therefore cannot be properly used to perform any communicative act.[4] I shall call expressions that can be properly used to perform a communicative act 'sentences'.

The communicative function of a given sentence will depend on recognizable features of the sentence: its semantically significant features. For example, 'Sam smokes.' can be properly used to assert that Sam smokes, because it is made up of certain words in a certain order, and features a certain kind of punctuation (in spoken language: inflection). Among the semantically significant syntactic features of a natural language sentence are therefore features such as (a) its constituent words, (b) its word order, (c) its punctuation, and for spoken language (d) its inflection (i.e. changes in intonation).

A theory of meaning for a language needs to correlate these syntactic features of a sentence with the sentence's semantic features, i.e. its meaning. To do so, it is useful to distinguish between two different elements in the meaning of a sentence. One element is the sentence's *illocutionary force*: a sentence can, for example, be assertoric or interrogative. If it is assertoric, then it is properly usable for asserting something; if it is interrogative, then it is properly usable for asking a question. The other element is the sentence's *content*: for example the sentence 'Sam smokes.' has the content that Sam smokes. Two sentences can have the same content and different force, as for example the two sentences 'The door is shut.' and 'Is the door shut?'. The first can be properly used to assert that the door is shut, while the second can be properly used to ask whether the door is shut. Similarly, two sentences can have the same force and different contents.

The task of a theory of meaning (of specifying the communicative function of each sentence) can be divided into two subtasks. The first subtask is to identify those syntactic features that indicate a sentence's illocutionary force (call these its 'force indicators') and to formulate a rule that states how these force indicators determine a sentence's force. The second subtask is to identify the syntactic features that indicate a sentence's content (call these its 'content indicators') and to formulate rules that state how a sentence's content depends on these content indicators.

The first subtask is comparatively easy. Each sentence has just one illocutionary force, so all one needs to do is find the force indicators of the language in question and define a function that assigns forces to sentences depending on the force indicator they feature. In English, for instance, assertoric force is indicated by a full stop (or the corresponding inflection) and a certain word order. It is the task of applied linguistics to discover the exact way in which assertoricity is indicated. In my sample language, there are only two force-indicating prefixes, '⊢' (assertoric force) and '?' (interrogative force). Natural languages allow more than these two illocutionary forces, but I shall not here enter the discussion on which these are.

The subtask of assigning forces to sentences is comparatively easy, because force indicators do not, arguably, have semantic structure. Each complete sentence is marked to have one illocutionary force.[5] Content indication, however, is more complicated. We can construct sentences with highly complex contents. The job of formulating axioms that formulate how the contents of sentences depend on their content indicators is a real problem. Not only are there many different ways of combining words and sentences (at least in any natural language), but these modes of construction can also be iterated. This makes it necessary to operate with recursive axioms.

## 4 Truth definitions 'serving as' meaning theories

This is the point where truth-conditional semanticists turn to mathematical logic, more specifically to the work of Alfred Tarski, the founder of model theory. Tarski devised a way of defining a notion of truth for a formal first-order language (Tarski 1956). A Tarskian definition of truth for a language $L$ allows one to prove a so-called 'T-sentence', i.e. a sentence of the form '$s$ is true if and only if $p$', for each sentence $s$ of $L$ so that '$p$' is the translation of $s$ into the language of the definition (the 'metalanguage').

Truth-conditional semanticists hope to exploit Tarski's technique for their own purposes. First, even though a T-sentence does not say what the content of the sentence in question is, it nevertheless allows one to infer what the sentence's content is, at least if it has been derived in a certain way from appropriate semantic axioms. Second, even though Tarski was defining truth for a formal language only, the truth-conditional semanticist hopes to adopt Tarski's technique for natural languages as well.[6] To get a concrete idea of how this might be done, let's consider a very simple propositional language, L1, which features both content indicators and force indicators:

### Syntax for L1

*Vocabulary:*

| | |
|---|---|
| Names: | a, b, c |
| 1-place predicates: | S, D |
| 2-place predicate: | L |
| Connectives: | &, ¬ |
| Force indicators: | ⊢, ? |
| Brackets: | (, ) |

*Definition of sentential phrase:*

For all $\Pi$, $\alpha \vdash$, $\beta$, $\theta$, $\rho$:
(1)   If $\Pi$ is a 1-place predicate and $\alpha$ is a name, then $\ulcorner \Pi\alpha \urcorner$ is a sentential phrase.[7]
(2)   If $\Pi$ is a 2-place predicate and $\alpha$ and $\beta$ are names, then $\ulcorner \alpha\Pi\beta \urcorner$ is a sentential phrase.
(3)   If $\theta$ and $\rho$ are sentential phrases, then so are $\ulcorner \neg\theta \urcorner$ and $\ulcorner (\theta \ \& \ \rho) \urcorner$.
(4)   Nothing else is a sentential phrase.

*Definition of* sentence:

For all θ:
(5)    If θ is a sentential phrase, then ⌜⊢θ⌝ and ⌜?θ⌝ are sentences and nothing else is.

Thus, ⌜¬(Da & ¬Sa)⌝ would for example be a sentential phrase of L1, ⌜⊢¬(Da & ¬Sa)⌝ a sentence. The definition of 'sentential phrase' is recursive: it allows repeated application of the two connectives to form a new sentential phrase each time. So there are infinitely many sentential phrases in L1. Nevertheless, we have tight control over the sentential phrases of L1, for they can be generated only in ways specified by the recursive definition of 'sentential phrase'. It is now the task of a theory of truth for L1 to make sure that truth is defined for each sentential phrase. This again is done recursively:

## Theory of truth for L I

*Definition of* reference:

(6)    The referent of a is Alfred, the referent of b is Bernard and the referent of c is Carl.

*Definition of* true:

For all α, β, θ, ρ:
(7)    If α is a name, then ⌜Sα⌝ is true iff the referent of α smokes.
(8)    If α is a name, then ⌜Dα⌝ is true iff the referent of α drinks.
(9)    If α and β are names, then ⌜αLβ⌝ is true iff the referent of α loves the referent of β.
(10)   If θ is a sentential phrase, then ⌜¬θ⌝ is true iff it is not the case that θ is true.
(11)   If θ and ρ are sentential phrases, then ⌜(θ & ρ)⌝ is true iff θ is true and ρ is true.

Given this theory of truth for L1, one can prove a T-sentence for each sentential phrase of L1. For example, one can prove the T-sentence

(T1)   ⌜¬(Da & ¬Sa)⌝ is true iff it is not the case that (Alfred drinks and it is not the case that Alfred smokes).

for the previous example sentence ⌜¬(Da & ¬Sa)⌝. In doing so, one retraces the syntactic operations by which the sentence has been compounded by applying the corresponding semantic axioms.

    How can this help in the task of formulating a theory of content, which can then feed into a theory of meaning that specifies the proper communicative

function of each sentence? All the T-sentences do is give a necessary and sufficient condition for the truth of a sentential phrase. The truth-conditional semanticist's idea is that the *right* T-sentences allow one to *read off* what the content of
the sentential phrase is. But not every T-sentence allows one to read off the content. To clarify this problem, let's define 'T-sentence' properly.

A *T-sentence* is a metalanguage sentence of the form:

　⌜θ is true iff $p$⌝

where 'θ' is replaced by a description of an object-language sentential
phrase, and '$p$' is replaced by a sentence that does not contain any reference
to object-language expressions.

Now suppose we wanted to exploit the T-sentences generated by our theory of
truth in order to assign communicative functions to sentences by adding one
more axiom and an inference rule:

(12)　If θ is a sentential phrase, then ⌜⊢θ⌝ can be properly used to assert the
content of θ.
(TM)　If ⌜θ is true iff $p$⌝ is a T-sentence, then θ's content is the content that $p$.

Then we could derive the following meaning-specifying theorem for ⌜⊢¬(Da &
¬Sa)⌝:

(M1)　⌜⊢¬(Da & ¬Sa)⌝ can be properly used to assert that it is not the case that
Alfred drinks and does not smoke.

This is as it should be: (M1) is the correct specification of the sentence's proper
communicative function. The problem is, however, that there are also uninterpretive T-sentences such as

(T2)　⌜¬(Da & ¬Sa)⌝ is true iff grass is green.

which might be true. If so, (12) and (TM) would permit derivation of a false
meaning assignment such as

(M2)　⌜⊢¬(Da & ¬Sa)⌝ can be properly used to assert that grass is green.

One might think that what is wrong with (T2) is that it is not derivable from the
theory of truth for L1. Clearly, in order to know (T2) one needs to know that
both its sides have the same truth value. This information cannot be derived from
the theory of truth for L1. So perhaps we need to modify (TM) in the following
way:

(TM*)　If θ is a sentential phrase, and if ⌜θ is true iff $p$⌝ is a T-sentence that can
be derived from the theory of truth for L1 by logic alone, then infer that
θ's content is the content that $p$.

(TM*) no longer applies to uninterpretive T-sentences such as (T2). However, there are still other uninterpretive T-sentences which *can* be proved from the theory of truth for L1 and logic alone. For example:

(T3)  $\ulcorner \neg(Da \ \& \ \neg Sa)\urcorner$ is true iff it is not the case that Alfred drinks and does not smoke, and if grass is green then grass is green.

Again, (TM*) would allow the derivation of a false meaning-specifying theorem.

So we need to modify (TM*) again. We need to exclude T-sentences that have been derived by inferential steps that make them uninterpretive. We can do so by describing a *canonical procedure* for proving interpretive T-sentences:[8]

> When deriving a T-sentence for a sentential phrase *s*, first apply the axiom that concerns the syntactic operation last used in constructing *s* to get a theorem of the form '*s* is true iff …'. For any object-language expressions mentioned in '…', repeat that procedure, and do so again for the resulting theorems until no more object-language expressions are mentioned. Then use the theorems derived, and the rule that equivalents may be substituted for one another to eliminate any object-language expressions mentioned on the right-hand side of the original theorem '*s* is true iff …'.

T-sentences derived in his way will be interpretive. So we can now use a new version of (TM):

(TM**)  If θ is a sentential phrase, and if $\ulcorner θ$ is true iff $p\urcorner$ is a *canonically derived* T-sentence, then infer that θ's content is the content that $p$.[9]

The theory of truth and the theory of force for L1 now permit the derivation of all and only correct meaning-specifying theorems for the sentences of L1. With the addition of (TM**), the theory of truth for L1 has in effect served as a theory of content.

Let me take stock. I have shown how a theory of meaning for the very simple language L1 can be constructed by first defining a notion of sentence and sentential phrase (syntax), then defining truth for sentential phrases, and formulating an inference rule (such as (TM**)) with which one can assign to each sentential phrase a content (or proposition). Finally, one can use (12) to assign to each sentence a communicative function. Thus, one can use this theory to derive for any sentence *s* of L1 a meaning specification of the form '*s* can be properly used to φ that *p*'. Let me call a meaning theory with this kind of architecture a 'truth-conditional meaning theory'.

L1 was just a propositional formal language, which simplified the task of formulating the definition of truth for L1. But the same could be done for languages containing quantifiers, as Tarski has shown. Now, even though Tarski's technique for defining truth for first-order formal languages is a crucial element of the truth-conditional paradigm, I do not want to clutter these pages with this relatively standard material.[10] The crucial point for the present discussion is that a truth-conditional theory of meaning for a first-order formal language is possible.[11]

## 5 Application to natural languages

I have now outlined the formal structure of truth-conditional theories of meaning for formal languages. But it is far from obvious whether and how the strategy outlined for formal languages can be made to work for natural languages. There are many natural-language constructions for which it is hard to find adequate semantic axioms that would fit into a truth-conditional theory. But during the last forty years or so many philosophers and linguists have spent time trying to make recalcitrant natural-language constructions workable within the truth-conditional framework—to discover their 'logical form', as this project is often described. Naturally, not every problem has been treated, nor is there even unanimity about many of the issues that have been debated. Nevertheless, the range of natural-language constructions for which logical-form proposals have been formulated is impressive. Broadly conceived, the truth-conditional para-digm is now the most successful and most widely pursued approach in natural-language semantics.

The topic of this book is a difficulty that would arise even if it could be shown that there are viable analyses of the logical form of all natural-language expres-sions and constructions. For that reason, I will not say anything here about my preferred solutions to the perennial problems in truth-conditional semantics, such as: proper names (e.g. 'Aristotle'), definite descriptions (e.g. 'the King of France'), indexicals (e.g. 'yesterday'), conditionals (i.e. if-sentences), indirect contexts (e.g. 'Sam believes that ...'), sentences describing actions (e.g. 'he de-fended himself passionately') and so on. Rather, I shall pretend that there are satisfactory solutions to all the problems to do with the susceptibility of natural languages to formal truth-conditional treatment. For example, I shall speak of the 'contents' of sentences as that which is captured by the interpretive T-sen-tences of a truth-conditional meaning theory, without presupposing any particu-lar view as to what kind of object a content is (if at all). Whenever details of the account are relevant for my argument, however, I will draw attention to this fact.

## 6 Proper communicative function

Even if we assume that questions of logical form can be settled, a lot remains to be explained, if the possibility of formulating truth-conditional theories of meaning for natural languages is to shed any light on the nature of linguistic communication via natural languages. First, I have used unexplained notions of communicative acts such as the notions of assertion and question. What is it for someone to assert or ask something? Secondly, I have not said how the meaning specifications a truth-conditional theory of meaning yields are to explain language use. The specifications make use of the notion of proper use. What does it mean to say that a sentence 'can be properly used' to perform a certain communicative act?

When a theory of meaning yields a meaning specification for a given sentence type $s$, then this is supposed to license a redescription of utterances of that sentence type (by users of the language in question) as communicative (illocutionary) acts. Thus if the theory specifies '$s$ can be properly used to assert (ask) that $p$', then utterances of $s$ may be redescribed as (literal) assertions that, or questions whether, $p$. Together with an account of the communicative acts of assertion and question, this will (eventually) allow us to explain how people can communicate by uttering and hearing sentences.

There are good reasons why it is helpful to speak of 'proper' use and 'literal' assertion. Speakers often use sentences non-literally or non-properly. The sentence 'The door is open.', for example, is assertoric, because it can be properly or literally used to assert that the door is open. However, it can also, in a sense, be used to issue a command. Similarly, the interrogative sentence 'Do fish ride bicycles?' can be used to answer a question rather than to ask one (e.g. to answer the question whether philosophers ever agree on anything). It would be very difficult to formulate a meaning theory the meaning specifications of which anticipate all possible communicative uses to which sentences may be put. The next best thing is a theory that predicts the literal or proper use to which sentences are put and leaves an explanation of non-literal uses for a separate theory. Even pretheoretically it is not implausible to say that any utterance of the sentence 'Do fish ride bicycles?' is a literal question whether fish ride bicycles, even if asking that question is presumably never the ultimate point of such an utterance. Suppose that the ultimate point of one particular utterance of the sentence is to communicate that the answer to a previously asked question is obviously 'no'. Then this aspect of the utterance should be explicable by recourse to the communicative act literally performed. This additional explanation might proceed along the lines of Grice's theory of implicature (Grice 1989).[12]

Let me use an analogy to illustrate and justify the concentration on literal or proper use. Suppose we wanted to shed light on the function of screwdrivers, perhaps as part of a general theory of domestic tools. Suppose further that we agreed that the function of screwdrivers was somehow based on the use people make of screwdrivers. Then surely we wouldn't be making much progress by claiming that the function of screwdrivers consisted in all the ways in which screwdrivers are actually used. Even if it were possible to specify all those ways, that would not tell us what their function is. For not all uses of screwdrivers are relevant to their function. It is the *proper uses* that are most telling. The proper uses are those uses that serve the purposes for which screwdrivers are designed, namely the purposes of screwing and unscrewing screws. We can explain the essential features of screwdrivers by recourse to these purposes (not the inessential features, such as a screwdriver's colour). In this way, we could gain an understanding of the function of screwdrivers and use it to explain and predict people's screwdriver-related behaviour.

Not all the improper uses of screwdrivers are wholly independent of their proper function. Some of the essential features may be exploited for purposes more or less similar to the proper purpose. I recall once using a screwdriver as a chisel. One could also use one for peeling oranges or for scratching one's back. Sometimes, it may even be unclear whether a use is proper, as for instance when I hold a bolt, instead of turning it, so that I can tighten a nut. In other cases, inessential features may be exploited in improper uses. For example, a screwdriver's colour might be used ostensively to identify a certain colour.

How does this analogy shed light on the notion of the meaning of an expression? The idea is that the meaning of a sentence consists in its proper use or proper function, and that by specifying the proper function of the sentences of a language we can predict and explain utterances of the sentence. The hypothesis is that after the proper function of sentences has been specified, we can also gain a better understanding of improper uses, much in the way in which an understanding of the proper function of screwdrivers might help in understanding improper uses of screwdrivers. Let me stress that in this connection the word 'improper' is not derogatory. There is nothing wrong in using language for purposes that diverge from proper function. There is nothing bad in using 'The door is open.' in order to issue a command, or in uttering 'Do fish swim?' not in order to ask a question. The priority of proper or literal function over improper or nonliteral use is merely explanatory priority in a theory that is intended to explain the workings of a language.

So how does one decide what the proper function of a given sentence is? In the case of the screwdriver, it is easy, because the proper function of screwdrivers is determined by the intentions of the makers or designers of screwdrivers. With language, the situation is different. Although it seems to me promising to start from the assumption that language is a *tool* of communication, this tool does not have a designer or inventor (at least not in the case of natural languages). If we cannot ask 'the inventor of a language' what the proper function of its sentences is, how can we find out? My suggestion is that we should use observations of language use in order to construct a theory that explains language use. There may be many such theories, each differing in respect of which uses of language are classified as proper, but not all of these theories are equally good theories. A theory that renders all uses as proper, for example, would not be very good, because it would lack systematicity. The best theory will provide an explanation of a maximum range of uses while being simple, systematic, integrated into other theories and using pre-theoretically familiar concepts (compare Thagard 1978).

On some such theory, I think, deviant uses will no longer be a problem. They will either be so deviant that they do not fall into the range of uses covered by the theory, or they will occur as non-basic uses that can be explained by recourse to the proper, basic function of the expressions used.

On this view, the literal meaning of a sentence, or its proper communicative function, therefore enjoys theoretical priority over the specific non-literal uses to which it may be put by language users. Is this methodologically justified? After all, a theory of meaning for a particular language should be based on the use people make of that language. The sentence 'Do fish ride bicycles?' has presumably never been used, in the pre-theoretical sense, to ask whether fish ride bicycles. So with what justification can one say that it can be *properly* used to ask whether fish ride bicycles? How do the data of language use confirm that the sentence has this communicative function if no one uses it to fulfil that function? Can reasons of theoretical simplicity justify this apparently blatant disregard for (or perhaps even inconsistency with) the data?

The answer is that the sentence's force indicators and content indicators are used as part of other sentences in ways that confirm that this is the sentence's proper function. Its word order and introduction with the auxiliary verb 'to do', as well as the question mark (or a certain inflection in spoken English), are syntactic devices that are used in countless other sentences that do in fact get used to ask questions—for example the sentence 'Does Sam smoke?'. The prediction that the sentence's proper function is interrogative is based on these data. The sentence's content indicators 'fish', 'ride', 'bicycle' and the way in which they are compounded are also devices that display their proper function in other sentences—for example 'Dutchmen ride bicycles.' or 'Fish have scales.'.

The systematicity at which a theory of meaning of this kind aims should therefore reflect the systematic, repeatable role each syntactic device displays in many different contexts. This methodological maxim serves an explanatory aim of a meaning theory. As I have mentioned earlier, one of the aspects of language use that needs explanation is the ability of language users to use novel sentences. If a theory of meaning for a language systematically describes the repeatable contribution each syntactic part makes to the proper function of the sentences in which it may feature, then such a theory can serve as a model for the cognitive processes by which language users compute the proper function of sentences of their language. Thus the division into uses that manifest a sentence's proper communicative function directly and those for the explanation of which we need to appeal to additional principles governing improper uses (e.g. a theory of implicature, ellipsis or metaphor) is a distinction that should be anchored in the actual linguistic behaviour of speakers.

Let me, once again, take stock. A truth-conditional theory of meaning for a language will yield, via axioms concerning all the content indicators and force indicators of the language, meaning specifications for all the sentences. These meaning specifications take the form '$s$ can be properly used to $\phi$ that $p$'. These specifications in turn license the redescription of utterances as (proper or literal) communicative acts, e.g. '$A$ has (literally) asserted that $p$'. Thus someone who possessed the theory could derive, for each utterance of a sentence of the language, which (literal) communicative act it serves to perform.[13] In this sense he or she would possess the ability to understand the language.

## 7 Communicative acts

Finally, I need to explicate the notion of a communicative act itself, i.e. the notions of assertion and question and perhaps further types of communicative act if necessary. These notions are no doubt pre-theoretically familiar. But some explication of the notions is needed to make their theoretical role clear. In §6, I said that a theory of meaning for a natural language can be empirically confirmed by data of language use. In that connection I talked as if we could observe directly that some sentence is used on some occasion to perform a certain communicative act. Thus a speaker's uttering a sentence s and thereby asserting that p confirms, to some degree, any theory of meaning that entails that s can be properly used to assert that p. Obviously, this can work only if there is some way of knowing that the speaker asserted that p by uttering s independently of having a correct meaning theory for the language in question. What we need is an explication of the notion of assertion, and of other kinds of communicative act, in independent terms.

In the literature, this problem is often discussed in the guise of the quest for an adequate characterization of the 'actual language relation'.[14] A theory of meaning of the kind I have outlined can be viewed as the description of an abstract object—a complex function that assigns meanings to sentence types. So conceived, there are countless theories of meaning that describe countless ('possible') languages. Only very few of these possible languages are actual languages, i.e. languages used by some population of language users.[15] The actual language relation is the relation in which a possible language stands to a population when, and only when, that population uses that language. What does this relation consist in?

I shall not here address the problem of the actual language relation directly, but rather approach the problem from the angle already mentioned, i.e. by looking for an account of the various communicative acts. I shall briefly outline an account of the sort I favour.

What we need is an account of assertion that makes it possible to judge whether it is likely, given general psychological assumptions, that an agent is intending to assert a certain content when uttering a given sentence type. One account of assertion (Brandom 1983) describes the linguistic practice of making assertions as a kind of game. In any game, there is a number of possible moves, and each move has a significance within the game. According to Brandom, to assert is to make a move in the social game of communication, a game the rules of which are ultimately underpinned by social norms and sanctions. The significance of making an assertion can be described as follows: to assert that p is (1) to undertake a responsibility to justify p if challenged to do so, and (2) to issue a licence to use p as a premise. Thus if one participant makes an assertion, other participants may challenge it. Since the asserter has, by making the assertion, undertaken a responsibility to justify his or her assertion if challenged, he or she is then obliged to justify the assertion. This justification can take the form of a further assertion which, if true, would confirm the original assertion, or the asserter may invoke an assertion made by another participant. If the asserter fails to comply with this obligation, he or she will normally suffer negative sanctions (e.g. his or her status in the community may suffer in some way). Since an asserter is under an obligation to provide justifications, other participants will frequently rely on an assertion and take it as evidence that what has been asserted is true—especially if they believe that the asserter would not have made the assertion, and risked sanction, unless he or she was in possession of good justification). Thus agents who make assertions will often bring it about that their addressees acquire new beliefs or at least change the likelihood they assign to what has been asserted. This is how participants in the game of assertion use language to communicate.

If this account is correct, then it provides a way of using general psychological principles to judge whether a given population with the patterns of its speech behaviour is in fact using a certain language. Suppose a participant utters a sentence the utterance of which counts as an assertion that $p$ in a language $L$, and that general psychology renders it likely that he or she would want to undertake the responsibilities and issue the licences that making the assertion involves. Then the view that members of that population use $L$ would be confirmed to some degree. Similarly, the participants' responses to assertions can provide evidence as to whether the population uses $L$: if the assertion is followed by what counts as a challenge in $L$, and this is then followed by what counts as a justification in $L$—or by a failure to justify and ensuing sanction—then this equally confirms the hypothesis that the population uses $L$.

An account of the communicative act of questioning could follow similar lines. By asking a question, a participant imposes an obligation on his or her addressee to answer the question or else give an excuse for failing to answer the question. More precisely, to answer a question whether $p$ is to assert either $p$ or the negation of $p$. A typical excuse for failing to answer a question is an assertion that one doesn't know whether $p$. Again, if this account of the communicative act of asking a (yes/no) question is correct, then it provides a basis for judging whether a given utterance is likely to have been intended as a question.

Of course this is only the barest outline of an account. Our actual communicative practices are far more complicated and allow for many exceptions. For example, under certain conditions, the obligation to answer a question may be overruled by other considerations, e.g. of secrecy. Similarly, some assertions are in no further need of justification, e.g. because their content is taken to be obviously true, or because the asserter has special authority or expertise. Moreover, the rules of the game do not only serve the aim of spreading information. Occasionally, participants will lie, or otherwise rely on the rules of the game, in order deliberately to mislead or deceive other participants. In those cases, participants run an (often calculated) risk of discovery and subsequent negative sanctions.

The general idea, however, is clear: communicative acts such as asserting and questioning have a certain social significance among users of the language and this allows us to judge from their linguistic behaviour and general psychological principles whether the hypothesis that they use a given language $L$ is a good one.

There are some more general problems with the empirical evidence for the hypothesis that a certain population uses a certain language. As far as I can see, these are general problems concerning the relation of theory to evidence. The data of language use that could be used to justify the view that a population uses some language $L$ are necessarily restricted to a small subset of the sentences of $L$. For the most part, the sentences of $L$ will never be used. There will be many alternative languages that concur with the meaning assignments of $L$ in the used range of sentences but differ from them in the unused range. How do we know that the population speaks $L$ and not one of $L$'s alternatives (Schiffer 1993)? This looks like a classic case of underdetermination of theory by evidence. Even if that were so, it would not be a special problem for the hypothesis that a population uses a given language, but rather a general problem faced by many empirical hypotheses. The situation isn't, however, as bad as it may at first appear. Even though there are many languages whose use would explain the speech behaviour of a population, not all these explanations are equally good. One hypothesis may be more economical or more comprehensible than another. One set of semantic axioms that generates meaning specifications that accord with actual use may provide a psychologically more plausible account of language processing than another set of axioms that generates meaning specifications that also accord with actual use.

## 8  Summary and conclusion

My sketch of the form and methodology of a truth-conditional meaning theory for a natural language is now complete. It takes the form of a set of semantic axioms about the primitive expressions of the language in question. These axioms allow the derivation of an interpretive T-sentence for each sentential phrase of the language, and moreover generate a meaning-specifying theorem for each sentence by recourse to the sentence's force indicator and the appropriate T-sentence of its constituent sentential phrase. Whether such a theory correctly describes the language of a given population can be gathered, via an account of the various communicative acts (assertion, question, etc.), from the communicative practices of the population. If it is true that this is a good way of constructing a theory of meaning for any particular natural language, then it also sheds light on the workings of natural-language communication in general.

The truth-conditional approach is inspired by Tarski's formal semantics. It is therefore not surprising that the approach incidentally makes the logical relations among sentence contents (sentential phrases) perspicuous and describable with precision. In order to make natural languages susceptible to Tarski's formal semantics the truth-conditional semanticist uncovers the logical form of sentences by formalizing them as sentences in a formal language of predicate logic. The original motivation for this was just that it seemed to be the only available way to formulate a compositional meaning theory with any precision. But if this project of formalization succeeds, it has the added advantage that it provides a logic of natural language—a means of judging the validity of a certain range of natural-language arguments.

# Chapter 2

# Excess Objectivity

## 1 Excess objectivity

Truth-conditional semantics, the approach I have introduced in the last chapter, is arguably the dominant approach not only in the philosophy of language but also in theoretical linguistics. The core and strength of truth-conditional semantics lies in its treatment of the compositionality of meaning, i.e. of the fact that the meaning of a complex expression must in some way depend on, and be determined by, the meanings of its constituent parts, and the way these parts are put together. Because the truth-conditional semanticist assumes that the central element of the meaning of each sentence is its truth-conditional content, he or she can exploit Tarski's recursive technique for stating in a precise way how the meaning of sentences depends on their parts. The assumption that the central semantic feature of a sentence is its truth-conditional content is therefore the key to the success of truth-conditional semantics. Thus truth-conditional semantics presupposes that the content of every sentence is truth-evaluable.

The theory of meaning is not the only area where it is convenient to assume that sentence contents are candidates for truth and falsehood. First, standard logic employs a notion of validity that presupposes that the premises and conclusions of valid arguments are truth-evaluable. Thus, if we denied global truth-evaluability and restricted the range of sentences whose contents are evaluable in terms of truth, we would thereby also restrict the range of sentences to which our standard logic applies. The assumption of global truth-evaluability is therefore convenient from the point of view of the range of applicability of logic.

Second, global truth-evaluability is also suggested by considerations about the function of the truth predicate. There is a very good reason why truth should be attributable to the contents of all sentences. We often need to attribute truth in order to endorse contents we cannot explicitly assert (compare, e.g., Quine 1970 and Horwich 1998). I might, for example, need to say that some of the things Wolfgang says are true. This need might arise whatever the subject matter of those of Wolfgang's enunciations that I have in mind. The usefulness of referring to the content of what someone says and then calling it true is independent of the subject matter of that content. Suppose that, say, contents concerning matters of taste were not capable of being true or false. Then I could not, for example, say that all Wolfgang says on matters of taste is true. I would have to look for different ways of expressing my agreement with Wolfgang. Thus, a denial of the assumption of global truth-evaluability would deprive us of an important linguistic tool. [1]

Despite its convenience, however, the assumption of global truth-evaluability is contentious. Three concrete example sentences may serve to illustrate why:

(1)    Licorice is tasty.
(2)    Popocatépetl will probably erupt within ten years.
(3)    Cheating on one's spouse is bad.

These three assertoric sentences have, respectively, the content that licorice is tasty, the content that Popocatépetl will probably erupt within ten years and the content that cheating on one's spouse is bad. According to the assumption in question, all three are truth-evaluable. This is controversial, because, roughly, it bestows too much objectivity on moral, probabilistic and aesthetic[2] questions. Only a moral, aesthetic and probabilistic objectivist, it seems, can accept the assumption of global truth-evaluability.

Arguably, not all natural-language sentences concern objective matters. Many philosophers, and indeed non-philosophers, would deny that it is an objective matter whether a work of art is beautiful. Many would deny that it is an objective matter whether a stew is tasty. Still many, though fewer, would deny that it is an objective matter whether an act is morally bad. Again, some people would deny that there are objective probabilities. Nevertheless, it can be the content of utterances that something is probable, bad or tasty. Does it follow that all these people have to abjure truth-conditional semantics? Does it follow that they must all restrict the range of applicability of logic? Do they have to stop calling certain contents true? The aim of this book is to show how the assumption of global truth-evaluability *can* be made compatible with the view that not everything is objective.

But what is meant by 'objective' and why does truth-evaluability seem to entail objectivity? One line of thought is the following. Truth is objective, because to be true is to describe reality correctly, to state how the world really is. But values and probabilities aren't part of reality; there are no evaluative or probabilistic facts. So whether something has a certain value or probability is not an objective matter. If someone says that something is valuable or probable, he or she is therefore not aiming at truth, not trying to describe or represent reality. The content of what he or she says is not evaluable in terms of truth. So the thesis of global truth-evaluability is false, at least in so far as those sentences are concerned that say that something has or lacks value, or that something is probable or improbable.

Who is to decide whether there are facts of a certain kind, or what sorts of aspects of reality are there to be described? Are we to trust our intuitions? I believe that we must not uncritically follow intuitions about the nature of reality and about what facts there are if this leads us to dismiss truth-conditional semantics, to restrict the applicability of logic, and to revise our ordinary practice of attributing truth.[3] So, before drawing radical conclusions, we must consider carefully how the difficulty might be circumvented. I shall briefly review three different options.

## 2  Three ways of solving the problem of excess objectivity

Let us call the general problem I have identified the 'problem of excess objectivity'. Then the conjunction of the following three claims can be made responsible for the problem of excess objectivity in the case of sentence (1):

(a)   (1)'s content is completely described as the content that licorice is tasty.
(b)   All contents are truth-evaluable
(c)   (For any $p$) if the content that $p$ is truth-evaluable, then it is an objective matter whether $p$.

As it follows from (a)–(c) that it is an objective matter whether licorice is tasty, we need to deny at least one of (a)–(c), if we want to be able to reject objectivism in aesthetics. The situation will be similar with (2), (3) and other problematic sentences. So presumably there are generally three strategies for solving the problem, namely those corresponding to the denial, respectively, of (a), of (b) and of (c).

How could one deny (a)? For example, by claiming that (1) is an elliptical sentence synonymous with 'I find licorice tasty.'. If this were true, (1)'s content would no longer be correctly described as the content that licorice is tasty. Rather, when someone utters (1), he (or she) asserts that he himself (or she herself) finds licorice tasty.[4] But for this revised content to be truth-evaluable, the objectivity of aesthetic judgements would no longer be required and the problem of excess objectivity would be solved. Let's call this view 'revisionism'. I shall examine and discard revisionism in Chapter 3.

To deny (b) is to deny the assumption of global truth-evaluability directly. On this view, it is not a question of truth or falsehood whether licorice is tasty. Therefore, sentences like (1) are an exception to the doctrine that the contents of sentences are candidates for truth. An alternative theory is then needed to account for the meaning of such sentences (and perhaps for the validity of arguments involving them). For example, it might be claimed that in uttering a sentence like (1), rather than asserting a truth-evaluable content, one expresses a non-truth-evaluable attitude. This view is usually called 'expressivism'. It will be treated in depth in Chapter 4, where I shall argue that it is extremely difficult to give a *separate* semantic treatment for problematic sentences like (1).

Assuming that I am right about revisionism and expressivism, we are left with the possibility of denying (c): even though it may be true or false that licorice is tasty, it nevertheless is not an objective matter. Let's call this view the 'soft-truth approach'. How could it be true that licorice is tasty, or that it is not tasty, without it being an objective matter? We first need to know more about the apparent connection between truth and objectivity. In the remainder of this chapter I shall try to define an appropriate notion of objectivity and point the way towards a notion of soft truth, i.e. a notion of truth that is such that global truth-evaluability and local lack of objectivity are no longer in conflict.

## 3 Kinds of objectivity

'Objectivity' is a philosophical term that has been used to express a whole range of different metaphysical and epistemological ideas. One such idea is the idea of something that is independent (or exists independently) of human thought, as opposed to something that would not be so (or would not have existed) without human intellectual activity. Let's call this 'ontological independence'. On this notion of objectivity, a foul in football, for example, is a non-objective matter. Another idea is that of something that is publicly accessible, as opposed to something accessible only to individual subjects. Let's call this 'public accessibility'. On this notion of objectivity, phenomenological qualities, for example, might be thought to be non-objective.

The notion of objectivity I have been talking about is neither objectivity in the sense of ontological independence nor objectivity in the sense of public accessibility. There is no prima facie incompatibility between truth-evaluability and ontological non-independence. The fact that nothing would be a foul without human thought is not in conflict with the possibility of it being true that someone committed a foul. There is no prima facie incompatibility between truth-evaluability and public inaccessibility either. Without further assumptions there is nothing wrong in thinking that something is true yet can be known only by one person or only via one person.

The sense of objectivity I am concerned with has to do with the idea of independence from individual viewpoints or personal preferences. Our judgements on objective matters, on this view, all answer to the same reality (or at least to the same standard), while the correctness of a judgement on a non-objective matter can depend on the preferences or standards of the person making the judgement. Thus, for example, most people would take it to be an objective matter whether Canary Wharf is taller than St Paul's Cathedral. By contrast, they would take it to be non-objective whether Johnny Depp is more handsome than Brad Pitt. Some people would say that Canary Wharf's being taller is a fact of reality, while there are no facts concerning the aesthetic value of things. But whether or not we adopt this metaphysical mode of speaking, the intuitive distinction between the objective and the non-objective remains.

One observation may help to make this notion of objectivity more precise. When two people are disagreeing on whether Canary Wharf is taller than St Paul's Cathedral, we automatically assume that one of them must be in error. However, when two people are disagreeing on who is more handsome, Depp or

Pitt, we leave room for the possibility that neither of them is in error. That's why some people say 'there is no disputing tastes': why dispute if there is no error. I shall give a lot of weight to this observation and ultimately base my definition of objectivity on it: a content $p$ is non-objective just if it is not a priori (in a sense still to be explained) that disagreements on whether $p$ or not-$p$ are a sign of error on one side of the disagreement. This should provide enough of a pre-theoretical grasp.

## 4 Wright's criterion of cognitive command

Why should truth-evaluability automatically lead to objectivity in this sense? Some say it need not. The so-called 'minimalists' about truth propose a notion of truth that is metaphysically non-committal, and thus frees us from unwanted objectivistic consequences of the assumption that all contents are truth-evaluable. Crispin Wright is one proponent of this view.

Wright's project in his book *Truth and Objectivity* (1992) is to develop a new framework for 'realist/antirealist debates'. For Wright, a realist about a given subject is someone who believes that our judgements or statements on that subject represent, and answer to, the external world 'as independently of the beliefs about it which we do, will, or ever would form' (1992: 2) and that we are, under favourable circumstances, capable of making judgements (statements) on this subject that represent the world *correctly*, i.e. are true. Wright recognizes that there are many subject areas where realism is legitimately controversial, notably the area of judgements (statements) that concern whether something is funny. Other examples are moral, aesthetic and modal discourse. He is dissatisfied with the fact that discussions of realism have often taken the form of debates on whether judgements of a certain sort are candidates for truth, and whether sentences that serve to express such judgements count as assertoric. He therefore calls for a new framework for discussing realism (1992: 7–12).

Within this new framework, realists and anti-realists (in Wright's sense, explained above) should be able to discuss their concerns in terms other than those of truth-aptness or assertoricity. He therefore proposes

> a conception of assertoric content which views it as something ensured by a discourse's satisfying constraints of internal discipline and surface syntax. ... Any of the areas of discourse which historically has provoked, or is likely to provoke, a realist/anti-realist debate is also likely to satisfy these constraints. And assertoric content, so ensured, suffices for the definability upon the discourse of a predicate which, by dint of its satisfaction of certain basic platitudes, qualifies ... as a truth predicate. (1992: 140)

These platitudes include the thesis that to assert is to present as true, the disquotational principle (that any sentence '$p$' is true just if $p$) and the thesis that every assertoric content has a negation that is also an assertoric content (see e.g. 1992: 34 and 72). Truth, on this view, is 'not intrinsically a metaphysically heavyweight notion' (1992: 72) and thus permits that even anti-realists concede the truth-aptness of all superficially assertoric sentences.

But what about all the perceived contrasts between those subject areas that are objective, where we represent an objective reality, and those that are not objective, where an anti-realist attitude is appropriate? If the difference is not to do with truth-evaluability or assertoricity, what does it consist in?[5] Wright provides several criteria for classifying discourses as more or less realist, criteria that are supposed to be independent of truth-evaluability. One of them, the criterion of 'cognitive command', exploits the idea that some areas of discourse are properly representational while others aren't. This criterion is particularly interesting for our purposes of characterizing objectivity.[6] A discourse exerts cognitive command, Wright says, if and only if:

> It is a priori that differences of opinion formulated within the discourse, unless excusable as a result of vagueness in a disputed statement, or in the standards of acceptability, or variation in personal evidence thresholds, so to speak, will involve something that may properly be regarded as a cognitive shortcoming. (1992: 144)

In the background is a comparison with representational devices, devices whose function is the production of representations, such as a camera or fax machine. If such devices diverge in the representations they produce, then that must be due either to malfunction or to difference in input. Similarly, if a discourse is in a strong realist sense representational, i.e. if the judgements and statements that are part of it function to represent independent reality, then any divergence in judgement between two believers must be due to a difference in input or malfunction: at least one of the two must have insufficient or misleading evidence, or have made a mistake in processing the evidence; in short, at least one is guilty of cognitive failure. The qualifications about vagueness and differences in personal evidence thresholds serve to accommodate obvious special cases of disagreement.

I believe that this criterion captures an important aspect of the ordinary concept of objectivity I have been discussing.[7] If two thinkers disagree on an objective matter, then that shows that one of them has made a mistake. Presumably it is an objective matter whether I have switched off the lights in the living-room: if I believe I have switched them off and you think I haven't, one of us has made a mistake somewhere. We cannot both be right. Presumably it is not an objective matter whether licorice is tasty: if I believe that licorice is tasty and you believe that it is not, then that does not yet show that one of us has made a mistake. Possibly neither of us has made a mistake. But if it were an objective matter whether licorice is tasty (as some would argue), then our disagreement would surely show that one of us is making a mistake. The criterion fits very well with the ordinary concept of objectivity, and I believe that either side of a given dispute about whether some topic is objective can agree on a criterion of this sort.[8]

Two features of Wright's criterion require brief comment at this point. First, Wright's formulation makes use of the notion of the a priori. A discourse exerts cognitive command just if *it is a priori* that disagreements within it involve cognitive shortcoming. I take Wright to be expressing a fairly obvious point: if a discourse is objective, we know that disagreements involve cognitive failure *without any further investigation about the particular circumstances of the disagreement, or about the disputants in question*. In other words, information on which discourse or topic it is (e.g. discourse about whether the lights have been switched off) and *that* there is disagreement already suffices for knowledge that cognitive shortcoming is involved. If finding out that a cognitive mistake has been made requires further information on the particular disagreements in question, then the discourse is not objective. In particular, if further investigation were to reveal that, as a matter of contingent empirical fact, disagreement in a given discourse is always down to cognitive failure, then that alone would not be sufficient for cognitive command. In §7 below I shall say more about the source of this aprioricity.

Second, Wright's criterion is a criterion for the objectivity of a *discourse*, not of individual questions. Intuitively, this makes a lot of sense. Objectivity is a matter of the *topic* concerned, and presumably discourses are in part individuated by topic. On the other hand, the cognitive command criterion also provides a criterion for the individuation of discourses. A range of contents does not qualify as a discourse, if its fulfilment of, or failure to fulfil, the cognitive command criterion is not uniform. In the following discussion I shall not dwell upon the issue of the individuation of discourses. I shall often speak of cognitive command as a criterion for the objectivity of a single question (i.e. the limiting case of a disourse: one that consists only of a content and its negation).

I have, so far, signalled sympathy with Wright's approach, and in particular with his criterion of cognitive command as a criterion for objectivity. Acceptance of the criterion, however, leads to a profound difficulty. As I shall now show, it seems that minimal assumptions about truth will ensure that any truth-apt discourse will exert cognitive command. If this were correct, the whole strategy of providing a metaphysically neutral notion of truth, i.e. one that allows truth-evaluability not to entail objectivity, would fail. It is in the response to this difficulty where I part company with Wright.

## 5 The problem of a priori error

Minimalists about truth, such as Wright, subscribe to the view that every substitution instance of the schema 'It is true that *p* if and only if *p*' is true. Let us follow Wright in calling this schema the 'equivalence schema' and formalize it as follows:

(ES)   $T(p) \equiv p$

If every instance of (ES) is correct, then so is every instance of the following two schemata:

(ES*)  not-T($p$) ≡ not-$p$
(ES**)  T(not-$p$) ≡ not-$p$

(ES*) is the result of negating both sides of (ES), and (ES**) is a special case of (ES). By transitivity it follows that instances of the following schema (Negation Equivalence) are also correct:

(NE)  not-T($p$) ≡ T(not-$p$)[9]

Finally, negating both sides of (NE) yields

(NE*) not-not-T($p$) ≡ not-T(not-$p$)

This little derivation shows that any disagreement in any discourse that is truth-apt will involve at least one mistake, namely the mistake of believing something not true. For consider any disagreement: one thinker, $A$, believes that $p$, another thinker, $B$, believes that not-$p$. Now suppose that B's belief is true. Then, according to (NE), A's belief is not true. But if it's not the case that A's belief is not true, then, according to (NE**), B's belief is not true. Thus, either way, one of the two believes something that is not true.

Within any discourse that admits a truth predicate, it is a priori that disagreement involves error, namely the plain error of believing something not true. Does this show that all truth-apt discourses also exert cognitive command? Not quite. Strictly speaking, Wright's notion of cognitive command requires that the involvement of *cognitive shortcoming* be a priori guaranteed for any disagreements within the discourse in question. Thus, if belief in something not true were to constitute a cognitive shortcoming, then the argument would have shown that cognitive command is exerted by every truth-apt discourse. In other words, the criterion would be trivially fulfilled, and thus useless as a crucial mark of realism or objectivity.[10]

## 6 Does plain error amount to cognitive failure?

Wright's response is to deny that belief in something not true amounts to cognitive shortcoming (1992: 148–57). This, of course, raises the question what exactly cognitive shortcoming is. Truth, as Wright himself takes great care to argue (1992: 15–18), is a norm. If we take this norm to require that one believe only what is true, then belief in something not true must amount to shortcoming of *some* kind. Why not a cognitive kind? Is truth not a cognitive norm? It would seem that Wright owes us an account of the notion of cognitive shortcoming that shows that mere failure to comply with the truth norm does not yet amount to cognitive failure. Wright, however, turns the tables. He claims that it is those who want to claim that mere violation of the truth norm qualifies as cognitive shortcoming who owe a proof (1992: 149). Taking discourse about what is funny as an example, he argues that it would be extremely difficult to defend the view that disagreements within this discourse must involve cognitive failure on the part of one of the disputants. Such a defence, he suggests, would need to invoke 'the idea of a *sui generis* cognitive sense or faculty of comedy, sensitive to *sui generis* states of affairs' (1992: 150). But such an idea would presumably be very difficult to sustain.

I do not wish to decide the issue of which side owes a proof here. But I do want to argue that Wright's interpretation of the notion of cognitive failure throws doubt on the usefulness of cognitive command as a criterion for objectivity. I have two arguments to this effect. The first casts doubt on its status as a criterion. The second shows that Wright cannot avoid the problem of a priori error, even if he claims that untrue belief may not amount to a cognitive shortcoming.

The first argument. The point of a criterion for something is to provide a way of recognizing that thing. Normally, a criterion is a condition the fulfilment of which reliably indicates that for which it is a criterion. A criterion that deserves the name, however, will not only be a condition that reliably indicates the presence of that for which it is a criterion, it will also be a condition the fulfilment of which is *more easily* recognized than that for which it is to serve as a criterion. The colour of litmus paper, for example, is a good criterion for the acidity of a liquid. That's because the colour not only reliably indicates acidity, but is also easier to recognize than the acidity of the liquid. By contrast, the concentration of H+ ions (i.e. positively charged hydrogen ions) is not a good criterion for acidity, because recognizing H+ concentration isn't any easier than recognizing acidity, even though H+ concentration reliably indicates acidity.

Another way in which a criterion may fail to be a good criterion is by requiring another criterion for its application, where this other criterion would provide more direct evidence. An example is the noise of raindrops on the roof as a criterion for rain. This may well be a good criterion in some situations. But consider this situation: my upstairs neighbour often waters the plants on his roof-garden, when it's not raining. The noise produced by the watering is indistinguishable from the noise caused by raindrops. Being offered the noise as a criterion for rain, I object that the same noise is produced by the watering. In reply, I am told that it is only the noise of *raindrops* that was to be the criterion. I continue to be sceptical and ask how I can know that a given noise is the noise of raindrops and not the noise of my neighbour watering his plants. The reply to this is: 'Well, just look out of the window, and check whether it's raining'. Clearly, the noise of raindrops is not a good criterion for rain in this situation, even though the noise of *rain* drops is a reliable indicator of rain. The problem is that in order to be able to apply the criterion, I need a criterion for the noise being caused by raindrops rather than by my neighbour. If this second criterion is whether it looks like it is raining outside my window, then I might as well have used that criterion as a criterion for rain in the first place.

I believe that Wright's criterion of cognitive command, as a criterion for objectivity, suffers from an analogous defect. We are to check whether it is a priori that disagreements within a given discourse involve cognitive shortcoming. If so, we know that the discourse is objective. An objector remarks that it is a priori in any discourse that disagreements involve untrue belief, and wonders how we know whether untrue belief amounts to cognitive shortcoming in any given case. Wright's reply is, in effect, that we ought to find out whether the processes by which we acquire beliefs of the sort in question are properly regarded as cognitive.

The problem is that applying the cognitive command criterion requires application of a further criterion, namely some criterion for the cognitiveness of the belief-producing faculties of a discourse. But if we were already in possession of this further criterion, then we would not need a criterion of cognitive command for objectivity. Rather, we would say that a discourse is objective if and only if its associated belief-forming faculty is cognitive. In fact, we don't know what it is for a faculty to be cognitive, nor do we have any good idea what these faculties are in the interesting cases. Non-cognitivists and realists in ethics, for example, notoriously disagree on just this: whether there is a cognitive faculty for producing moral judgements. Thus introducing the cognitive command criterion does not help in any of Wright's realism/anti-realism debates, nor does it help us in coming to grips with the notion of objectivity: *either* we have an independent criterion for the cognitiveness of a belief-forming faculty, in which case cognitive command is useless because we could define objectivity directly in terms of the notion of the cognitiveness of a faculty, *or* we do not have an independent criterion for the cognitiveness of a faculty, in which case cognitive command is useless, because it cannot be applied without having such an independent criterion for cognitiveness.

Before I present the second argument, a little recapitulation. My aim is to find a suitable account of objectivity in order to find out what a notion of truth must be like if every content is to be truth-evaluable without this having controversial objectivistic consequences. We want to be able to say that the contents of all sentences are truth-evaluable without thereby pre-deciding issues such as the objectivity of matters of taste or the objectivity of probability. One candidate for such an account is Crispin Wright's criterion of cognitive command. It could be shown, however, that there is a difficulty with this criterion if plain error (untrue belief) is to count as cognitive shortcoming. For in that case, any truth-apt discourse can be shown to exert cognitive command. Wright's response to this difficulty was to insist that untrue belief may not amount to cognitive failure. My first argument showed that Wright's response renders cognitive command useless as a criterion for distinguishing between objective and non-objective topics. My second argument is now going to show that Wright's response to the problem of a priori error does not really solve that problem.

By any standards, truth is a norm governing belief (and assertion). To believe (or assert) something not true is to commit a mistake of *some* kind. A purported notion of truth that doesn't meet this constraint is not a notion of truth at all.[11] Now, since untrue belief ('error', for short) is a mistake, the two schemata (NE) and (NE\*) derivable from the equivalence schema show that any disagreement on any topic must involve a mistake on the part of at least one of the disagreeing parties. But someone who denies the objectivity of some area of discourse, aesthetic discourse, say, will insist that there can be aesthetic disagreement without anyone making any kind of mistake. If I say that a picture is beautiful and you say it is not, it doesn't yet follow that one of us is making a mistake, or so the aesthetic anti-realist will claim. He or she will not be appeased by Wright's assurances that even though a mistake is involved, no *cognitive* mistake need be involved. Rather, the aesthetic anti-realist will draw the conclusion that aesthetic judgements are not evaluable in terms of truth.

Might Wright not say that untrue belief isn't really a very serious mistake? No, for that would conflict with the role of truth as a norm. In what sense could truth be a norm if believing something untrue were not really a very serious mistake?

One could put the point by saying that Wright faces a dilemma. If he claims that truth is a norm (as he rightly does), then his project of providing a metaphysically neutral notion of truth fails. For a notion of truth that entails that disagreements are always the symptom of someone's being mistaken is not metaphysically neutral. If, on the other hand, he plays down the seriousness of the mistake one makes when believing something untrue, then it looks as if his notion of truth is not really a norm.[12]

The difficulty raised by (NE) and (NE\*) is profound. It suggests that no truth notion could be metaphysically neutral, because mere truth-aptness will always ensure that disagreement is down to someone's error. In the next section we shall see that this suggestion is wrong. There is a truth notion that avoids the connection between truth-evaluability and objectivity.

## 7 A new criterion for objectivity

In the last section I argued that the problem of a priori error cannot be circumvented by stipulating that cognitive command requires more than it being a priori that disagreement guarantees untrue belief. The second argument in particular showed that if cognitive command requires more than a priori untrue belief, then the compatibility of truth-aptness with lack of cognitive command will not yet suffice to make truth-aptness compatible with non-objectivity in the appropriate sense. The possibility of a discourse that is truth-apt yet lacks cognitive command will not be enough to free the assumption of global truth-aptness from unwanted objectivistic consequences. For even a discourse that lacks cognitive command in Wright's sense will be objective in the sense that any disagreement within the discourse is necessarily the symptom of one party making a mistake.

Nevertheless I believe that the basic idea of the cognitive command criterion is useful. There is a difference between those topics on which we think we may legitimately disagree and those where mere disagreement shows that someone has made a mistake. This is manifest in our discursive behaviour. Suppose you and I have just departed on a journey and I assert that the lights are still on in the living-room while you deny it. It would be absurd to suppose that neither of us has made a mistake, and that we are therefore both right. Only one of us *can* be right, and we know that. It is also clear that if the lights are still on, then we ought to turn back to switch them off. So we will try to find out who is right and who is in error and perhaps compare the reasons we each have for our belief, i.e. argue about the matter. The fact that we do argue shows that we take it for granted that only one of us can be right. Now suppose that we are in a restaurant and deliberate about what to order, planning to share a meal. I assert that haggis is tasty, you deny it. In this situation we will not necessarily take it for granted that one of us must be in error. Perhaps we will assume that neither of us is in error about the taste of haggis. In this case, we will not argue about it, at least not about the question of whether haggis is tasty, though we might argue about what to order, whose preference ought to be taken into account, etc. Thus, in this case we do not take it for granted that only one of us can be right. I think that one would not misdescribe this difference by saying that we take it to be an objective matter whether the lights are off, while we take it to be non-objective whether haggis is tasty.

Are there any stronger reasons for adopting the impossibility of blameless disagreement as our mark of objectivity? One problem that makes it hard to argue about this matter is the fact that 'objectivity' is used in so many different senses. I have already discerned ontological independence and public accessibility as senses of objectivity I am not going to discuss. I indicated that the relevant sense of objectivity is one according to which objective propositions represent an independent reality. This, however, is not a helpful account of objectivity as there is no way of ascertaining directly whether a proposition represents independent reality. Moreover, the distinction we pre-theoretically draw between those areas where disagreements indicate error and those where they don't seems to me to be closely aligned with the philosophical, or proto-philosophical, distinction between those areas where the judgements of all of us answer to the same reality and those where they don't. Thus it seems to me legitimate to call a proposition 'objective' just if disagreement about it indicates a mistake.

In addition, there are systematic reasons to operate with this notion of objectivity *in the current investigation*. The problem under investigation is the prima facie incompatibility of truth-aptness with non-objectivity. Thus the notion of objectivity we operate with ought to be one that is prima facie entailed by truth-aptness. The problem of a priori error showed that this is indeed the case: given minimal constraints on truth it seemed possible to show that blameless disagreement on a truth-apt proposition is impossible. But the problematic areas under discussion (probabilistic and evaluative propositions) are precisely the ones where, at least arguably, blameless disagreement *is* possible. Conversely, if it can be shown, for a given area of discourse, that blameless disagreement is not possible, then it is hard to see why that area should not be truth-apt.

Now, how do we know that a proposition is objective? We seem to know this a priori, that is, we need to know only what a disagreement is about, and that is enough for us to know whether error must be involved. But what is the source of this knowledge? Wright's comparison with representational devices is instructive here. Why do we know a priori that if two representational devices, two cameras say, yield conflicting representations, then one of them must be malfunctioning? It's because we know what the function of a camera is. It is part of the concept of a camera that well-functioning cameras cannot yield diverging outputs. Someone professing to know a priori that two cameras with conflicting outputs are not both functioning properly is not boasting to have magical powers. Rather, he or she thereby shows a good grasp of the function of a camera. Cameras are designed to serve a certain purpose, to fulfil a certain function. That's why we can know a priori what it is for a camera to function properly. The same goes for our a priori knowledge that disagreements on certain topics must be the result of some mistake. For this is part of the function of certain beliefs, and of their linguistic expression. It is part of the function of beliefs on whether the lights are on that if two such beliefs are contradictory, a mistake has occurred. It is not part of the function of judgements of taste that divergences are the symptom of some mistake.

In fact, these functional constraints on beliefs arise within a complex interpersonal functional system of belief acquisition, reasoning, communicative belief expression and action. Let me sketch this out a little bit. Some beliefs, such as beliefs on matters of taste, have an intrinsically motivational role. Constraints concerning the acquisition of such beliefs are therefore different from those governing beliefs that are motivationally inert. Part of these constraints governing belief acquisition are constraints on communicative processes. Thus, the status of a communicative situation in which two speakers assert contradictory contents[13] will vary depending on the subject matter, because beliefs on different subject matters may have fundamentally different functions. In some subject areas, two contradictory assertions by different speakers will therefore count as the symptom of error and warrant discussion or further investigation. In other areas, contradiction among different thinkers will not count as a sign of error. Thinking and communicating agents know these differences in subject matter just in virtue of being competent thinking and communicating agents.

I have offered no adequate support for this view of judgement and communication, nor have I described it in much detail. Chapter 6 will make up for this deficiency. For present purposes, it suffices merely to point at the sort of theory that grounds the claim that there are a priori differences in the status of disagreements. The a priori character of these differences in status stems from certain functional constraints on belief formation and communication. Some evidence for this is provided by the manifestation of these differences in our communicative practices.

On this theoretical background, I now want to put forward a new criterion of objectivity, one that leaves no room for Wright's response to the problem of a priori error. For any $p$: it is an objective matter whether $p$, just if:

(CO)  For all thinkers $A$ and $B$: it is a priori that if $A$ believes that $p$ and $B$ believes that not-$p$ then either $A$ has made a mistake or $B$ has made a mistake.

There are clear cases of contents that are objective and also clear cases of contents that are not objective according to this criterion. For instance, my earlier example of the content that the lights are off is a clear case of an objective content. My example of the content that licorice is tasty is a clear case of a content that is not objective (or so I hope). There are also cases that are not so clear-cut, such as moral contents. It is not immediately clear, I think, whether of two thinkers who contradict each other on a moral point, one must have made a mistake. Similarly, it is not immediately clear whether it is a priori that disagreements on matters of probability must involve a mistake. The fact that cases such as these appear at first unclear should not discourage us. On the contrary, it reflects the notorious controversies that arise over the objectivity of moral issues and of probability. If these areas were to come out as more objective than matters of taste yet less than fully objective, this would be a desirable result. In Chapter 6, §6, I will show how (CO) can be refined in order to allow a gradual, multidimensional classification of topics into more or less objective ones.[14] For the moment, however, I shall operate with (CO) in examining what a notion of truth must be like if it is to leave room for truth-apt contents that are nevertheless not objective. This is the task of the next section.

## 8 How to solve the problem of a priori error

We now have a clearly defined aim: a notion of truth that is such that the mere truth-evaluability of a content does not yet guarantee its objectivity in the sense of (CO). On the other hand, we are now back to where we were in §5 of this chapter: the problem of a priori error. The new criterion for objectivity doesn't yet bring us any closer to solving this problem. On the contrary, it momentarily intensifies the difficulty in that it precludes the move that allowed Wright seemingly to evade the problem of a priori error. The problem is clear-cut: if we are to accept each instance of (ES):

(ES)  $T(p) \equiv p$

and consequently each instance of (NE):

(NE)  not-$T(p) \equiv T(\text{not-}p)$

then it seems inevitable that of any two thinkers $A$ and $B$ who believe contradictory contents, one must have made the mistake of believing something untrue.

There thus seems to be no room for contents that are candidates for truth but are nevertheless not objective according to (CO).

Only a radical manoeuvre can make room for contents that lack objectivity, the manoeuvre of making the evaluation of contents as true or false *relative* to something. Suppose that contents are evaluated as true or false only in relation to entities of a certain sort—entities that I will call 'perspectives'. Suppose further that thinkers possess perspectives at times, and that truth is a norm in the sense that one ought to believe only what is true in relation to one's own perspective. Then we can avoid the problem of a priori error. When thinker $A$ believes that $p$ and thinker $B$ believes that not-$p$, it is now possible that neither $A$ nor $B$ has made a mistake, for $p$ might be true in $A$'s perspective and not true in $B$'s perspective.

I am well aware that many readers will find the idea of relative truth not worth serious consideration. If relativism about truth is the only way in which it can be denied that truth-evaluability entails objectivity, then doesn't that amount to a *reductio ad absurdum* of the idea of truth without objectivity? Doesn't that show that we must look elsewhere for a solution to the problem of excess objectivity? The next three chapters are devoted to the exploration and criticism of the two alternative ways of solving the problem of objectivity mentioned in §2 of this chapter. But before I go on, I'll begin work on the difficult PR job of promoting the view that relativizing truth is a legitimate, well-motivated move.

First, I would like to make a methodological point. My reasons for advocating a form of relativism can be put into an argument of roughly the following form. At the beginning stands the realization that the following set of attractive assumptions yields a contradiction:

(A1)   The content of each sentence is evaluable in terms of truth.
(A2)   For all $p$: if it is true that $p$, then it is not true that not-$p$; and if it is true that not-$p$, then it is not true that $p$. ((NE), (NE*))
(A3)   Believing something that is not true constitutes a mistake.
(A4)   Some topics are non-objective; i.e. for some $p$, $A$, $B$: it is possible that A believes that $p$, B believes that not-$p$, but neither $A$ nor $B$ has made a mistake.

Each assumption can be independently motivated. (A1) is motivated by my considerations in Chapter 1 and §1 of this chapter. (A2) follows from a minimal assumption about truth, namely the assumption that each instance of (ES) is correct. (A3) follows from an equally minimal assumption about truth, namely that it is a normative notion. (A4) is not only intuitively compelling, but, moreover, denying it would show many of our cognitive practices to be fundamentally misguided. Nevertheless, (A1)–(A3) jointly entail the negation of (A4).

It seems as if one of the assumptions must go. But a more subtle move is available. Instead of denying one of the attractive assumptions, we can introduce a conceptual refinement: contents get evaluated as true or false only in relation to a perspective. Short of denying any of the assumptions, we need only to reinterpret them in the light of the conceptual refinement. In particular, throughout (A2) 'true' needs to be understood as making reference to the same perspective:

(A2*) For all contents $p$ and all perspectives $s$: if it is true in relation to $s$ that $p$, then it is not true in relation to $s$ that not-$p$; and if it is true in relation to $s$ that not-$p$, then it is not true in relation to $s$ that $p$.

(A3) requires reinterpretation of the normativity of truth. This is where the idea of perspective possession comes into play: thinkers *possess* perspectives, so the prohibition of untrue belief gets restricted to beliefs that aren't true in the thinker's own perspective:

(A3*) Believing something that is not true according to one's own perspective constitutes a mistake.

Under the conceptual refinement, the assumptions are no longer incompatible. Two thinkers can have contradictory beliefs without it being a priori that one of them has made a mistake. For as long as their perspectives are distinct, a disagreement between them may be blameless. The motivation for the refinement is that it allows us to save versions of all four assumptions.

Secondly, in order to win sympathy for this form of argument, I want to present an analogous argument that I believe will be acceptable to all readers. This is the argument for the relativity to times of temporary features. Some Presocratic philosophers saw a great problem in the fact that the occurrence of change requires that the same thing possess and lack a certain feature. Something's turning pink, for example, requires that the same thing is and is not pink—a contradiction. Unlike Parmenides, who (seems to have) concluded that change is impossible, we tend to make the less radical Aristotelian move: the same thing is not pink at one time and pink at a later time. No contradiction is required. Whether something is pink is relative to times.[15] In fact, the Aristotelian point of view is now taken for granted—so much so that we find it difficult to understand how Presocratic philosophers could have been puzzled by the problem.

Why do we go along with Aristotle on this matter and dismiss Parmenides' view as absurd? In order to save the phenomena: we want to save the possibility of change and the impossibility of true contradictions. So we make the relativistic concession that features such as pinkness are relative to times. Relativity saves the common-sense assumption that change is possible.

I did not bring up the example of relativism about temporary features because I regard it as a particularly interesting or controversial form of relativism. Rather, I wanted to win the reader's agreement that the kind of reasoning by which I propose to arrive at a form of relativism about truth is a perfectly legitimate one: we motivate a form of relativism by the fact that this form of relativism allows us to save some common-sense assumptions. Similarly, my earlier argument used the fact that the relativization of truth to standards can save assumptions (A1)–(A4).

Of course, these arguments do not prove conclusively that truth is relative or that the possession of temporary features is relative to times. Nor do these arguments suffice to justify, by themselves, the conceptual change they are used to motivate. What is needed in addition is that the new conceptual framework be theoretically fruitful. Relativism about temporary features has already proved, over more than two thousand years, that it is a fruitful framework. Relativism about truth, however, is still associated with a highly unsuccessful paradigm, namely Protagorean relativism, which is widely (and in my view rightly) regarded as absurd and unviable. Protagorean relativism has highly counter-intuitive consequences, for example the consequence that error is impossible.[16] This consequence alone is enough to render this form of relativism a theoretical dead end. But Protagorean relativism is not the only form of relativism about truth. The form I advocate does leave room for error. I therefore ask the reader not to dismiss relativism about truth out of hand.

In this section, I have given a preliminary sketch of the relativistic position I am going to develop in Chapters 5–7. In Chapter 6, for example, I present a more detailed theory of perspectives and perspective possession to back up my proposed form of relativism. Certain restrictions on perspective possession ensure that relativity to perspectives not only makes room for truth-evaluable contents without objectivity but also leaves room for contents that *are* objective according to (CO). Before setting out my own account, however, I need to address rival solutions.

# Chapter 3

# Revisionism

In the last chapter, I set out the problem of excess objectivity and began to unfold my own strategy for solving it: denying that truth-evaluability entails objectivity. I argued that this strategy ultimately leads to relativism about truth. This is likely to provoke the response that we'd better look for a different solution. If a view leads to relativism, isn't that tantamount to reducing it to absurdity? An important part of my case for relativism is therefore to demonstrate that no other solutions are available, or at least that other solutions are less attractive. In §2 of Chapter 2 I mentioned two other ways of solving the problem of excess objectivity: revisionism and expressivism. In this chapter I present my case against revisionism. In the next, I shall discuss expressivism.

## 1 How to revise a content ascription

The problem of excess objectivity arises from three assumptions: that truth-evaluability entails objectivity, that all contents are truth-evaluable and that some contents are not objective (see Chapter 2, §2). In the case of a sentence like

(1)    Licorice is tasty.

the problem is that we want to say, on the one hand, that its content is truth-evaluable and therefore objective, but, on the other hand, find fault with the consequence that it is an objective matter whether licorice is tasty. A common response is to deny that (1) expresses the content that licorice is tasty. If (1) had a different content, perhaps the content that its utterer likes licorice, no problem would arise. Even if it is non-objective whether licorice is tasty, it may well be objective whether someone likes licorice. Generally, whenever a sentence appears to have a content that is not objective, we must look again and revise our content ascription. In other words, since contents are truth-evaluable and objective, there are no non-objective contents. If our content ascription suggests otherwise, it is therefore the content ascription that must be revised.

However, the decision as to the content a theory of meaning assigns to a given sentence (utterance of a sentence) is not arbitrary but heavily constrained in ways outlined in Chapter 1. A sentence's content is given by the right-hand side

of its interpretive T-sentence, and this T-sentence will be generated by the semantic axioms of the theory. It therefore seems that a different content ascription
can be achieved only by a change in the semantic axioms, and this change will in
turn cause further changes in the contents ascribed to other sentences. It looks as
if it would be difficult to find acceptable changes in the semantic axioms,
changes that would generate exactly the revised content ascriptions we need
from the point of view of the problem of excess objectivity. How could the
axioms for 'licorice', 'is' and 'tasty' be changed in such a way as to yield 'an
utterance of "Licorice is tasty." can be properly used to assert that the utterer
himself likes licorice'? Any general change in the basic axioms will have further
unwanted changes in content ascription as a consequence.

I can see two ways of getting around this problem—but both eventually face
the same objection. Suppose we want to achieve that the theory ultimately assigns to utterances of (1) the same content as to utterances of 'I find licorice
tasty.'. First, one could locally revise the semantic axiom for 'is tasty' in such a
way that '... is tasty' in effect receives the same interpretation as 'I find ...
tasty'. On this view, the apparently simple predicate '... is tasty', would function
as if it were an abbreviation for the semantically complex expression 'I find ...
tasty'.

Second, one could invoke the extra-semantic phenomenon of ellipsis. Consider a typical example of ellipsis: I utter the incomplete sentence 'Not always.'.
If this follows the question 'Do you pay your phone bill on time?', then my utterance of the incomplete 'Not always.' should be interpreted as would have
been an utterance of the complete 'I do not always pay my phone bill on time.'.
The extra-semantic version of revisionism invokes the same phenomenon. On
this view, 'Licorice is tasty.' is an incomplete sentence in need of completion.
The theory of content does not generate a T-sentence for (1), but only for 'I find
licorice tasty.'. Since there is no appropriate T-sentence for (1), speakers and
hearers automatically interpret utterances of it as if they were utterances of some
contextually appropriate complete sentence such as 'I find licorice tasty.'.

The extra-semantic solution might not work as easily for every content revision the revisionist might envisage. Consider, for example, interpreting an utterance of (1) as having the content that the utterer himself or herself likes licorice, where the expression 'is tasty' gets lost completely. The semantic solution
might have its own disadvantages to do with its consequences for language
processing. But whichever of the two routes the revisionist takes, the outcome is
the same at the level of ascribing contents to utterances. My objections to revisionism will be aimed at that level, so I will ignore the differences between the
two routes.[1]

## 2 The attraction of revisionism

Once the revisionist has achieved his or her revision of content ascription, he or
she seems to have an attractive solution to the problem of excess objectivity. In

effect, the revisionist claims that there are no non-objective contents. But he or she does so without having to declare aesthetic and other controversial matters to be objective. For he or she denies that there are genuine sentence contents whose truth would require there to be objective probabilities, aesthetic values, etc. What *appear* to be utterances expressing such contents are really utterances expressing different contents.

But having decided *that* he or she wants to revise away problematic contents, the revisionist still needs to make up his or her mind on *which* revised contents to assign. In my current example, problematic sentences are to be interpreted as making implicit indexical reference to the speaker. Thus I proposed that (1) should be interpreted as

(1*)  I find licorice tasty.

A similar suggestion would be 'Licorice is tasty on my standard of taste.'. In the area of probability, the revisionist might propose that probability-ascribing sentences should be interpreted as making implicit reference to the speaker's evidence. Thus a sentence of the form

(2)  It is probable that $p$.

might get reinterpreted as

(2*)  Given my evidence, it is probable that $p$.

In the area of sentences attributing moral value, the implicit reference might be to the speaker's set of moral principles or standards. Thus a sentence of the form

(3)  $X$ is morally good.

would be reinterpreted as

(3*)  According to my principles, $X$ is morally good.

Other kinds of revision, even non-indexical ones, are possible. But let us suppose for the time being that these are the revisions proposed by the revisionist. Then the revisionist proposal is in effect that every apparent assertion of a moral, aesthetic or probabilistic content is in fact an autobiographical assertion about the speaker's moral, aesthetic or probabilistic evaluations.

At this point, it is worth explaining how revisionism differs from expressivism. According to expressivism about matters of taste, a sentence like 'Licorice is tasty.' serves not to assert that licorice is tasty, but rather to express one's attitude towards licorice. Expressing such an atitude is not a kind of assertion, but a *sui generis* communicative act. By contrast, the revisionist I have described holds that the sentence is indeed asssertoric and serves to assert that the speaker himself or herself finds licorice tasty. Thus, in a way, the revisionist could also be viewed as saying that one expresses one's attitude towards licorice by uttering

'Licorice is tasty.' But the revisionist, unlike the expressivist, believes that this is done via asserting the autobiographical content that the speaker himself or herself finds licorice tasty.

The distinction between asserting that one has an attitude and merely expressing it without asserting that one has it may seem spurious. But it is an important distinction that needs to be made even independently of the current problem. If someone utters '$p$.' and thereby asserts that $p$, he or she is often thereby also expressing his or her belief that $p$. But there is a clear difference between thus expressing one's belief that $p$ and asserting that one believes that $p$. For in order to assert that one believes that $p$, one would normally need to use the sentence 'I believe that $p$.'. Such an assertion might then (if sincere) express one's belief that one believes that $p$. But it may or may not be an expression of one's belief that $p$.

A further difference between the revisionist and the expressivist is that the revisionist, unlike the expressivist, holds that the sentence 'Licorice is tasty.' is either incomplete (on the extra-semantic route) or an abbreviation for a more complex sentence (on the semantic route). In either case, the sentence is dispensable, as there are alternative ways of communicating what can be communicated by it. According to the expressivist, however, the sentence has a meaning in its own right, one that involves a special communicative or illocutionary force and a special content that is not truth-evaluable, and there may be no alternative sentence with which to communicate what can be communicated by it.

## 3  Objection to revisionism: denial

However intuitively appealing revisionism may seem as a solution to the problem of excess objectivity, it is also fraught with intuitive difficulties. What one properly communicates by uttering (1) is clearly different from what one properly communicates uttering (1*). There is an intuitive difference between saying that licorice is tasty and saying that one finds it tasty. One difference is that in doing the latter, one is talking about oneself, making an autobiographical remark, something one clearly doesn't do when one is doing the former. Intuitively, uttering (1) does not involve making reference to oneself.

In this form, however, the objection is in danger of begging the question. The revisionist believes that the problem of excess objectivity shows that a sentence such as (1) cannot have the content it intuitively appears to have. Thus to insist that (1) expresses the content it intuitively appears to have is simply to ignore the revisionist's reasoning. To make the objection stick, we thus need some further evidence that (1) and (1*) differ in meaning (or, more precisely, are properly used to perform different communicative acts).

Such further evidence can be found, for (1) and (1*) do not behave as one would expect them to behave if the revisionist's hypothesis were correct. For the revisionist, (1) functions in effect like an indexical sentence. The content one asserts by uttering it varies with the context of the utterance, in particular with the utterer. Now, consider the following plausible view about denial. One can deny what someone has said by retorting, for example, 'No, you are wrong there.' or 'What you have said isn't true.' or the like. Plausibly, such a denial should be interpreted as equivalent to an assertion of the negation of what was originally asserted. Thus if you say 'It's a little baby boy.' and I retort 'No, you are wrong there.', then I should be interpreted as having asserted that it is not a little baby boy, i.e. the negation of the content you asserted. In particular, if the sentence originally uttered is indexical, any denial should be interpreted as an assertion of the negation of the content asserted by the original utterer, and *not* of the content the denier would have expressed had he or she uttered the same sentence. For example, if I say 'I make the best pancakes in the western hemisphere.' and you retort 'No, you are wrong there.' then your denial is equivalent to you uttering '*You* do not make the best pancakes in the western hemisphere.'. Your denial does *not* amount to you saying about yourself that you do not make the best pancakes in the western hemisphere. The original assertion as well as the denial are about the same person, namely me.

Now apply this theory of denial to (1) and (1*). According to the revisionist, utterances of (1) and (1*) count as assertions of the same content. Thus according to our theory of denial, utterances of (1) and (1*) should behave in the same way under denial. But this patently is not the case. Compare the following two exchanges:

(D1)   A: 'Licorice is tasty.'
       B: 'No, you are wrong there.'
       ($\approx$ 'No, licorice is not tasty.')

(D2)   A: 'I find licorice tasty.'
       B: 'No, you are wrong there.'
       ($\approx$ 'No, you do not find licorice tasty.')

Our theory of denial together with the revisionist hypothesis leads us to expect that B's denial in (D1) should be interpreted in exactly the same way as B's denial in (D2). It seems undeniably clear, however, that B's denial in (D2) is equivalent to 'No, you do not find licorice tasty.', while B's denial in (D1) is equivalent to 'No, licorice is not tasty.'—which according to the revisionist is again equivalent to either 'No, I find licorice not tasty.' or 'No, I do not find licorice tasty.'.[2]

This objection to the revisionist proposal is not yet decisive. The revisionist might claim that B's denial in (D2), and denials of statements of taste generally, are an exception to my proposed theory of denial. B's utterance of 'No, you are wrong there.' should be interpreted as 'No, I do not find licorice tasty.'. Perhaps this is dictated by a special rule about the denial of statements on matters of taste (e.g. 'interpret a denial as an assertion of the negation of the content the *denier* would have asserted had he or she uttered the sentence type originally uttered'). Under this rule, the denials in (D1) and (D2) would again receive identical interpretations, in accordance with the revisionist thesis that (1) and (1\*) have identical communicative functions.

But such a manoeuvre would be highly unattractive. The revisionist would have to deny that the correct interpretation of B's utterance in (D1) is different from the correct interpretation of B's utterance in (D2). This clearly runs against the intuitions of speakers of English. Moreover, the move involves a separate treatment of the denial of indexical utterances when matters of taste are involved. Normally denials of indexical utterances function differently. In order to appreciate the absurdity of the special rule in non-taste cases, consider a situation where I say 'Hello, my name is Max.', addressing Paul. It would be very strange indeed if Paul were to answer 'No, it's Paul.'—unless he wanted to accuse me of pretending to be someone I am not. Thus, on the revisionist proposal, denial would no longer be a uniform phenomenon, contrary to all appearances.[3]

I conclude that the current revisionist proposal of viewing (1) as elliptical, or an abbreviation, for (1\*) is not viable. The same objection can be applied, *mutatis mutandis*, to the envisaged revisions for probabilistic and moral sentences. Just replace A's utterance of (1) and (1\*) in (D1 and D2) by (2) and (2\*) or (3) and (3\*). B's denials in (D1) and (D2) will again receive diverging interpretations.

## 4 Revising revisionism

The objection of §3 has shown that someone who utters (1), (2) or (3) is not making implicit indexical reference to himself or herself. Such an utterance may reveal something about its utterer, but the utterer is not thereby *saying* anything about himself or herself—just as someone who says 'Cloning humans is possible.' might, under certain circumstances, be revealing his or her knowledge, even though he or she isn't talking *about* his or her own knowledge.

This, however, is not yet the end of revisionism. My objection turned on the assumption that the revisionist treats utterances of problematic sentences as involving implicit indexical reference to the speaker himself or herself. More to the point, the indexical elements my revisionist read into utterances of problematic sentences were such that their reference varied from one speaker to another and thus from an original speaker to someone denying what the original speaker asserted. For example, the reference of 'I' in (1\*) is the speaker, and the reference of 'my moral principles' is the moral principles of the speaker. If the indexical (or even non-indexical) element the revisionist incorporates into his or her revision were such that its reference did not vary between the original utterer and the denier, then the objection would not get started.

Can the revisionist revise his or her position in such a way as to avoid my objection? Let me examine some options. Consider first the taste case. One suggestion as to the content expressed by (1) might be the content that licorice is tasty on the standards prevailing at the time and place of utterance, so that (1) comes out as elliptical (or an abbreviation) for

(1**)   Licorice is tasty according to the standard of taste that prevails here and now.

At first sight, this proposed new content assignment avoids my objection: under normal conditions, i.e. when asserter and denier are located at the same time and place, there will be no discrepancy between denials of (1**) and denials of (1).

There are two problems, however. First, the proposal presupposes that there is such a thing as standards of taste that (objectively) prevail at times and places. To the extent to which the objection can be avoided because the asserter and the denier are normally at the same time and place, taste is assumed to be objective. This defeats the purpose of defending the conceptual possibility of taste being non-objective. If we are prepared to make that concession, we might almost concede the objectivity of taste outright, and in that case no problem of excess objectivity arises in the first place. Second, the revised proposal doesn't avoid my objection in all cases. The problem with denial recurs whenever the asserter and the denier fail to share the same time and place (they might be communicating in some mediated way, e.g. by telephone or e-mail). The two problems interact as a catch-22 trap: if the revisionist reduces the number of cases where the denial problem arises, he or she increases the amount of objectivity simultaneously. If he or she diminishes objectivity by allowing more situations where standards of taste vary, he or she increases the number of cases where the denial problem arises.

The same goes for revised revisionist proposals in the area of probabilistic sentences. If the proposal is, say, that (2) serves to assert the content that on the best available evidence it is probable that $p$, i.e. that (2) is equivalent to

(2**)   According to the best available evidence, it is probable that $p$.

then the revisionist comes dangerously close to an objectivist view of probability. But the aim of the whole exercise was to find a way of avoiding excessive objectivist consequences of global truth-evaluability.

The only area where the new revisionist strategy cuts any ice at all is morality. Consider the view that (3) is equivalent to

(3**)   According to my culture, $X$ is morally good.

This view avoids the denial problem in those cases where the asserter and the denier belong to the same culture. Unlike (1**) and (2**), (3**) is not a complete non-starter. This proposal reflects a view that is at least worth some consideration, namely cultural relativism about moral values. However, it still faces the problem of denial in cases where the asserter and the denier belong to different cultures. Moreover, it is *only* acceptable to cultural relativists about moral values. It will not appeal to those who want to combine global truth-evaluability with lack of moral objectivity even within the same culture.

Finally, I need to consider the possibility of regarding problematic sentences as elliptical for (or an abbreviation of) sentences that aren't indexical at all. Any such suggestion would avoid the problem with denial altogether. But no such suggestion can avoid a fairly strong form of objectivism in the area concerned. Consider just one non-indexical proposal: (1) is elliptical for (an abbreviation of) (1***):

(1***)   On the standard of Paul Bocuse, licorice is tasty.

If this proposal were correct, it would remove the problem. But, again, it would throw the baby out with the bathwater, for the proposal is in effect a species of objectivism: in matters of taste, it claims, Paul Bocuse is the objective standard. Of course, the proposal is also highly implausible. But it serves to illustrate that it is impossible to remove the denial problem. Suppose we found a plausible physiological reduction of the concept of tastiness and translated it into a non-indexical improvement of (1*). The resulting view would unavoidably be objectivist and no problem of excess objectivity would arise in the first place.

I conclude that revisionism fails as a way of solving the problem of excess objectivity.

# Chapter 4

# Expressivism

The problem of excess objectivity arose from the assumption that all contents are truth-evaluable and therefore objective, together with the view that not all sentences concern objective matters. Revisionism is the view that we ought to reassign contents in such a way that there are no longer any contents that may be argued to be non-objective. In the last chapter I presented my case against revisionism. I now turn to the second strategy for avoiding the problem (see Chapter 2, §2): the strategy of denying that all contents are truth-evaluable and providing a non-truth-conditional account of the meaning of those sentences whose contents are claimed not to be truth-evaluable. I call this view 'expressivism'.

Expressivism is widely known as a thesis that semantically complements non-cognitivism in meta-ethics: if there are no moral facts to be known, if moral judgements or statements are not capable of being true or false, then the meaning of morally evaluative sentences cannot centrally consist in their having a truth-evaluable content. Non-cognitivists are therefore called upon to offer an alternative theory of meaning for moral sentences. What they frequently offer is expressivism, the view that the meaning of moral sentences must be analysed in terms of special kinds of illocutionary act, for the performance of which these sentences serve. To utter the sentence 'Gambling is bad.', for example, is not to assert the truth-evaluable content that gambling is bad (there is no such truth-evaluable item), but rather to condemn gambling and thereby to *express* one's moral attitude towards gambling.

Whether or not 'expressivism' is a good label for this view ('speech-act analysis' might be a better one), there are highly analogous views about sentences other than moral ones, which we might conveniently label in the same way. Thus, as there are expressivists about morals, there might be expressivists about truth, about negation, about causality, about taste, about probability, about modality, about conditionals and more. All these views share the combination of two claims: a denial of the truth-evaluability of (the contents of) the sentences in a certain class $X$ combined with a speech-act analysis to account for the meaning of the sentences in $X$. So it would seem to be reasonable to assume that expressivism can be discussed in general for variable $X$.

The plan of this chapter is to re-examine and to generalize a certain line of objection against expressivism, a line prominently taken by Searle (1969) and Geach (1960, 1965). I shall return to my previous examples and discuss expressivism about morals, taste and probability. The outcome of my re-examination will be that expressivists of these sorts must give up truth-conditional semantics across the board (not just for the problematic sentences). In §1 I very briefly introduce expressivism about morals, about taste and about probability. In §2 I discuss the difficulties Searle and Geach raised for expressivism, and in §3 I consider how they could be circumvented. In §4 I use and generalize an argument by Bob Hale (1986) to show that any expressivist semantics for the problematic sentences must be extended to cover all sentences for reasons of grammatical uniformity. In §5 I discuss how this uniformity could be achieved. Finally, in §6, I put this result into perspective and draw my conclusion from the point of view of the problem of excess objectivity.

## 1 Some expressivists

Unlike revisionism, expressivism has been hotly debated for decades. Perhaps the most famous statement of expressivism about morally and aesthetically evaluative sentences is Ayer's in chapter VI of his *Language, Truth and Logic* (1946).[1]

> The presence of an ethical symbol in a proposition adds nothing to its factual content. Thus if I say to someone, 'You acted wrongly in stealing that money', I am not stating anything more than if I had simply said, 'You stole that money.' In adding that this action is wrong I am not making any further statement about it. I am simply evincing my moral disapproval of it. It is as if I had said, 'You stole that money', in a peculiar tone of horror, or written it with the addition of some special exclamation marks. The tone, or the exclamation marks, adds nothing to the literal meaning of the sentence. It merely serves to show that the expression of it is attended by certain feelings in the speaker.
>
> If now I generalize my previous statement and say, 'Stealing money is wrong', I produce a sentence which has no factual meaning—that is, expresses no proposition which can be either true or false. It is as if I had written 'Stealing money!!'—where the shape and thickness of the exclamation marks show, by a suitable convention, that a special sort of moral disapproval is the feeling which is being expressed. It is clear that there is nothing said here which can be true or false. (1946: 107)

Ayer is not interested in a detailed account of the meaning of evaluative sentences. His main concern is the verificationist one of ruling out that evaluative sentences can express propositions and therefore admit of truth or falsehood (see Ayer 1946: 14–15 and 22). This does not mean that he wants to do away with evaluative statements altogether. They do, for him, serve the function of allowing people to express their moral sentiments. However, if two people contradict each other on a pure matter of value, then 'there is plainly no sense in asking which ... is in the right. For neither of [them] is asserting a genuine proposition' (1946: 108)—evaluative matters are non-objective in the sense of Chapter 2, above. Nevertheless, Ayer's account contains the germ of a more positive expressivist account of the meaning of evaluative sentences which others have later attempted to provide. Most prominent in this respect are Richard Hare and Simon Blackburn. Hare claims, for instance, that an explanation of the meaning of 'good' must include the fact that 'good' is standardly used to perform the speech act of commendation (Hare 1970). His account is therefore often called a 'speech-act analysis' or 'pragmatic account' of moral discourse. The linguistic function of the predicate 'is good' is not to describe things, but rather to commend them.

For Blackburn (1984: chapters 5 and 6), too, moral sentences are properly used to express certain moral attitudes and this exhausts their linguistic function. Blackburn stands out in that he is the first expressivist to have made efforts towards developing a systematic positive account of the meaning of the sentences in question. He takes seriously Hare's idea that evaluative sentences are designed for the performance of particular speech acts, and treats the predicates 'is good' and 'is bad' as if they were special force indicators (I shall say more about Blackburn's account in §3).

Just as Ayer's verificationism gave rise to his expressivism about evaluative sentences, Keynesianism and subjectivism about probability can give rise to expressivism about sentences ascribing probabilities. Keynesians about probability believe that probability ascriptions express the speaker's degree of belief in some proposition, and whether that proposition merits that degree of belief is a relative matter, relative to the evidence available. A probability judgement may be correct on one background of evidence and incorrect on another. Subjectivists about probability, such as Ramsey or De Finetti, go even further. They too believe that probability ascriptions express a speaker's degree of belief. But unlike the Keynesians, they believe that the degree to which the speaker believes a given proposition is not subject to any norm of correctness beyond certain norms of coherence. Thus even thinkers with the same evidence may legitimately have diverging probability assignments if their initial probability assignments were different. Both Keynesians and subjectivists thus deny that probabilistic sentences are truth-evaluable and are therefore called upon to provide an account of the meaning of such sentences that does not presuppose their truth-evaluability.

Huw Price is an example of a highly articulate expressivist about probabilistic sentences, who does provide such an account. In his 'Does "Probably" Modify Sense?' (1983), he argues that in sincerely using what he calls 'single-case probability sentences' (SP sentences), one is not asserting, i.e. expressing full belief in, a specifically probabilistic, truth-evaluable proposition, but is rather partially asserting, i.e. expressing one's partial belief in, a non-probabilistic proposition.[2]

For example, the sentence 'Whirlwind will probably win.' is not an assertoric sentence with the content that Whirlwind will probably win, but rather a partially assertoric sentence with the content that Whirlwind will win. The same goes for the corresponding judgements: judging that Whirlwind will probably win is not to form a belief with the truth-evaluable content that Whirlwind will probably win, but rather to form a partial belief (with high degree of confidence) with the content that Whirlwind will win.[3]

I am not, in this chapter, discussing Alan Gibbard, who in his excellent book *Wise Choices, Apt Feelings* (1990) defends what seems to be a version of expressivism. The last section of Chapter 6 is devoted especially to Gibbard's theory. This is for two reasons. First, I believe that it is unclear whether Gibbard's theory is a form of expressivism in the sense in which I have defined it, namely as the view that some class of problematic sentence, which cannot be analysed as having truth conditions, should be analysed as having a special kind of illocutionary force. On my own interpretation Gibbard does not fit this description. Second, it will be much easier to explain why Gibbard isn't an expressivist, and how my own position differs from his, at the end of Chapter 6.

## 2 Unendorsed contexts

A typical expressivist about sentences on matters of taste will claim that the meaning of the sentence

(1)    Haggis is tasty.

is constituted by the fact that it can be properly used to present oneself as aesthetically approving of haggis.[4] This suggestion runs into immediate difficulties, if one considers what one might call 'unendorsed' occurrences of (1). For while the phrase 'haggis is tasty', when used on its own, can indeed be used to express approval of haggis, this is obviously not the case when it occurs in sentences such as

(2)    I wonder whether haggis is tasty.

or

(3)    Either haggis is tasty or what I had wasn't haggis.

The meaning of the embedded occurrences of 'haggis is tasty' in (2) and (3) can obviously not consist in the fact that they can be used to express approval of haggis, or, in Hare's terms, to commend haggis. Utterances of (2) might serve the expression of the speaker's uncertainty about whether he or she approves of haggis, which is quite opposed to an expression of approval. Similarly, utterers of (3) in no way commit themselves, by their utterance, to an approval of haggis: were they to learn that it wasn't haggis, they could quite consistently maintain that haggis isn't tasty, i.e. express their disapproval of haggis. We can say that by uttering (1), a speaker endorses the suggestion that haggis is tasty, while by uttering (2) or (3) one does not. Accordingly, we can call the occurrence of 'haggis is tasty' in the first 'endorsed' and its occurrences in the other two 'unendorsed'.

Unendorsed occurrences represent a difficulty for expressivists because their meaning analysis only fits endorsed occurrences, but does not fit unendorsed ones. However, the meaning of the relevant phrases seems to remain constant across both kinds of occurrence, just as the meaning of the phrase 'haggis is tasty' does not appear to change from (1) to (2) and (3).

The natural reaction for the expressivist might be to insist that, despite appearances, the meaning of the phrases in question varies and that the expressivist account of their meaning applies only to their endorsed occurrences. Therefore I now want to consider two reasons why the expressivist ought not to make this move — the first inconclusive, the second conclusive.

### Searle's adequacy condition

The first reason has been put forward by John Searle in his *Speech Acts* (1969). Searle emphasizes that we must distinguish the *use* to which a word or sentence may be put on some occasions from that word's or sentence's *meaning*. Expressivists, he thinks, do not pay sufficient attention to this distinction. By saying that the meaning of, for instance, (1) consists in its proper use for expressing approval, expressivists do point to a fact about the *use* of the sentence on certain, namely endorsed, occasions, but this fact does not constitute the sentence's meaning. Searle supports this view by his adequacy condition for the meaning analysis of words:

> Any analysis of the meaning of a word (or morpheme) must be consistent with the fact that the same word (or morpheme) can mean the same thing in all the grammatically different kinds of sentences in which it can occur. Syntactical transformations of sentences do not necessarily enforce changes of meaning on the component words or morphemes of those sentences. (1969: 137)

Expressivist analyses of meaning of the form given earlier generally violate this condition. For example, if it were part of the meaning of 'is tasty' that it can be used to express aesthetic approval in endorsed contexts such as (1), but it did not have this meaning in unendorsed contexts such as (2) and (3), then Searle's adequacy condition would be violated. For certain syntactical transformations would alter the meaning of 'is tasty'. And they would do so necessarily, because it is in the nature of, for instance, embedding in the context 'I wonder whether ... .' that one does not, in uttering such contexts, endorse the embedded sentence separately.

In Searle's view, the origin of the expressivist's mistake lies in a wrong under-standing of the principle that meaning is use (1969: 146–8 and 152). According to Searle's own account, the predicate 'is tasty', like all predicates, has the function of determining which proposition is expressed, no matter in what context it occurs. That (1) can be used to commend haggis is due to the fact that in (1) that proposition occurs *assertorically*. So the commendatory use of (1) is due to the meaning not only of 'is tasty', but to that of 'is tasty' *together with* that of what-ever indicates assertoric illocutionary force in (1). Thus for Searle, the expres-sivist attributes to 'is tasty' alone a meaning that it has only in combination with assertoric force.

Searle's adequacy condition appears to be at least a useful hermeneutic prin-ciple, which ought to guide meaning analysis. It is better to attribute meanings that can explain the use of words in every context than to attribute meanings that vary with context. But can we always adhere strictly to Searle's adequacy condi-tion? After all, there are lexically ambiguous words, i.e. words that have dif-ferent meanings in different contexts, as, for example, the English words 'bill' and 'coach'. Admitting such ambiguity does complicate theories of meaning, and they would doubtless be prettier without it. However, we must acknowledge the fact that there are these lexical ambiguities. So why couldn't there also be more systematic phenomena of ambiguity, words that systematically change their meaning with syntactic transformation? After all, this form of ambiguity would be much more systematic and tractable than ordinary lexical ambiguity.

Hare points out that Searle himself violates the adequacy condition in his analysis of the meaning of so-called performatives, such as the verb 'to promise' (see Hare 1970: 9–10; and Searle 1969: 30–3). Searle claims that 'promise', al-though it is a verb, and therefore appears to function as a predicate, really is an illocutionary force indicator. Thus the speech act performed by uttering 'I promise to come.' is not the act of asserting the proposition that the speaker promises to come, but rather the act of making a promise concerning the propo-sition that the speaker will come. Similarly, uttering 'I don't promise to come.' does not constitute an autobiographical assertion but the act of refusing to make a certain promise.[5] But if we subject such a sentence to a syntactical transforma-tion, such as putting it into the past tense ('I promised to come.') or into the third instead of the first person ('He promises to come.'), then 'to promise' will sys-tematically change its meaning, i.e. become a predicate used for reporting the performance of the speech act of promising.[6]

Of course, Searle has reasons for violating his adequacy condition in this case. Nevertheless, Hare's point shows that—even for Searle—there may be cases where there are reasons for violating the condition. Expressivists have their rea-sons for being expressivists. So if expressivists could not avoid violating Searle's condition, then these reasons would perhaps suffice to justify the viola-tion. Searle's objection is therefore inconclusive.

### Geach and his Frege-point

There is, however, a more conclusive reason why we ought not to attribute different meanings to endorsed and unendorsed occurrences of the same word or phrase. It has been put forward by Peter Geach (1960, 1965) in an attempt to refute expressivism in general (he dubs it the 'Frege-point'). Switching the example, consider the following argument:

(4)    <u>Gambling is bad</u>.
(5)    If <u>gambling is bad</u>, then *inviting others to gamble is bad*.
(6)    Therefore: *Inviting others to gamble is bad*.

This argument is obviously formally valid and its validity depends crucially on the fact that the two underlined occurrences of 'bad' have the same meaning. Had they not the same meaning, the argument would equivocate. The same applies to the two italicized occurrences of 'bad'. An expressivist about 'bad', like Hare, however, would claim that 'bad' in (4) is not used to describe an action as bad, but to condemn it. But in (5), where 'bad' occurs unendorsed (twice), it obviously does not have this condemning function. Thus the meaning of 'bad' cannot consist in its condemning function and the expressivist thesis must be false.

I regard Geach's objection as decisive against the formulation of expressivism discussed so far. It is undeniable that (4)–(6) is a formally valid argument whose validity depends on the sameness of meaning of the two occurrences of 'gambling is bad' (and of the two occurrences of 'inviting others to gamble is bad'). So the positive expressivist account of the meaning of the sentences whose truth-evaluability it denies needs to be modified. To see how this could be done, let us consider how standard non-expressivist theories of meaning, such as Searle's, Geach's or Frege's would avoid the same problem. For on the face of it, the problem can also be posed against these theorists: they claim that it is part of the meaning of 'gambling is bad' in (4) that it can be used to assert that gambling is bad. But the embedded occurrence of the same phrase in (5) cannot be so used, thus seems to have a different meaning. But then Geach's argument (4)–(6) would equivocate. Does the standard theory face a problem of unasserted contexts where the expressivist faces a problem of unendorsed contexts?

The standard theorist will reply that all that is required to avoid equivocation is that the *proposition* asserted in (4) be the same as the *proposition* occurring unasserted as the antecedent of (5). So, strictly speaking, it is only a proper part of the meaning of (4) that needs to be the same as a proper part of the meaning of (5). But this part, namely the proposition that gambling is bad, does not include (4)'s assertoric force as applied to that proposition. So, the fact that the meaning of (4) consists partly in its appropriateness for asserting that gambling is bad, while this is not part of the meaning of the occurrence of 'gambling is bad' in (5), does not have the consequence that Geach's argument equivocates.

The standard theorist even has a detailed account that explains why the argument is valid and why its validity requires the sameness of the proposition asserted in (4) with that occurring as the antecedent of (5). He or she might define a notion of logical entailment thus: a set of propositions $P$ logically entails another proposition $c$ if and only if the occurrences of *logical constants* in the propositions in $P$ guarantee that $c$ is true if each proposition in $P$ is true. Now he or she can easily say what it is for an argument to be valid: if 'argument' is taken to refer to a sequence of propositions, as is often done in logic, then an argument is *valid* if and only if its premisses logically entail its conclusion. If, on the other hand, one takes 'argument' to refer to a sequence of complete assertoric sentences, i.e. sentence-types that can properly be used, as they stand, to assert something, then an argument is defined as *valid*, iff the propositions assertable by its premisses logically entail the proposition assertable by its conclusion.

With this apparatus, the standard theorist can explain why it is required, in order for (4)–(6) to be valid, that the proposition asserted in (4) be the same as the proposition that constitutes the antecedent of (5): (4)–(6) is an argument in the latter sense of 'argument', i.e. it is a sequence of complete assertoric sentences. The propositions assertable by uttering (4) and (5) logically entail the proposition assertable by uttering (6). This is so because (5) is assertoric of a compound conditional proposition whose antecedent is assertable by (4). By the meaning of the conditional connective (one of the logical constants), conditional propositions are not true exactly if their antecedent proposition is true and their consequent proposition false (assuming a material treatment of conditionals). So, if both the proposition that gambling is bad and the proposition that if gambling is bad, then inviting others to gamble is bad are true, then the proposition that inviting others to gamble is bad must also be true. This would not be the case if the proposition expressed by (4) wasn't the same as that expressed by the antecedent of (5).

In a further step, this account of validity can be developed into a fully-fledged logical theory. Such a theory may consist of axiom-schemata and rules of inference that enable the logician to derive all and only valid argument forms, i.e. those argument forms each instance of which is a valid argument. In such a theory, (4)–(6) may turn out to be an instance of the valid argument form of modus ponens, here displayed for both senses of 'argument':

$(MP^P)$     $A$                              (for sequences of propositions)
$\phantom{(MP^P)}$   $\underline{\text{if } A \text{ then } C}$
$\phantom{(MP^P)}$   $C$

$(MP^S)$     $\vdash A$                       (for sequences of complete sentences)
$\phantom{(MP^S)}$   $\underline{\vdash \text{if } A \text{ then } C}$
$\phantom{(MP^S)}$   $\vdash C$

(In $(MP^S)$, the turnstile ('$\vdash$') symbolizes assertoric force.) The use of the same propositional letters at different places of an argument schema, of course, makes it obvious which parts of the meaning of an argument must coincide in order for that argument to be unequivocatingly of that argument form.

Clearly, the standard theorist is well prepared to deal with the validity of Geach's argument. The question I want to raise now is whether it is essential to the standard solution to the problem of unendorsed contexts that the sentences in question are treated as expressors of truth-evaluable, assertable propositions, or whether the same *kind* of solution would be available to the expressivist.

It is fairly obvious that the key element of the solution lies in the standard distinction between the assertoric illocutionary force and the proposition asserted. This distinction allows the bipartite theorist to avoid the problem by saying that only a *part* of the meaning of (4) is identical with a *part* of the meaning of (5). Since this part does not include (4)'s illocutionary force, it does not matter for the validity of Geach's argument that the occurrence of 'gambling is bad' in (5) is unasserted, that in (4) asserted. Thus, it seems that the same kind of solution might be available to anyone who distinguishes, in the meaning of (4), between the commitment that an utterance of (4) constitutes and the item to which the utterer is committed: (4)'s content. The expressivist could, for instance, distinguish between a certain attitude towards gambling and the endorsement of that attitude, indicated by an illocutionary force. He or she could then modify his or her semantic account in order to meet Geach's challenge and thus avoid the problem of unasserted contexts: while the meaning of (4) is constituted by the fact that it can be properly used to endorse an attitude of disapproval towards gambling, the occurrence of 'gambling is bad' in (5) shares only part of that meaning, namely the (now unendorsed) expression of, or reference to, the same attitude. This *partial* identity of the meaning of (4) and (5) suffices to ensure the unequivocating validity of Geach's argument.

My sketch of a solution, however, is still incomplete. The standard truth-conditional account could also give a detailed explanation of the validity of arguments. The expressivist can certainly not make use of this part of the standard theorist's solution, because it presupposes that the contents involved are truth-evaluable. And this is precisely what the expressivist wants to avoid. So the expressivist's version of the distinction between illocutionary force and assertable content will need to be part of a non-truth-functional account of the composition of contents that yields the desired logical relations among contents. I will explore the space of possibilities for such an account in the next section.[7]

Let me summarize. The unendorsed contexts problem, together with Geach's argument, imposes the following constraints on the positive account of any expressivist about a class of sentences X. First, it must allow for the sameness of meaning of endorsed and unendorsed occurrences of the same X-sentences. Second, it ought to provide an alternative explanation for the validity of arguments such as (4)–(6).[8] The first of these requirements is a must, for it rests on the undeniable assumption that the validity of (4)–(6) depends on the sameness of meaning of the two occurrences of 'gambling is bad'. Meeting the second requirement is strongly recommended. For as long as the expressivist cannot explain the validity of arguments involving premises from X, his or her account will fall significantly short of the standard one.

# 3 Two ways of meeting Geach's challenge

The problem of unendorsed contexts discussed in the last section imposes certain constraints on a successful positive expressivist account of the meaning of those sentences whose truth-evaluability the expressivist denies. At the very least, the expressivist's account must incorporate a distinction analogous to the standard distinction between the force and the content (proposition) of a sentence. This analogue needs to be part of an account of the composition of sentences to form compound sentences that explains why some arguments are formally valid.

Given the diversity of discourses about which one might have reason to be an expressivist, it is difficult to give a general treatment of the options an expressivist has in developing such a positive semantic account. I do believe, however, that we can initially discern two very general routes any such account might take, and that there are interesting things to be said about them. In order not to operate in too abstract a realm, let us again consider three sample sentences from different areas of discourse:

(7)     Haggis is tasty.
(8)     Gambling is bad.
(9)     Popocatépetl will probably erupt within ten years.

To understand the two routes I have in mind, consider first how a standard bipartite theory of meaning would proceed with these sentences. On a standard account, all the constituent words of these sentences will be classified as *content indicators* (see Chapter 1, §3). That is, the meanings of the words in each sentence are viewed as contributors to the determination of the content of that sentence, while the assertoric force of each is indicated by other features, such as word order, punctuation, initial capitalization and inflection. In (7), for example, it is the job of the term 'haggis' to identify a dish, and that of the predicate 'is tasty', to identify a property. In combination, these two determine the content of (7), namely the content that haggis is tasty, a content that is true just if the dish identified by 'haggis' has the property identified by 'is tasty'. Moreover, (7)'s word order, punctuation and capitalization determine that the sentence is assertoric. A standard analysis of the other sentences would be very similar, though in the case of (9) more complicated.

Now, in introducing his own force–content distinction, the expressivist can proceed in either of two ways. Either he or she classifies sentence features into force indicators and content indicators in the same manner as on the standard account, or he or she does not. More concretely, he or she either counts the problematic expressions, e.g. 'is tasty', 'is bad', 'probably', etc. as pure content indicators, as in the standard account, or treats them as indicating illocutionary force, unlike the standard account. Let us call the first option *the content-indicator approach* and the second *the force-indicator approach*. These options arise for each discourse about which one can be expressivist, i.e. for each kind of expressivism. However, it seems that the force-indicator option has been taken more frequently. For example, Hare and Blackburn[9] pursue a force-indicator approach. For they would treat the predicate 'is bad' in (8) as a force indicator. Also, Price (1983) argues that 'probably' should be treated as modifying a sentence's force, rather than its content. I shall therefore now concentrate on the force-indicator approach and return to the content-indicator approach later.

## The force-indicator approach

In my above quote (p. 44) Ayer presents the prototype of an expressivist account that treats 'is wrong' as a force indicator:

> If ... I ... say, 'Stealing money is wrong', ...[i]t is as if I had written 'Stealing money!!'—where the shape and thickness of the exclamation marks show, by a suitable convention, that a special sort of moral disapproval is the feeling which is being expressed. (1946: 107)

Filling in the details in the manner of Hare and Blackburn, what Ayer is saying is that we ought to treat 'is wrong' as a force indicator that can be combined with an expression denoting an action-type to yield a sentence that can be used to perform a speech act of condemnation, or to express moral disapproval, of that action-type. Such a force indicator would be syntactically curious in that it would operate not on sentential phrases, but on denoting expressions. But I do not see why there could not be force indicators that behave in this—admittedly unfamiliar—way.[10]

We can easily imagine analogous accounts for our three sample sentences. In (7), 'is tasty' is the force indicator, which combines with denoting expressions to yield sentences that can be used to express aesthetic approval of the thing denoted. (8), of course, combines the force indicator 'is bad' with an expression denoting the action-type gambling, and can be used to express moral disapproval of gambling. In (9) 'probably' is the force indicator. Unlike the previous two, this force indicator seems to combine with sentential phrases. We could say that such sentential phrases serve to identify conventional contents, i.e. truth-evaluable propositions, and then sentences containing 'probably' could be viewed as expressing a high degree of belief, on the part of the utterer, in the proposition thus identified.

I shall now use the example of moral expressivism to discuss the force-indicator approach in more detail. After that, I will try to draw some conclusions about the force-indicator approach in general.

The force-indicator accounts sketched above are still unguarded against the problem of unendorsed contexts. Consider again sentence (8) and the conditional sentence (10) in which it occurs unendorsed:

(10)    If gambling is bad, then inviting others to gamble is bad.

As Geach's argument has shown (in the last section), the phrase 'gambling is bad' must have the same meaning in both (8) and (10). Thus, if 'is bad' in (8) is to function as a force indicator, then so it must in (10). So, if we represent the form of (8) as

(F8)   B!(gambling)

using Blackburn's Boo–Hooray notation, then we must equally represent the form of 'gambling is bad' on its occurrence in (10) as involving the force indicator 'B!( )'. Treating the second occurrence of 'is bad' in (10) in the same way, we then get something like the following as the form of (10):

If[B!(gambling), B!(inviting others to gamble)]

Now we face the problem of unendorsed contexts. All sides will agree that (10) is not properly usable for expressing disapproval of gambling: its antecedent is unendorsed. Nevertheless, the current analysis, forced by Geach's argument, attributes to the occurrence of 'gambling is bad' in (10) a meaning that makes it usable precisely for expressing that. So if the expressivist wants to maintain that 'is bad' serves as a force indicator, he or she must take care that on his or her analysis this force indicator somehow gets 'defused', or put out of operation, when embedded in unendorsed contexts. How can he or she do that?

I can, for example, defuse the abusive phrase 'You moron!' by putting it (as I just did) in quotation marks, thus not abusing you, the reader. It is part of the meaning of quotation marks that whatever appears between them loses many aspects of its normal meaning, including its abusive force in this case. Another example of a 'defuser' is 'that …'. By prefixing a sentence with 'that …', one can put that sentence's illocutionary force out of operation—this is why this word is often used to identify the content of, or the proposition expressed by, a sentence, as distinct from its illocutionary force.

In order to avoid the problem of unendorsed contexts, the expressivist therefore needs to attribute a defusing function to some features of those contexts embedding into which makes phrases unendorsed. In the present case, the expressivist could construe the compounding device 'if … , then --- ' as accomplishing the task of defusing 'B!(gambling)'. Alternatively, he or she could separate the compounding from the defusing function and introduce into his or her formalizations an extra sign, say '/…/', whose function it is to defuse anything occurring in place of the dots. This 'slash notation' has in fact been used by Blackburn in his attempt to solve the unendorsed contexts problem in his (1984: 194). Blackburn helpfully glosses the function of slash expressions as that of *denoting* the attitude a speaker normally commits himself or herself to when he or she utters the sentence within the slashes separately. For example, '/B!(gambling)/' denotes the attitude of moral disapproval of gambling. But what is the role of such denoting expressions in the context of a sentence such as

(10)? Obviously, (10)'s consequent also contains a defused occurrence of the force indicator 'is bad'. Thus we get something formally like

If[/B!(gambling)/, /B!(inviting others to gamble)/].

How is the context 'If[ ... , --- ]' to be understood? There are two distinct semantic functions we still need to assign to it. First, the two denoting expressions '/B!(gambling)/' and '/B!(inviting others to gamble)/' need to be compounded, and secondly the whole of (10) obviously has some illocutionary force. In the formalization, we can either keep these functions separate or assign them both to the context 'If[ ... , --- ]'. Blackburn separates them. On the one hand, he introduces a two-place nominal connective ';', which takes slash expressions as arguments and yields another compound expression denoting a combination of moral attitudes. For instance,

/B!(gambling)/; /B!(inviting others to gamble)/

denotes the combination of disapproval of gambling with disapproval of inviting others to gamble. More precisely, it denotes an *attitudinal disposition*: someone who has that disposition would disapprove of inviting others to gamble, were he or she to disapprove of gambling itself. On the other hand, Blackburn introduces another force indicator 'H!( )' (for 'Hooray'), which functions syntactically like 'B!( )', and can be used to express moral approval of whatever the expression it is applied to denotes. If we apply 'H!( )' to the above compound, we get Blackburn's full formalization of (10):

(F10)  H!(/B!(gambling)/; /B!(inviting others to gamble)/).

So (10) is viewed as a sentence expressive of moral approval of a certain attitudinal disposition, namely approval of the disposition one has if one tends to disapprove of inviting others to gamble, should one disapprove of gambling itself.

This account already meets the first requirement imposed by Geach's objection (see end of last section): (F8) and (F10) display how endorsed and unendorsed occurrences of (8) coincide in meaning. It also begins to meet the second requirement, that of an explanation for the validity of the Geach argument. For the account explains why someone who has the attitude expressible by (10) and that expressible by (8), but fails to hold that inviting others to gamble is bad, is committing a mistake of inconsistency of some sort. As Blackburn says, such a person's attitudes 'clash' in the sense that his or her evaluative attitudes 'cannot fulfil the practical purposes for which we evaluate things' (1984: 195). For Blackburn, this inconsistency amounts to *logical* inconsistency. In support of Blackburn, one could add that, as holding clashing attitudes defeats the purpose of having such attitudes, it is irrational to do so, on a instrumental view of rationality.[11]

This account of the meaning of moral sentences, of the connective ';' and of the two force indicators 'B!( )' and 'H!( )' should also explain the *formal*

validity of arguments such as Geach's. That is, it ought to show that the
argument from (8) and (10) to 'Inviting others to gamble is bad.' is an instance
of a valid argument *form*. But this requirement is easily met: (8)'s meaning is
part of (10)'s meaning, and this is what a formal account of validity needs to
require in order for Geach's argument not to equivocate. Blackburn can claim
that Geach's argument is an instance of the following valid argument form of
Moral Modus Ponens:

(MMP)      $x$
           $\underline{H!(/x/;/y/)}$
           $y$

where '$x$' and '$y$' are schematic for complete moral sentences, i.e. sentences
formed by applying one of the indicators 'H!( )' or 'B!( )' to an expression denoting an action-type. It can hardly be denied that this is sufficient to render the
Geach argument *formally* valid—at least relative to Blackburn's formal language
which includes the constants 'B!( )', 'H!( )', '/' and ';'. But any notion of formal
validity is, I believe, relative, so this should not be a problem. [12]

Another issue is the semantic explanation an expressivist like Blackburn can
offer as to why certain argument forms rather than others are valid. On the standard truth-conditional account, this can be explained nicely. Validity is defined
in terms of the impossibility of the conclusion's not being true if the premises
are true. Since the connectives, such as 'if ... , then --- ', were interpreted as
truth functions, it can then be shown why arguments of certain forms are valid.
The expressivist cannot use the standard definition of validity in terms of truth,
for he or she denies that the premises and conclusions of valid arguments are
always truth-evaluable, as, for example, those of the Geach argument are not.
Blackburn thus needed to appeal to a different notion of validity, characterized
in terms of the 'clashing of attitudes', which is presumably best understood as a
failure of some kind of instrumental rationality. [13]

Blackburn's account of the validity of Moral Modus Ponens, however, makes
specific reference to the situation in moral discourse. Thus it is not immediately
clear how his strategy could be extended to other expressivisms. The specificity
of the explanation of the validity of MMP, and the fact that its schematic letters
range over complete moral sentences, also make it hard to see how MMP can be
viewed as a kind of modus ponens. [14]

We have now seen how, roughly, an expressivist about moral sentences can
construct a semantics that complies with the requirements imposed by the unendorsed contexts problem. We have also seen that there are different ways of pro-
ceeding. It was, for instance, only a peculiarity of Blackburn's account that the
overall illocutionary force indicator of (10) was also one of the moral force indicators 'B!( )' and 'H!( )'. It was also, for example, a matter of choice whether
the defusing function was to be separated from the compounding device 'if ... ,
then --- '. Moreover, there are questions I didn't even address, e.g. the questions

whether there are further embeddings, how they work, whether embeddings can be iterated, etc.

What I have said about the force-indicator approach to *moral* sentences cannot easily be generalized for force indicator approaches in general. However, I believe that the space of options is similarly structured for all expressivists who want to treat the problematic words as force indicators. Analogous issues will arise for any expressivist who opts for the force-indicator approach. It seems, then, that the two requirements posed by Geach's objection can be met on a force-indicator approach. However, as we'll see in §4, there is a general difficulty with incorporating such an expressivist semantics for moral (aesthetic, probabilistic, etc.) sentences into a general semantics for all sentences of a natural language.

### The content-indicator approach

What if an expressivist takes the other route, that of maintaining the conventional classification into force indicators and content indicators? The proposal, on this route, is to treat all those sentence features as content indicators that standardly count as content indicators, and to treat those features as force indicators that standardly are so treated. A fortiori, the problematic expressions, such as 'probably', 'is tasty', etc. will be treated as content indicators. At first, it seems that this will create much more trouble than the force-indicator approach, since it requires a new notion of content as well as a novel kind of illocutionary force. In (8), for example, the phrase 'gambling is bad' will then express some content, let us say the content that gambling is bad. This content must be of a new sort, for it is, according to the expressivist's conviction, not truth-evaluable, i.e. it has no truth condition. On the other hand, (8)'s word order, capitalization, full stop and inflection indicate some illocutionary force. But which force? For a sentence to have a certain illocutionary force is for it to have a certain communicative function in relation to some content. For example, it is the function of assertoric sentences to permit utterers to assert the relevant content. What, according to the expressivist, could that communicative function be in the case of (8)? Since the contents operated upon are of a novel sort, the force needed in the case of (8) will also have to be a novelty.[15]

However, once we know what sorts of content and force we are talking about, we no longer have an unendorsed contexts problem. Since the content-indicator approach shares the force–content structure of standard semantics, the force of a sentence is not part of what gets embedded when that sentence occurs embedded. For this reason, there is no problem with the fact that, in the embedded context, the sentence no longer has the same force.[16]

What would an expressivist account of the meanings of our samples (7)–(9) look like on the content-indicator aproach? (7) will have the content that haggis is tasty, (8) that gambling is bad, (9) that Joan is probably asleep. Each will have some illocutionary force, indicated implicitly in its word order, punctuation and capitalization. This illocutionary force will in each case, presumably, correspond to some communicative act of acceptance, since all of (7)–(9) are declarative. For example, uttering (7), one can present oneself as, in some sense, accepting that haggis is tasty. This view is supported by the fact that each of the samples has counterparts with different, non-accepting forces, but intuitively the same content: e.g. 'Is haggis tasty?' is such a counterpart of (7). But what exactly are these contents and what exactly do these novel illocutionary forces of acceptance involve?

On a standard truth-conditional account, the function of (7), for example, might be stated as follows: (7) can be properly used by a speaker to assert, i.e. present himself or herself as believing, that haggis is tasty. The standard account would thus make use of a certain psychology of belief and desire. This psychology, however, presupposes that beliefs are to be characterized in relation to certain theoretical entities: truth-conditional contents. If the expressivist on the content-indicator approach could deploy a similar belief-psychology that didn't presuppose that belief contents, such as the content that haggis is tasty, have truth conditions, then he or she could pursue the old strategy: specifying for each sentence that it can be properly used by speakers to present themselves as $\phi$-ing a certain content that is expressed by the complex of that sentence's content indicators (where $\phi$-ing is a belief-like attitude that relates thinkers to contents of a not necessarily truth-apt variety).

Let us call the requisite belief-like attitude 'opining' (having an opinion). A person can opine that $p$ for any content that $p$. Someone sincerely uttering (7), for instance, will be said to express his or her opinion that haggis is tasty. How can this notion of opining and that of a (not necessarily truth-evaluable) content be elucidated? As the expressivist cannot characterize these contents in terms of truth conditions, he or she should use some kind of conceptual role characterization. Let me give a brief sketch of such an account.

First, an opinion is something one can have or not have. Having or not having an opinion will make a difference for the possessor's dispositions to act. Obviously, having the opinion that haggis is tasty will give rise to different behavioural dispositions from those arising from an opinion that haggis tastes disgusting. Second, there are reasoning processes in which opinions, and possibly other cognitive states, play a role. Opinions can be the input as well as the output of a reasoning process. For example, my opinion about Cumberland sausages might be part of the input of a reasoning process that results in my decision not to buy any. This opinion about Cumberland sausages, again, might have been the result of a reasoning process that started from my awareness of certain repeated experiences with Cumberland sausages. Third, opinions can be characterized and differentiated in relation to *contents of opinion*. Contents of opinion are theoretical entities that can be compounded, using certain operations of composition, to yield new, compound contents of opinion. According to whether and how such contents of opinion are compounded, they stand in logical relations. (There will be logical relations, analogous to those of the propositional calculus, that arise from the composition of simpler contents into compound contents. Other logical relations will arise from the way in which contents are built up at the sub-sentential level—these are analogous to the logical relations described by the predicate calculus, and perhaps by the logics of particular words.) These logical relations among contents of opinion give rise to norms of rationality as to how reasoning processes involving opinions are to proceed, and what combinations of opinions one ought not to have. Moreover, contents of opinion can be considered, rejected, supposed or accepted. To accept a content of opinion is to have the corresponding opinion.

Contents of opinion are invoked in the theory, because they provide a way of systematically describing opinions. They provide, as it were, a scale one can use for measuring opinions.[17] Now, in so far as we want to construct an expressivist account of the meaning of sentences about taste, we need to ask how each content indicator in such a sentence contributes to determining that sentence's content. But since contents are primarily invoked as units of measurement for opinions, we can ask directly how the content indicators of a sentence about taste determine the opinion one can present oneself as having by uttering that sentence. Let's look at our sample (7). It is the sentential phrase 'haggis is tasty' that determines (7)'s content. This phrase decomposes into the grammatical subject 'haggis' and the grammatical predicate 'is tasty'. Now, the expressivist cannot treat 'is tasty' as a genuine predicate, at least not if to be a genuine predicate is to identify a property that things can be described as having by affirmatively applying the predicate (and if things' possession of properties is an objective, factual matter). On the other hand, the phrase 'is tasty' is *grammatically* a predicate: it is constructed in a typical way from an adjective and a copula, its complements are noun-phrases, which apparently serve to identify an object of reference; and if so complemented, it yields a sentential phrase, i.e. something that can, if further complemented by a force indicator, be used to perform a speech act. Let us therefore cautiously call 'is tasty' a *quasi-predicate*.[18] (7)'s subject 'haggis', by contrast, seems to present no problem at all. It can be treated just as it would be treated in conventional semantics, namely as identifying, or referring to, an object, namely in this case the Scottish dish haggis.[19]

We are now in a position to adumbrate an expressivist semantics of sentences about matters of taste, or at least of those that share (7)'s simple subject–predicate structure. If a sentence $s$ has the form '$!Fa$', where '$!$' indicates an illocutionary force of acceptance, '$F$' is an aesthetic quasi-predicate, and '$a$' is a denoting expression, then $s$ can be properly used by speakers to present themselves as having that kind of opinion about the thing denoted by '$a$' that is associated with the quasi-predicate '$F$'. If a sentence $r$ has the form '$?Fa$', where '$?$' indicates some interrogative sort of force, then $r$ can be used to present oneself as wishing to make up one's mind whether or not to adopt an opinion with the same content.

A word on my phrase 'that kind of opinion … that is associated with the quasi-predicate so-and so'. Such kinds of opinion differ from one another in their conceptual role: they differ in the kind of 'evidence', or motivation, that would lead one to adopt them towards something, and they also differ from one another in the kinds of action they tend to lead their possessors to take. For example, the quasi-predicate 'is beautiful' is associated with one kind of opinion. It takes a certain perceptual or intellectual response to something for someone to adopt that kind of opinion about that object. Having adopted such an opinion of an object, i.e. judging it to be beautiful, will make a difference to one's actions. The quasi-predicate 'is loathsome' is obviously associated with a different kind of aesthetic opinion.

In the next step, the expressivist about matters of taste will have to introduce the compositional devices that can be used to construct compound sentential phrases about matters of taste from simple ones, such as 'or': 'either haggis isn't tasty, or labskaus tastes divine'. For instance, he or she might introduce a disjunctive connective with the same inferential properties as the truth-functional disjunctive connective. Of course, he or she could not introduce it *as* a truth-functional connective, since its complements will not have truth values. But he or she could nevertheless endow it with the same logical properties as any truth-functional connective by laying down appropriate inference rules. In this way, he or she could try to make just those arguments (involving premises about matters of taste) come out formally valid that already seem so pre-theoretically. The compound sentential phrases that result from applying the new compositional devices will presumably also be appropriate for combination with the same illocutionary force indicators that combined with the simple ones. If iteration of the compounding operations is to be made possible, this is the best way of ensuring it.

This sketch of an expressivist semantics for sentences about matters of taste should be fairly typical of what any expressivist on the content-indicator approach needs to do. The remaining problem for such expressivists is to show that their semantics can explain why certain inferences are logically valid. Again, they will have to use a notion of validity different from the standard one that defines validity in terms of truth preservation.

## 4 Hale and the grammatical uniformity of declarative sentences

If an expressivist about a class of sentences $X$ is able to give an account of the meaning of $X$-sentences, of their communicative function within a limited $X$-discourse, then that has some merit, no doubt. Focus on $X$-sentences alone, however, may not suffice to secure the success of the account. For the discourse in question may comprise expressions that are also used, with the same meaning, outside that discourse, i.e. in sentences that are not in $X$. Whenever there are such expressions shared across the border of $X$, the success of the local account of $X$-sentences can depend on how well the local account of the shared expressions can be applied outside the borders of $X$. High time for an example: suppose I have an account of the meaning of moral sentences. This account will have to include something about the word 'gambling', because this word can occur in moral sentences, such as our old friend 'Gambling is bad.'. This word, however, is what I have just called a 'shared' expression. For it is an expression that is not only used within moral discourse, as a constituent of moral sentences, but also in other sentences, such as 'Gambling is popular.' or 'Gambling is the pillar of Las Vegas's economy.'. Now since the word appears not to change its meaning according to whether it occurs in moral or non-moral sentences, an overall theory of meaning of the language in question ought to allow for this sameness of meaning across the boundaries of moral discourse. If the local account attributes to 'gambling' the function of referring to an action-type, then it ought to be possible to explain extra-moral occurrences of the word by the same function.

Now, while 'gambling' doesn't appear to present any difficulty in this respect, there are other 'shared' expressions that do create a problem. We have seen that an expressivist about $X$ pursuing a force-indicator approach is forced, by the unendorsed contexts problem, to give a *special* account of unendorsed contexts. He or she is forced to do so because the standard account involves, in our example, treating 'if' as a truth-functional connective.[20] This is not open to the expressivist, because for him or her, the elements combined by 'if' aren't truth-evaluable. On Blackburn's (1984) account of 'if' within moral discourse, it turned out to be a two-place nominal operator, something that combines two expressions each denoting a moral attitude, and yields an expression that also denotes such an attitude, though of a complex sort. The same goes for other connectives on Blackburn's account.[21]

The special treatment of shared compositional devices such as 'if', 'not' or 'and' does create problems for expressivists like Blackburn (1984).[22] In effect, Blackburn is proposing a complete semantic split between moral and non-moral language. While the standard truth-conditional account with truth-functional compositional devices applies to non-moral sentences, the iterated force-indicator approach with nominal connectives applies to moral discourse. Moral and non-moral discourse are treated as semantically fundamentally different. On the surface, however, moral and non-moral sentences share many of their characteristics: there are moral and non-moral declarative, interrogative, imperative sentences. Composition by 'if', 'not', 'or' and other compositional devices seems to function exactly the same way in moral and non-moral discourse. To propose a separate semantics for moral sentences is to ignore this grammatical uniformity of declarative sentences across the board. Thus, Blackburn's semantic split is unattractive: it renders heterogeneous what seems homogenous.

Unattractive does not mean false—often the truth is unattractive—nor does it mean impossible. Perhaps the reasons for being a moral expressivist are serious enough to justify even an unattractive semantic account. However, while a semantic split might be justifiable in principle, it leads to more difficulties than are at first apparent. The reason is that it is not always possible cleanly to separate an X-discourse from other discourses. A case in point is the following example of a 'mixed' sentence, put forward by Bob Hale:[23]

(H)    If Ed stole the money, he ought to be punished.

Blackburn's semantic split account does not provide for cases like (H). For the consequent of (H) belongs to moral discourse, while its antecedent does not. Thus, neither Blackburn's semantics of 'if' in moral contexts, nor his standard semantics of 'if' in non-moral contexts can be applied to (H). It can't be the special moral 'if' of the form 'H!( ... ; --- )', because that operates only on expressions denoting moral attitudes, and (H)'s antecedent cannot be so construed. It cannot be an ordinary truth-functional 'if', because that attaches only to sentential phrases with truth conditions, and according to the expressivist, (H)'s consequent is not truth-evaluable. In other words, had the standard account of 'if' been applicable to moral sentences as viewed by the expressivist, then he or she wouldn't have had to introduce a special moral 'if' in the first place. Conversely, had the expressivist's account of *moral* conditionals been applicable to conditionals in general, then there would have been no need for a semantic split either, for the expressivist's account of conditionals would then have qualified as a general account of conditionals. Since there are countless 'mixed' sentences that are compounds from moral and non-moral sentences, the semantic-split theorist would have to introduce yet a third sense of 'if' and other connectives, for mixed sentences, if he or she wants to maintain the semantic split. Perhaps mixed sentences can again be compounded with mixed, moral or non-moral sentences. Will the expressivist carry on introducing new senses of connectives for each possible combination? I think that he or she ought to look for a unified interpretation of the compositional devices in at least the mixed contexts. But once he or she has such an interpretation, it could also apply to purely moral and purely non-moral sentences, and make for a superior alternative to the semantic-split account. This shows that even if the proposed semantic split account can do justice to our actual linguistic practice by covering all mixed sentences with a unified account, it is still inferior to an alternative, more unified overall account that does not introduce a semantic split. If no unified account of all mixed contexts is available, then this also discredits the semantic split account, for it then becomes too complex. Thus, Blackburn's semantic split cannot be effected in the presence of compositional devices that 'mix' across the moral/non-moral border and iterate.

As no semantic split is viable, there is only one possibility for rescuing Blackburn's expressivism: generalize his expressivist semantics of moral sentences to cover non-moral sentences as well. Hale's example shows that Blackburn cannot remain merely a *classical* expressivist, who claims that moral sentences are an exception, while all other sentences have the meanings the standard account says they have. Rather, Blackburn is forced to adopt a *radical* expressivism, i.e. the view that the standard truth-conditional account misrepresents not only moral sentences, but *all* sentences.

I shall shortly discuss the prospects for such a generalization. But before that, I want to generalize the argument against Blackburn's semantic split to hold for all expressivisms of a certain kind. A generalization of the point will be an important result, for it will show that expressivisms of the sort so far discussed cannot take the *classical* form, the form of proposing an alternative semantics for the problematic sentences *only*, while maintaining the standard account of all other sentences. Instead, any expressivism would have to take a *radical* form and propose the alternative account for all sentences.

The difficulties for the semantic split arose from the presence of a certain kind of compositional device, which I shall call a 'globalizer'. A two- or more-place compositional device is a globalizer relative to a class of sentences $X$ just if it can be used to compound sentences from inside and outside $X$ and, moreover, can be iterated and embedded into other sentences in the usual ways.

Now suppose we want to be expressivists about sentences that are problematic in some way, for example evaluative or probabilistic ones. Suppose also that there is a globalizer $d$ relative to these problematic sentences. Then it will not be immediately clear whether we count sentences that are $d$-compounds of problematic *and* unproblematic sentences as problematic or as unproblematic. But suppose that it is clear which $d$-simple sentences (sentences that are not $d$-compounds) are problematic and which aren't. We can then start by defining two classes of sentences: first, the class of $d$-simple sentences that are problematic together with all the $d$-compounds from problematic $d$-simples (call this class '$X$') and secondly, the class of those $d$-simples that are not in $X$ together with all the $d$-compounds from those $d$-simples (call this class 'not-$X$'). Now, because $d$ is a globalizer, there will be sentences that are neither in $X$ nor in not-$X$—call these 'mixed sentences'.

Now, a semantic-split account $S$ of the globalizer $d$ would be an account that attributes different meanings to $d$ depending on whether it occurs in sentences in $X$ or not-$X$. Say it attributes $M_X$ to $d$ in $X$-sentences and $M_{not-X}$ to $d$ in not-$X$-sentences. Such a semantic-split account faces the following trilemma:

Either

(i) $S$ attributes $M_X$ to mixed occurrences of $d$. In this case, it is possible for $d$ to attach to not-$X$-sentences and still be interpreted by attributing $M_X$ to it. Thus we could have attributed $M_X$ to *all* occurrences of $d$ in the first place, in which case a uniform treatment of $d$ as having $M_X$ would have been available and preferable to $S$.

Or

(ii) $S$ attributes some further meaning $M_M$ to *all* mixed occurrences of $d$. In this case, there is a meaning $M_M$ for $d$ that permits $d$ to be attached to both $X$- and not-$X$-sentences (and mixed sentences). Thus $M_M$ should have been the uniform meaning of $d$ in the first place, which would have made for a better account than $S$.

Or

(iii) $S$ attributes *varying* meanings to mixed occurrences of $d$, according to the exact 'mixture' (e.g. sentence from $X$, combined with sentence not from $X$, etc.). In this case, S is an impractically complicated account of $d$, because for any type of mixture, there will be other, more complicated types of mixture. There would have to be indefinitely many different interpretations of $d$ for the indefinitely many different mixtures.[24]

This trilemma shows that, generally, a semantic account of a globalizer $d$ of a class of problematic sentences cannot be split along the borders of that class. For doing so would either result in a far too complicated account that splits the meaning of $d$ along many more borders, or, if a further and further splitting can be avoided, a better, more uniform account is available. Thus, any such account must treat $d$ uniformly across the borders of $X$. For example, Blackburn must give a uniform account of 'if', if 'if' is a globalizer of the class of moral sentences. He cannot split the semantics of 'if' along the boundaries of moral discourse. The same goes for most expressivists about other classes of sentences. If, say, the probabilistic expressivist wants to give a separate account of 'or' in probabilistic contexts, then he or she can coherently do so only if 'or' is not a globalizer of the class of probabilistic sentences.

This result has immediate consequences for any expressivist about a class $X$ of sentences of which there are globalizers. His or her account of $X$-sentences will only be acceptable, if he or she can assimilate the overall treatment of any globalizers of $X$ to the special treatment he or she has given them within $X$. For it is already clear that he or she could not assimilate the other way, i.e. assimilate the special $X$-treatment of the globalizers to their truth-functional treatment outside $X$. Thus the only remaining possibility is to assimilate the overall treatment of the globalizers to the expressivist treatment within $X$.

## 5  Resolving Hale's problem

Can an expressivists on the force-indicator route assimilate the treatment of all globalizers to their own expressivist local treatment of the globalizers? Let us take Blackburn (1984) as our example again. Blackburn's account of 'if' in moral contexts is highly unorthodox, for he treats it as a nominal functor, yielding an expression denoting a complex moral attitude from two expressions denoting simpler moral attitudes. How could this account be generalized and extended to cover all conditionals? In the first place, Blackburn would have to treat all potential antecedents and consequents as denoting expressions, and then he would have to explain what sorts of thing they denote, and what sort of more complex thing is denoted by conditional denoting expressions. Probably he would need to introduce as many force indicators as there are predicates, each appropriate for the expression of some particular attitude. He might claim that the sentence

(11)    If Ruben is three years old, then Linda is two years old.

has the following form:

(F11)   X!(/Y!(Ruben)/;/Z!(Linda)/).

It is not clear to me how exactly Blackburn's account of the moral conditional is best extended to cover all conditionals, e.g. what sorts of force indicators 'X!(...)', 'Y!(...)' and 'Z!(...)' would be. But perhaps it can be done. It is, however, clear that no one aiming at a limitation of damage should pursue this any further, since Blackburn's treatment of moral 'if's in *Spreading the Word* (1984) is tailored to fit only moral conditionals, especially as far as the iterative aspects of the proposal are concerned.

   Nevertheless, let me discuss one suggestion for an extension of Blackburn's expressivist semantics (which is inspired by Hale, 1986). The suggestion is this: For any $x$ which is denoted by the expression to which 'Y!( )' or 'Z!( )' get attached respectively, 'Y!( )' could be a force indicator expressive of the attitude of believing that $x$ is three years old, and 'Z!( )' a force indicator expressive of the attitude of believing that $x$ is two years old. For example, 'Z!(Linda)' would be a sentence by which one could express the attitude of believing that Linda is two years old. Each non-moral predicate could be treated as a force indicator expressive of an epistemic attitude in this way. Thus, 'is round' would be expressive of the attitude of believing that something is round, 'is square' of the attitude of believing that something is square, and so on for all non-moral predicates. Then '/Y!(Ruben)/' would denote the attitude of believing that Ruben is three years old (following the rule that slash-expressions denote the attitude standardly expressible by the sentence within the slashes). We could then write:

/Y!(Ruben)/;/Z!(Linda)/

and thereby denote a certain complex attitude, following the rule that '$A; C$' denotes the complex dispositional attitude of tending to have the attitude denoted by '$C$', should one have the attitude denoted by '$A$'. The dominant operator 'X!( )' could then be some force indicator expressive of epistemic approval. We would then arrive at the following proposal for (11):

(F'11)   X!(/Y!(Ruben)/;/Z!(Linda)/).

The same procedure would also allow us to formalize Hale's problematic mixed sentence (H): 'If Ed stole the money, he ought to be punished.'. For simplicity, let us assume that 'ought'-sentences can be translated into equivalent 'is good'-sentences in such a way that 'he ought to be punished' can be read as 'punishing him is good'. Then (10) could be formalized as follows:

(F'10)   H!(/SM!(Ed)/; /H!(punishing Ed)/)

where 'SM!( )' is of course the appropriate epistemic force indicator.

Up to this point we are distinguishing epistemic from moral approval and moral from non-moral predicates. If we abstract from these differences, we get a uniform expressivist semantics. Introduce a general declarative force indicator indicating general approval, i.e. either epistemic or moral approval: 'D!( )'.[25] Then, (10) and (11) appear, finally as having the same form:

(F''11)   D!(/Y!(Ruben)/;/Z!(Linda)/)
(F''10)   D!(/SM!(Ed)/; /H!(punishing Ed)/).

For both have the form 'D!(/$p$/;/$q$/)', where '$p$' and '$q$' are placeholders for complete sentences, fit for performing a speech act. More specifically, both have the form 'D!(/ $\Phi$!( $\alpha$)/;/ $\Xi$!($\beta$)/)', where '$\Phi$!( )' and ' $\Xi$!( )' are placeholders for force indicators, and ' $\alpha$' and '$\beta$' are placeholders for denoting expressions.

The account sketched shows how a force-indicator expressivist like Blackburn (1984) could assimilate his or her overall semantics to match his or her special expressivist local semantics of the problematic discourse. In this way, even an expressivist on the force-indicator route could be a radical expressivist, as he or she ought to be in the presence of globalizers (if the result of §4 is correct). I shall now demonstrate that this radical force indicator account is structurally equivalent to radical content-indicator accounts.

Compare what the form of (10) and (11) would be on a standard, truth-conditional account. Each of the two would be viewed as having assertoric force, here symbolized by '⊢', operating on a conditional content constructed from two simple contents by the conditional connective ' → ':

    ⊢ that $p$ → that $q$.

Here '$p$' and '$q$' are again placeholders for complete sentences. A structural similarity with 'D!(/$p$/;/$q$/)' is already obvious. But now consider how the standard account would break down the subsentential phrases within (10) and (11):

(C11)   ⊢3Y(Ruben) → 2Y(Linda)
(C10)   ⊢SM(Ed) → G(punishing Ed).

Thus on the standard account (10) and (11) would both have the form ' ⊢$F(a)$ → $G(b)$', where '$F$( )' and '$G$( )' are placeholders for predicates, and '$a$' and '$b$' placeholders for denoting expressions.

It becomes clear now that the defused force indicators '/$\Phi$!( )/' of the generalized force-indicator account are just like the predicates '$F($ )' of the conventional account. This is not surprising, if we recall that the development of the details of the force-indicator approach was a response to the difficulty posed by Geach's objection to expressivism (see §2). Geach pointed out that typical expressivist speech act analyses of 'non-descriptive' adjectives such as 'good' didn't match certain unasserted, embedded occurrences of these adjectives. His diagnosis, in 'Ascriptivism' (1960), is that the expressivist confuses predication with assertion, i.e. that he or she fails to distinguish the constant function of *predication* that predicates have on *all* their occurrences from the function they have only on asserted occurrences: that of *asserting* something of something. Assertion is related to predication in that one can assert something of something else by assertorically predicating the former of the latter.

The expressivist's remedy was the introduction of the 'defusing' slashes, which remove a sentence's illocutionary force by turning it into a designation of the attitude expressible by the sentence. I have now generalized the expressivist's account to cover all predicates, reinterpreting them as force indicators. Thus it was to be expected that *defused* force indicators are very similar to predicates.

Now consider that the expressivist content-indicator approach was the attempt to maintain the same force-indicator and content-indicator classification as conventional semantics, but to reinterpret the notions of content and force involved. Thus, the content-indicator approach will also yield something like (C10) and (C11) as formal representations of (10) and (11), under a reinterpretation of '⊢' and '→' that does not require them to operate on truth-evaluable contents only, and under a reinterpretation of predicates as quasi-predicates (see §3). Therefore a generalized content-indicator approach and a generalized force-indicator approach will yield structurally equivalent analyses of (10) and (11). This suggests that there is not much more than terminological difference between the two.

## 6 Concluding remarks

Let me take stock. Hale's objection from 'mixed' compounds showed that a moral expressivist cannot give a separate semantics of moral sentences, while sticking to standard semantics for non-moral sentences. My generalization of Hale's point makes clear that the same holds for expressivists about any class $X$ of sentences that admits composition with globalizers. Any such expressivist must offer a general, unified expressivist semantics, i.e. become a radical expressivist. As my suggestion for a plausible such unified theory on the force-indicator approach leads us to an account that is structurally equivalent to a unified expressivist account on the content-indicator approach, a reasonable conclusion is that any expressivist affected by the globalizer problem ought to pursue a unified content-indicator expressivism in the first place, in order to save himself or herself the trouble of introducing force indicators and slashes globally. According to my suggestion in §3, the content-indicator approach amounts to a unified conceptual role semantics.

One might be tempted to conclude from my argument in §4 that *any* expressivism must take the form of radical expressivism, i.e. that expressivism about *no* class of sentences *X* can take the classical semantic-split form. That would be too rash. My conclusion was restricted to those expressivisms that are affected by globalizers. Any expressivism unaffected by globalizers, i.e. any expressivism about a class of sentences without globalizers, will escape the conclusion.[26]

Now, it is easy to see that most expressivisms *will* be affected. Typically, expressivisms are about classes of sentences that are identified by a topic — a topic that renders them non-truth-evaluable for reasons of non-objectivity. Thus moral expressivism is about moral sentences, sentences that predicate (apparent) properties such as moral goodness or badness, and sentences whose content is that something ought or ought not to be done. Probabilistic expressivism is about sentences that ascribe probabilities, or perhaps about those sentences that contain the phrase 'it is probable' or the word 'probably' in a crucial way (where 'crucial' is meant to exclude occurrences within propositional attitude constructions and quotation marks).

The reason why any such expressivism *will* be affected by globalizers is simply that the property by which sentences are classified to belong to the problematic class is *syntactically irrelevant* in the sense that that property does not place any limits on how sentences in the class can be compounded and embedded. The presence of predicates like 'is good' or adverbial constructions like 'probably' does not affect the syntactic status of a sentential phrase according to which it may or may not be compounded in certain ways. The predicates 'is good' and 'is popular', when combined with a noun phrase, such as 'gambling', will yield sentential phrases that are embeddable in exactly the same ways, for example within a 'that ... ' construction or as part of a disjunction. As long as the sentences are classed as problematic by dint of a syntactically irrelevant property, there will be globalizers. It is not surprising, then, that most expressivisms are about sentences that are identified in a syntactically irrelevant way. For most expressivisms are metaphysically or epistemologically motivated, and natural language grammar is notoriously insensitive to metaphysico-epistemological distinctions.[27] This is where the trouble started in the first place.

The conclusion of this chapter is therefore that expressivism, the strategy of denying the truth-evaluability of problematic contents, leads ultimately to a semantics that does not rely on truth conditions at all. Thus expressivism leads us away from truth-conditional semantics. This does not show that expressivism is wrong. But it does show that expressivism is not a solution to the problem of excess objectivity, which arose within truth-conditional semantics because it presupposes global truth-evaluability. Expressivism, however, leads to an entirely new, non-truth-conditional approach to meaning.

# Chapter 5

# Soft Truth

In Chapters 3 and 4 I rejected revisionism and expressivism as solutions to the problem of excess objectivity. I rejected revisionism because it falsely identifies contents that are demonstrably distinct. Expressivism (at least the radical form I proposed) may not be false, but it leads away from truth-conditional semantics to a completely new approach to semantics, while the task of this book is to find a solution to a problem arising *within* truth-conditional semantics. I have therefore eliminated two out of the three possible solutions mentioned in Chapter 2, §2. We are left with what I called the 'soft-truth option'.

Consider again the sentence 'Licorice is tasty.'. Suppose its content is the truth-evaluable content that licorice is tasty and that what is truth-evaluable is objective. It follows that it is an objective matter whether licorice is tasty. The last two chapters dealt with the possibility of avoiding this consequence by denying the first of these suppositions. The soft-truth strategy avoids it by denying the second, i.e. by claiming that there may be contents that are truth-evaluable yet non-objective.

In Chapter 2, I introduced a notion of objectivity according to which a content is objective just if it is a priori that any disagreements over that content are a symptom of someone having made a mistake. More precisely, I used the following definition:

(CO) For any $p$: it is an objective matter whether $p$, just if: for all thinkers $A$ and $B$: it is a priori that if $A$ believes that $p$ and $B$ believes that not-$p$, then either $A$ has made a mistake or $B$ has made a mistake.[1]

There may be other senses of 'objective'. But whichever other senses there are, a solution to the problem of excess objectivity must avoid global objectivity *at least* in the sense of (CO). For there are areas of discourse where it is arguably not the case that of two contradictory contents only one can be believed without mistake. To assume that if I believe that licorice is tasty and you believe it isn't, one of us must be mistaken is to assume excessive objectivity.

Having settled upon the relevant notion of objectivity, I now need to consider whether there can be a notion of truth that makes room for truth-evaluability without objectivity and can play the requisite role in semantics—a notion of soft

truth. I argued in Chapter 2 that soft truth must be relative, for only a relativization of truth can make room for truth-evaluability without objectivity. I shall unfold the details of this relativization in the next chapter. In the present chapter I
want to address more fundamental issues concerning the possibility of a notion
of soft truth and of invoking such a notion in semantics. First, there is a long-
standing philosophical debate about truth and it is necessary to locate the notion
of soft truth here envisaged in relation to this debate. Second, it is necessary to
examine the view, held by many truth-conditional semanticists, that *the* notion of
truth plays a central explanatory role in semantics, and that it is therefore not a
matter of discretion which notion of truth is invoked in a semantic theory.

## I  The traditional debate

The traditional debate concerns the nature of truth, i.e. the question of what truth
really is. Participants in the debate generally assume that there is exactly one
notion — *the* notion — of truth which it is their ambition to analyse or define.
Some believe that no analysis or definition is possible and that truth is an unusual, primitive property. Deflationists believe that even though we can define
the truth predicate and explain its function, it expresses no genuine or interesting
property. Coherence theorists hold that the truth of a proposition consists in its
membership in a coherent class of propositions. Correspondence theorists believe that truth consists in a kind of correspondence with reality or with the facts.
Pragmatists regard those propositions as true that are useful in a certain way, or
are in a certain way conducive to success in action.

It is not necessary to review all these positions in detail, or even to make a decision as to which of them is correct. From the point of view of the present project, the interesting question is which of the positions allows truth-evaluability
not to entail objectivity. To examine this issue, we need to connect the notion of
truth with that of making a mistake (for objectivity is present, according to (CO),
whenever mere disagreement is a sign of a mistake). The connection was introduced already in Chapter 2, §8, above: to believe something not true constitutes
a mistake.

Now coherentists and pragmatists are presumably quite at ease with the idea
that a content may be truth-evaluable yet not objective. To see this, consider a
disagreeing pair of thinkers A and B: A believes that *p*, B believes that not-*p*. It
is clearly possible that both A's belief and B's belief are members of a coherent
set of beliefs. So coherentism does not rule out soft truth. It is also possible that
both A's belief and B's belief are conducive to successful action. Suppose A
happens not only to believe that licorice is tasty (as we are already assuming) but
does so because he or she likes licorice, and that B not only believes that licorice
is not tasty but does so because he or she loathes licorice. Then both A's belief
and B's belief are conducive to success in action, as A will try to get licorice,
because he or she believes it to be tasty, and B will try to avoid it, because he or
she believes it not to be tasty. A thus successfully promotes his or her pleasure

and B successfully avoids his or her displeasure. In this situation, both beliefs are true according to the pragmatist and neither of the disagreeing thinkers is committing a mistake. So for pragmatists too, there is no obstacle to regarding truth-evaluability as compatible with non-objectivity.[2]

There are good reasons too why deflationists should allow truth without objectivity. Deflationists ususally describe the function of the truth predicate and the truth concept as follows. It is sometimes impossible for a thinker to believe or assert some content because the thinker can only obliquely refer to the proposition in question without being able explicitly to state or think it. Typical examples are 'Everything the Pope says is true.' or 'What the policeman said is true.'. The thinker may be unable explicitly to think or state what the policeman said or everything the Pope says. But he or she can use the truth predicate and some description of the contents in question to think or assert something equivalent (see Quine 1970: 12 and Horwich 1998: 2–5). This rationale for a truth predicate, however, is equally useful and necessary for all contents of thought and speech, regardless of their topic. The deflationist is therefore committed to global truth-evaluability and faces the problem of excess objectivity unless he or she concedes that truth-evaluability and non-objectivity are compatible. In other words, for deflationists, expressivism does not even offer itself as an alternative solution, because they are directly committed to global truth-evaluability on account of their view of the function of truth. Thus deflationists must also allow truth-evaluability without objectivity.

This only leaves us with the correspondence theory of truth. Correspondence theorists will indeed put up resistance against the view that something may be true yet non-objectively so. They believe that what makes beliefs or their contents true is their correspondence to reality or to the facts. Typically, this relation of correspondence is some kind of representation: true contents represent reality correctly, or as it really is. On some theories, this involves an exact match between the constituents of the content and the constituents of a corresponding fact. Now the correspondence theorist might argue that we all face the same reality, the same facts. So if two thinkers have contradictory beliefs, one of them inevitably must have misrepresented reality, for contradictory beliefs represent reality in mutually incompatible ways. They can't both represent reality correctly. Therefore disagreements must be the symptom of error and there is no room for truth without objectivity.

But on second thoughts, even a correspondence conception need not be incompatible with non-objective truths. Let's grant that we all face the same reality and that it is some representational relation between contents and reality that makes contents true. But suppose that for different thinkers different ways of representing reality may be correct. Then it would be possible for each of two disagreeing thinkers to be correctly representing reality, and the content in question would be non-objective.

Clearly, most correspondence theorists would insist that the correspondence relation that makes contents true is as objective as reality itself. And they are entitled to this view. For nothing obliges them to concede global truth-evaluability. Those who regard truth as an objective representational relation to objective reality do not easily afford the status of truth-bearer. If there is doubt as to whether a given content concerns an objective matter of fact, the correspondence theorist will deny that this content is the sort of thing that can be true or false. The objective correspondence theorist thus restricts the range of applicability of his or her truth notion. Not all contents are evaluable in terms of correspondence truth. If my arguments against revisionism and expressivism are correct, this means that correspondence truth cannot be the notion used in truth-conditional semantics.

## 2 Two notions of truth

I said earlier that I do not need to settle the question as to which of the traditional views of truth is correct. Now, one of these views turned out to be incompatible with soft truth. There are two reasons why I don't consider myself to be obliged to rule out the correspondence view of truth. First, I believe that the notion of truth invoked in truth-conditional semantics need not be any particular notion of truth, or even *the* notion of truth, as long as it can fulfil its function in the machinery of a semantic theory. Second, I do not share the above-mentioned presupposition of the traditional debate that there is exactly one notion of truth—*the* notion of truth—which should be the object of our efforts of analysis. I will shortly return to the first point. As for the second point, it relies on observations of our use of the truth predicate. As I shall now argue, there is no single notion of truth that would make coherent sense of all aspects of our use of the truth predicate, so the best way to make sense of our usage is to assume that there are two distinct but related notions at work.

One aspect of our use of the truth predicate is clearly related to the deflationist's theory of its function. On this theory, the point of a truth predicate is to permit the assertion or acceptance of contents equivalent to contents the thinker cannot explicitly assert or accept. I can obliquely assert or accept Fermat's theorem by asserting or believing that Fermat's theorem is true. Similarly, I can compendiously assert or accept what the Pope declares *ex cathedra* by simply asserting or believing that everything the Pope says *ex cathedra* is true. Without the truth predicate this would not be possible. I could try to say: I agree with everything the Pope says *ex cathedra*. But that would not be the same. I may agree with everything the Pope says *ex cathedra* without it being true, and vice versa. This is also clear if one compares the following two conditionals:

(1)    If everything the Pope says *ex cathedra* is true, then abortion is wrong.
(2)    If I agree with everything the Pope says *ex cathedra*, then abortion is wrong.

Clearly, (2) expresses something quite different from (1). Thus 'I agree with … ' cannot do the job ' … is true' does.

This indispensable function of the truth predicate is equally useful for the oblique expression of contents on any topic. Correspondingly, we can observe that language users have a tendency to use the truth predicate across the board, i.e. to treat all contents of thought and speech as truth-evaluable. People do say such things as 'Everything the Pope says is true.' regardless of the objectivity status of the contents the Pope asserts. And they do so because the purpose served by the truth predicate is independent of the objectivity status of contents.

Confusingly there are also language users, even in some cases the same language users who manifest the global use of 'true', who are selective in the topics they regard as appropriate for evaluation as true or false. It is quite common for people, not only philosophers, to express their doubts about the objectivity of a topic by saying that it isn't really a matter of truth and falsehood. My quotation from Ayer in Chapter 4 (p. 44) illustrates the use:

> If ... I ... say 'Stealing money is wrong', I produce a sentence which has no factual meaning—that is, expresses no proposition which can be either true or false. (1946: 107)

This second aspect of the use of 'true' is clearly incompatible with the first. One cannot coherently both use the concept of truth globally *and* be selective about its proper range of applicability. I have no proper experimental evidence that language users do in fact use 'true' (or its equivalent in other languages) in the two conflicting ways.[3] But my own anecdotal evidence suggests it, and I believe that most people are in possession of similar anecdotal evidence.

There are three ways of responding to this situation. One can (a) dismiss the global use as misguided and endorse the selective use, or (b) dismiss the selective use and endorse the global use, or (c) claim that there are two distinct notions at work, both misleadingly expressed by the same word. On my view, (a), i.e. banning the global use, is not an option, because it would deprive us of an important linguistic tool in those areas of discourse from which the selective notion bans the truth predicate. Banning the selective use, i.e. (b), may not ultimately lead to a loss of expressive power, because there are presumably different expressions that could replace 'true' in its selective use. Nevertheless, I regard this response as patronizing. Why should selective users not carry on in their practice if there is still option (c), and if they take care not to confuse the two distinct notions? My conclusion is therefore that our use of the predicate 'true' is associated with two distinct notions of truth, one with a restricted range of applicability, the other globally applicable. It may be that the global use is associated with a metaphysically neutral deflationary truth notion, while the selective use is associated with a metaphysically loaded correspondence notion.

Since I am arguing that truth as invoked in truth-conditional semantics must be a soft notion (i.e. admit non-objectivity), it will come as no surprise that on my view this notion is not the one associated with the selective usage described above. Truth as invoked in semantics is more akin to the other, non-selective notion. However, I shall now argue that there is no need to identify truth as invoked in semantics with any independently accessible truth notion. The notion expressed by the predicate 'is $T$' in a theory of meaning can be taken to be implicitly defined and to have a purely instrumental role.

Many truth-conditional semanticists believe that the notion of truth plays a crucial explanatory role in semantic theories. I believe that this widespread misconception results from a misunderstanding of Davidson's original idea of a truth-conditional semantics for natural languages.

The doctrine that truth has an explanatory role in theories of meaning is closely linked to another Davidsonian doctrine: the prima facie absurd view that a theory of meaning for a language does not say what any sentence of that language means. More precisely, this is the view that the target theorems of a theory of meaning for a language ought to take the extensional form of material biconditionals of the form '$s$ is true iff $p$', so that the theorems of a theory of meaning do not *say* what the sentences of the language mean (or what their truth conditions or contents are) but rather 'give the meaning' of sentences and allow us to interpret them if we have further information about these theorems. I shall call this the 'biconditional doctrine'. The biconditional doctrine can easily lead to the second doctrine: the view that *the* concept of Truth plays a central explanatory role in Davidsonian theories of meaning for a language. I shall call this doctrine the 'truth doctrine'.

I shall now argue that the original reasons for adopting these two doctrines are flawed, and that there are in fact good reasons for not adopting them. Both doctrines are often uncritically accepted and have almost become part of the Davidsonian legacy. In order to show that they are unjustified and that the main insights of Davidson's programme do not depend on them, I need to go back quite a bit.

## 3 Davidson's programme

In 'Truth and Meaning', Davidson sets out to describe the form a theory of meaning for a particular language should take if it is to show 'how the meanings of sentences depend upon the meanings of words' (1967a: 17, 23). This pretheoretical adequacy condition is dictated by the simple need to explain the fact that languages can be learned even though they contain an indefinite number of sentences, the meanings of which could not be learned one by one. Davidson proceeds by considering the form of the theorems that a theory of meaning would generate. He rejects theorems of the form '$s$ means $m$', where the replacement for '$m$' is an expression referring to a meaning (he uses a form of the slingshot argument). He also rejects theorems of the form '$s$ means that $p$', because it is reasonable to expect that in wrestling with the logic of the apparently non-extensional 'means that' we will encounter problems as hard as, or perhaps identical with, the problems our theory is out to solve. (1967a: 22)

Davidson's point here is that if we want a theory that entails theorems of the form '*s* means that *p*', then we need to know something about the logic of the expression 'means that': we need to know which inferences involving this expression are valid. But the expression is intensional, and the best available account of the logical properties of intensional contexts involves a notion of meaning or synonymy: within intensional contexts, the substitution of synonymous expressions preserves truth (see e.g. Frege 1892a and Carnap 1956). But if we are out to explain the notion of meaning in general, or in a particular language, we cannot employ a logic that presupposes the very same notion of meaning.

Because of these difficulties, Davidson then looks out for a different, extensional expression that is to fill the gap in theorems of the form '*s* ... *p*', so that these theorems can be derived in a purely extensional axiomatic system. He says that

the success of our venture depends not on the filling but on what it fills. The theory will have done its work if it provides, for every sentence *s* in the language under study, a matching sentence (to replace '*p*') that, in some way yet to be made clear, 'gives the meaning' of *s*. (1967a: 23)

His suggested filling is 'is *T* iff', i.e. some (initially uninterpreted) predicate 'is *T*' combined with the extensional sentential connective 'iff'. The adequacy of a theory of meaning for a language can now be captured by the requirement that the theory 'entail all sentences got from' (1967a: 23) the schema '*s* is *T* iff *p*' when '*s*' is replaced by a structural description of a sentence of that language and '*p*' by a translation of that sentence.

It then turns out that Tarski's recursive method of defining a truth predicate for a formal language provides a way of satisfying this adequacy condition on 'is *T*'. Thus Davidson's proposal is that at least one good way of explaining how the meanings of the sentences of a given language depend upon the meanings of words is to construct a Tarski-style recursive theory of truth that generates theorems of the form '*s* is *T* iff *p*' for every sentence of that language.[4] This is Davidson's basic idea: to exploit Tarski's recursive technique in order to do justice to the compositional requirements of a semantic theory. In subsequent works, he developed the details of this approach by (a) showing how some recalcitrant natural-language constructions could be forced into the tight corset of a Tarskian recursive structure, and (b) explaining how a theory of meaning thus understood could be confirmed by empirical data (radical interpretation). Many philosophers and theoretical linguists have since joined Davidson in this effort.

### The biconditional doctrine

The biconditional doctrine results from an obvious basic problem with David-son's approach. Suppose we have constructed a Davidsonian theory of meaning for a language, i.e. a theory that entails a theorem of the form '*s* is *T* iff *p*' for each sentence *s* of the language, such that what replaces '*p*' in each theorem is a translation of *s*. These theorems are, in common parlance, 'interpretive' ('give/show the truth condition of a sentence'), but they do not *state* what the mentioned sentence means (or what its truth conditions are). They are just mate-rial biconditionals: all that is required for the truth of a material biconditional is that both sides flanking the biconditional have the same truth value. If I know that a given sentence is true iff snow is white, I do not thereby know that this sentence means that snow is white, nor do I thereby know that its 'truth condi-tion' is that snow is white. An easy way to see this is to consider the two sen-tences

(T1)    'Snow is white' is *T* iff snow is white.
(T2)    'Snow is white' is *T* iff grass is green.

If we wanted to say that by knowing (T1), I know that 'snow is white' means that (or has the truth condition that) snow is white, then we would also have to say that by knowing (T2), I know that 'snow is white' means that (or has the truth condition that) grass is green.

Davidson sets himself this problem in 'Truth and Meaning', and his response (1976: 174; 1967a: 26; 1984: xiv and xviii) is to say that in order for (T1) to give me information on what 'snow is white' means, I need to know in addition that (T1) has the status of a natural law, i.e. is derivable from a truth theory that has been empirically confirmed in the right way (i.e. through a process of radical interpretation) and is maximally simple. (T2) is not so derivable—to derive it, one would need further, non-semantic information on whether the content that 'snow is white' is true and the content that grass is green have the same truth value.

This, however, does not remove all the problems. Consider

(T3)    'Snow is white' is *T* iff snow is white and either grass is green or grass is not green.

Just like (T2), (T3) is not interpretive, but unlike (T2), (T3) *is* derivable from a truth theory confirmed by a Davidsonian process of radical interpretation. At least it is thus derivable if (T1) is, because it is logically equivalent to (T1).[5]

Davidsonians normally respond to this new difficulty by introducing the no-tion of a 'canonical T-theorem'. A T-theorem is a metalanguage sentence of the form '*s* is *T* iff *p*' where '*s*' is a description of an object-language sentence and '*p*' is a metalanguage sentence that does not mention any object-language ex-pressions (see Chapter 1, §4, above). A canonical T-theorem, now, is a T-theorem that can be derived following a specified (canonical) procedure. Roughly, this procedure involves applying the semantic axioms concerning the syntactic constituents of *s* in an order that inverts the order in which *s* was constructed from its constituents and then arriving at a T-theorem by repeated application of the rule of substitution of material equivalents. [6] All canonical theorems are interpretive and are free from (T3)'s problem. Thus if one knows that a theorem has been derived in the canonical way, one thereby knows that the sentence mentioned on one side of it is interpreted by the sentence used on its other side.

A modified response is given by Larson and Segal (1995, §§2.2.1 and 2.2.2; repeated in Segal 1999). According to Larson and Segal, a theory of meaning is supposed to model the knowledge that explains speakers' linguistic behaviour, i.e. it models the 'semantic module'. On their view, such a semantic theory consists of a set of semantic axioms and a set of rules of inference ('production rules')—rules that permit fewer inferences than classical logic. These inference rules are designed to permit only the derivation of interpretive T-theorems. This is an improvement on the standard response, because it avoids the detour of first formulating a theory with general logical inference rules, and then restricting the use of these rules by introducing the notion of a canonical proof. If a semantic theory is to model the information contained in the semantic module, such a gratuitous detour ought to be avoided (Larson and Segal 1995: 559 note 14).

Both the standard and the modified response to the problem leave Davidsonians with the awkward biconditional doctrine: the theorems of a theory of meaning are material biconditionals that do not *state* what the sentences mentioned mean. They do, however, 'give' the meaning, or truth condition, of the sentence, and additional information on what constitutes a canonical proof allows one to use such a theory for interpretive purposes. In Larson and Segal's formulation, humans have a semantic module that can be modelled as a T-theory, and humans treat the theorems that can be generated by the theory *as* interpretive. (Larson and Segal 1995: 39; Segal 1999: 55).

It is surprising that the cumbersome biconditional doctrine has not received more critical attention. The view that a semantic theory, or a semantic module, does not, on its own, provide information on what sentences mean, should have been highly suspect. Larson and Segal, who are the only Davidsonians who take the problem seriously, improve upon the standard version of the doctrine. But their claim that by allowing only a restricted set of inference rules, one can avoid uninterpretive theorems should have led to further reflection: if the only T-theorems derivable in a semantic theory are interpretive ones, then it should have been possible to modify the theory in such a way that it generates genuinely meaning-specifying theorems of the form '*s* means that *p*' (or '*s*'s content is that *p*' or '*s*'s truth condition is that *p*').

It is easy to see that the unattractive biconditional doctrine is unnecessary, if one considers Davidson's original reason for introducing target theorems of the form '*s* is *T* iff *p*'. Davidson's reason, as mentioned above, was the intensionality of the expression 'means that'. He thought that the theorems of a theory of meaning could not take the form '*s* means that *p*' because in order to derive such theorems, he would need to know intensional logic, something he thought presupposed the notion of meaning. However, both the standard version and the modified version of the biconditional doctrine provide an easy solution to this problem of deriving intensional theorems, or so I shall argue in the next section.

### How to derive intensional theorems

Let me explore in more detail how genuinely meaning-specifying theorems of the form '*s* means that *p*' could be derived in a semantic theory of Tarski–Davidsonian cut.

Consider the standard version of the biconditional doctrine first. It says that there is a canonical procedure following which one can derive, from the semantic axioms of the truth theory, all and only interpretive T-theorems. It would seem that this provides us with all we need to know about the intensional logic of 'means that'. Can't we simply add an inference rule that permits one to move from

(P)   '*s* is *T* iff *p*' is a canonical T-theorem

to

(C)   *s* means that *p*?

Let me first make a general observation about the form of inference rules. Any inference rule for a theory of meaning $M$ would be formulated not in the language $L_M$ of $M$ itself but in a meta-theoretic language. It would take the form of an inference schema with schematic letters ranging over expressions of $L_M$ (not the object-language). The schema then indicates that certain inferential moves from sentences of $L_M$ to sentences of $L_M$ are permitted. This is not unusual: the inference rules of any theory can be formulated only meta-theoretically.

The suggested inference schema is not a rule of this sort: it permits inferences from sentences of the form of (P) to sentences of the form of (C). The former, however, are not sentences of $L_M$, but meta-theoretic. This is because instances of (P) mention $L_M$ sentences and ascribe to them the meta-theoretically defined property of being a canonical T-theorem.[7]

We need a proper meta-theoretic rule that permits a move within $L_M$ from a T-theorem to its meaning-specifying counterpart if the T-theorem is canonically derived. The following formulation uses an adapted version of a standard notation for schematically stating inference rules:

(R)    .

    .    (canonical derivation)

    .

$s$ is $T$ iff $p$

---

$s$ means that $p$.

Schema (R) shows that one may derive an $L_M$ sentence $\ulcorner s$ means that $p \urcorner$ if one has previously been able to derive an $L_M$ sentence $\ulcorner s$ is T iff $p \urcorner$ in the canonical way. The three dots, together with the specification in brackets, give a meta-theoretic instruction: they indicate that $\ulcorner s$ is T iff $p \urcorner$ needs to have been canonically derived if the move to $\ulcorner s$ means that $p \urcorner$ is to be legitimate.

This form of stating a rule of inference may appear unorthodox and therefore arouse suspicion. But a little reflection will show that it is not unorthodox. Consider, for example, a typical schematic formulation of the rule of conditional proof for the propositional calculus:

(CP)   $[p]$

    .

    .

    .

$q$

---

$p \to q$

Consider the role of the meta-theoretic instruction here: the three dots between the bracketed '$p$' and '$q$' indicate that if a formula $q$ has been proved on the assumption that $p$, then one may infer $\ulcorner p \to q \urcorner$. Standard formulations of other rules of inference, such as *reductio ad absurdum* and constructive dilemma, involve even more complex meta-theoretic instructions (compare e.g. Hodges 1983: 29–30). Thus, if these are legitimate formulations of inference rules (which I take it they are), then so is (R).

But if (R) is a legitimate form of characterizing a rule of inference, then all we need to make it work is a canonical procedure following which one can derive all and only interpretive T-theorems. As we saw, the standard move of Davidsonians in the face of Foster-type problems is to invoke the existence of precisely such a canonical procedure.[8] Thus there is no reason why these Davidsonians could not introduce a rule like (R), thereby generating intensional, meaning-stating theorems and giving up the biconditional doctrine.

Now consider Larson and Segal's modified version of the biconditional doctrine. They claim that the inference rules 'contained in the semantic module' allow the derivation of all *and only* interpretive T-theorems. If this is true, then there may be an even more direct way of deriving meaning-stating theorems: just add an inference rule that allows the move from any T-theorem to its meaning-specifying counterpart. Schematically:

(R*)    $s$ is $T$ iff $p$

---

$s$ means that $p$.

Since a Larson and Segal-style semantic module employs inference rules that do not allow the derivation of uninterpretive T-theorems we need no meta-theoretic instruction that restricts this move to cases where the premiss has been canonically derived (see Larson and Segal 1995: 40, note 15).

This is too simple, however. Not every properly derived $L_M$ sentence of the form '$s$ is T iff $p$' is a T-theorem, i.e. a theorem in which the right-hand side '$p$' is replaced by an $L_M$ sentence that does not mention any object-language expressions. As a consequence, (R*) allows too much. For example, the theory will allow the derivation of sentences of the form ' "$s$ & $r$" is true iff $s$ is true and $r$ is true.'. But '"$s$ & $r$" means that $s$ is true and $r$ is true.' is false. Our inference rule should be applicable only to T-theorems. This needs to be included in the meta-theoretic description of the premiss in (R*). So the following might be a correct formulation of the rule for Larson and Segal's theory:

(R**) $s$ is $T$ iff $p$

> (where '$s$' is a description of an object-language sentence and '$p$' is an $L_M$ sentence that does not mention object-language expressions)

---

> $s$ means that $p$.

Thus both on the standard view and on Larson and Segal's, there is a way in which a theory of meaning can have intensional, meaning-specifying theorems.[9]

All this, however, should not be taken to suggest that we can do without T-theorems or that we can replace '— is true iff ...' early on, or throughout, with '— means that ...'. In the derivation of a meaning specification of a sentence, application of (R) or (R**) is only the last step. The real work is done previously by the derivation of a T-theorem.

An example may illustrate why: consider the derivation of a T-theorem for some conjunctive sentence $\ulcorner s$ & $r \urcorner$. One would first use the axiom for '&' to derive

(i)    $\ulcorner s$ & $r \urcorner$ is $T$ iff $s$ is $T$ and $r$ is $T$,

then one would use independently derived theorems of the form

(ii)    $s$ is $T$ iff $p$
(iii)    $r$ is $T$ iff $q$

to derive something of the form

(iv)    $\ulcorner s$ & $r \urcorner$ is $T$ iff $p$ and $q$

using a rule of substitution of equivalents. No meaning-specifying theorems could play the role of (ii) and (iii) in this derivation. Of course, (R) could be applied to (ii) and (iii) directly, and would then yield the correct meaning specification for $s$ and $r$. But in order to derive the meaning specification for $\ulcorner s \And r \urcorner$, we need the original biconditional version of (ii) and (iii).

My proposal is therefore not intended as an objection to Davidson's view that 'we have no other idea how to turn the trick' (1967a: 23) of formulating a theory that allows one to generate pairings of object-language sentences with their metalanguage translations from information about simple sentence constituents. Tarski's machinery has an indispensable role in the theory (until we find a different idea how to turn the trick). What I object to is the unreflected upon doctrine that a theory of meaning cannot say what sentences mean because we lack information about the logic of the intensional phrase 'means that'.

Thus we know enough about the intensional logic of 'means that' to derive safely theorems of the form '$s$ means that $p$' as a final step. We *can* have a meaning theory that states what sentences mean. The cumbersome biconditional doctrine is an unmotivated dogma. We *can* after all utilize Tarski-style recursive machinery and still derive, in a second step, what sentences mean.[10]

### Davidson's programme before the truth doctrine

Once one has taken the step of recognizing that the biconditional doctrine is a dogma, it becomes easier to take an instrumental view of the role of the predicate 'is $T$' in some theorems of a theory of meaning: it enables the recursive machinery to generate interpretive T-theorems—and ultimately theorems of the form '$s$ means that $p$'. The important function of the predicate is that it allows us to generate theorems that pair object-language sentences with their metalanguage interpretations.

At the time of writing 'Truth and Meaning', Davidson was promoting this view himself, as is shown by the remark I quoted above (p. 75):

the success of our venture depends not on the filling but on what it fills. The theory will have done its work if it provides, for every sentence $s$ in the language under study, a matching sentence (to replace '$p$') that, in some way yet to be made clear, 'gives the meaning' of $s$. (1967a: 23)

Davidson continues in this vein later in his paper, when he discusses the problem of evaluative sentences. Evaluative sentences would constitute an obvious problem for Davidsonian meaning theories if the predicate involved in the T-theorems were thought of as expressing the notion of truth. For it is controversial whether evaluative sentences (or the contents expressed by utterances of them) can be evaluated in terms of truth at all. But Davidson brushes any such worries aside, asserting, once again, that all that counts is whether the theory can generate the right theorems from its axioms, implying that it does not matter whether the predicate involved expresses the notion of truth:

> If we suppose questions of logical grammar settled, sentences like 'Bardot is good' raise no special problems for a truth definition. The deep differences between descriptive and evaluative (emotive, expressive, etc.) terms do not show here. Even if we hold there is some important sense in which moral and evaluative sentences do not have a truth value (for example because they cannot be verified), we ought not to boggle at ' "Bardot is good" is true if and only if Bardot is good'; in a theory of truth, this consequence should follow with the rest, keeping track, as must be done, of the semantic location of such sentences in the language as a whole—of their relation to generalizations, their role in such compound sentences as 'Bardot is good and Bardot is foolish', and so on. What is special to evaluative words is simply not touched: the mystery is transferred from the word 'good' in the object-language to its translation in the metalanguage. (1967a: 31)

These remarks show that Davidson did not object to the concept invoked in the T-theorems being distinct from the concept of truth—or at least from truth in any sense in which it cannot be applied to evaluative sentences. As long as a theory of meaning delivers the needed T-theorems that permit us to interpret speakers, it doesn't matter what exactly we mean by 'true' in the theory of meaning. Thus, at the time of writing 'Truth and Meaning', Davidson did not subscribe to the truth doctrine—the view that the notion of truth plays a key explanatory role in theories of meaning for particular natural languages.

### The emergence of the truth doctrine

Davidson changed his view on this when he developed his theory of radical interpretation (See Davidson 1984: xiv–xv and 1990: 286 note 20). It was considerations about the explanatory aims of Tarski's project as opposed to the explanatory aims of his own meaning theories that prompted this change of view and gave rise to the truth doctrine. Davidson expressed the new view in many of his works after 1973. For example in the introduction to *Inquiries into Truth and Interpretation*:

> [W]hile Tarski intended to analyse the concept of truth by appealing (in convention T) to the concept of meaning (in the guise of sameness of meaning, or translation), I have the reverse in mind. I considered truth to be the central primitive concept, and hoped, by detailing truth's structure, to get at meaning. (1984: xiv)

In 'Radical Interpretation':

[A]ssuming translation, Tarski was able to define truth; the present idea is to take truth as basic and to extract an account of translation or interpretation. (1973: 134)

And in 'Belief and the Basis of Meaning':

Our outlook inverts Tarki's: we want to achieve an understanding of meaning or translation by assuming a prior grasp of the concept of truth. (1974: 150)

And more recently in 'The Structure and Content of Truth':

The theory is correct because it yields correct T-sentences; its correctness is tested against our grasp of the concept of truth as applied to sentences. (1990: 300)

[I]t is our grasp of [the concept of truth] that permits us to make sense of the question whether a theory of truth for a language is correct. (ibid.)[11]

Let me spell out some of the background of these remarks. In 'The Concept of Truth in Formalized Languages' (1956), Tarski formulated an adequacy condition for definitions of truth for a language. This condition requires that an adequate definition of truth for a language $L$ must entail for each sentence of $L$ a theorem of the form '$s$ is true in $L$ iff $p$', where '$s$' is a 'structural description' of that sentence and '$p$' is the translation of that sentence in the language in which the definition is stated. Thus, in order to apply this criterion for the adequacy of a definition of 'true in $L$', one needs to understand what it is for a sentence to be a translation of (or synonymous with) another sentence. Davidson proposed to construct a structurally similar theory, also entailing theorems of the mentioned form, but with the aim of 'giving' the meaning of each sentence of the language under discussion. In order to decide whether such a theory is adequate, Davidson cannot, obviously, presuppose knowledge of which sentences of the metalanguage are translations of which sentences of the object-language, as this is what the theory is supposed to yield knowledge *of*. So Davidson needs to apply a different criterion of adequacy for his theories of truth (which are to serve as theories of meaning). How could it be decided whether a Davidsonian theory of truth is adequate?

Davidson does in fact have a very good answer to this question. It is given by his methodology of radical interpretation. But he also uses the following line of thought to convince himself that he needs to presuppose the notion of truth as a basic explanatory concept: assuming what it is for one sentence to translate another, 'Tarski was able to define truth',[12] so if one wants to explain meaning (translation) using the very same theory, one obviously needs to be in possession of the notion of truth already. In Paul Horwich's words:

[W]e would be faced with something like a single equation with two un-knowns ... knowledge of the truth conditions of a sentence cannot simulta-neously constitute *both* our knowledge of its meaning *and* our grasp of truth for the sentence. (1998: 68)

Davidson concludes that the notion of truth must play a central explanatory role in the construction of theories of meaning.

The starting point of this line of thought is correct. But its conclusion is not. It is correct that Davidson needs a new criterion of adequacy, different from Tar-ski's. He cannot check whether all the theorems of a theory of meaning for a language are correct by checking whether their right-hand side translates the sentence mentioned on their left-hand side. But he does not need to check whether the theorems are correct by checking *immediately* whether their right-hand side gives sufficient and necessary conditions for the truth of the sentences mentioned on their left-hand side. If he needed to be able to know necessary and sufficient conditions for the truth of all the sentences *immediately*, then the pro-ject of interpreting an unknown language would be hopeless.[13] Instead, what Davidson can do (and what he in effect proposes to do in his methodology of radical interpretation) is to check whether the theorems, if taken as interpretive, allow one to make good sense of the linguistic behaviour of the speakers of the language.

John McDowell, in his reconstruction of the original Davidsonian project, ex-ploits just this idea. A theory of meaning for a language ought ultimately to pro-vide us with information that would be sufficient to interpret speakers of that language correctly. Now, a Davidsonian T-theory can take us part of the way. It can help us assign to every sentence a propositional content. But in addition to such a theory of content, we a need a theory of illocutionary force. These two elements together form what McDowell calls a 'bipartite' theory of meaning. If one knows such a theory for a language (and if one has sufficient time and pa-tience), then it allows one to redescribe speakers' phonetic acts, i.e. acts of emit-ting certain sequences of sounds, as propositional acts, e.g. acts of asserting that, or asking whether such-and-such. According to McDowell, the acceptability of such a theory, as an empirical theory about the language's speakers, is measured by the extent to which these redescriptions allow us to make sense of the lin-guistic and non-linguistic behaviour of the speakers (see McDowell 1976: 44–5). The working of such a theory, and the process of empirically confirming it, in no way depends on the interpretation of the predicate 'is T' that we are employing in our interpretive T-theorems and in generating them. Nothing prevents us from regarding 'is T' as a theoretical notion that is implicitly defined by the theory. Any (perhaps partial) coextensiveness between 'is T' and our ordinary notion of truth is something we discover afterwards, it's not something we need to assume before we start the project. In McDowell's own words:

> The thesis should be not that [meaning] is what a theory of truth is a theory of, but rather that truth is what a theory of [meaning] is a theory of. (1976: 30)

On McDowell's view, as long as we can make out a legitimate empirical methodology for constructing bipartite meaning theories, nothing obliges us to think of the T-notion employed in the theory of content as the notion of truth.

Again, rejecting the biconditional dogma puts one into a better position to see this. If we take a meaning theory for a language to yield predictions (theorems) of the form '*s* means that *p*', and not of the form '*s* is true iff *p*', then Davidson's motivation for the truth doctrine vanishes completely. Obviously, a radical interpreter is not required to know *immediately* whether the meaning-specifying theorems delivered by his or her theory of content are correct. He or she will test their correctness via further predictions these theorems allow us to make about speakers. Now, what further predictions these are will depend on how a theory of meaning *interacts* (to use a McDowellian expression) with other theories, i.e. theories that predict which sentences speakers will utter given that they have a certain meaning, or, in other words, theories that explain why speakers utter sentences with a certain meaning.

Since the truth dogma is deeply entrenched, these abstract and general considerations are likely to meet with scepticism. But it should be agreed even by sceptics that the method by which a Davidsonian theory of meaning is to be tested empirically should be our ultimate touchstone for the truth doctrine: if the methodology of radical interpretation requires explanatory use of the notion of truth, then the truth doctrine is justified. If it does not, then the truth doctrine can be thrown onto the scrapheap of unjustified dogmas together with the biconditional dogma. In the next section I shall therefore look in more detail at the details of a methodology of radical interpretation in which the notion of truth makes no appearance whatsoever.[14]

## 4  Radical interpretation without *the* notion of truth

How can a Davidsonian theory of meaning for a particular natural language be empirically tested? In order to do this, we need to know more about the *observable* consequences of such a theory. What observable consequences could a theory have that states what the sentences of a language mean? Intuitively, if the theory is correct, speakers of the language will use certain sentences under certain conditions. It would seem, for example, that if some sentence meant that snow is white, then speakers would have a tendency to utter that sentence when they wish to get across that snow is white. If they do in fact have this tendency, then this confirms the theory; if they don't, it disconfirms the theory.

This commonsensical strategy is in principle correct. But we need to add a bit of theory before we can make some such strategy work. We need to clarify the connection between facts of meaning, as specified in the theorems of the modified Davidsonian theory, and the behaviour of language users these facts should lead us to expect.

I have already said in Chapter 1 that by assigning to each sentence a meaning, or truth condition, via a Davidsonian theory, one has not yet captured all meaning features relevant for communication. Sentences can also be classified as having various communicative functions. Some sentences serve to make assertions, others to ask questions or to issue commands. Combining a Davidsonian theory with a theory of communicative function, one can say that a Davidsonian theory specifies what the *content* of each sentence is (or what *proposition* it expresses), while the theory of communicative function specifies for the performance of which communicative act (in relation to this content) the sentence serves. For example, uttering the English sentence 'Sam smokes.', one *asserts that* Sam smokes, while uttering the sentence 'Does Sam smoke?', one *asks whether* Sam smokes, performing a different communicative act on the same content.

Adding an assignment of communicative functions to a Davidsonian theory of content brings us closer to being able empirically to verify the now combined theory. The combined theory predicts that speakers perform certain actions of assertion, question, etc. when they utter sentences. But how do we test empirically whether a speaker is really performing such an action? We need a detailed account of the various linguistic acts, so that we can test the predictions the theory yields against general psychological assumptions concerning action.

The most promising accounts treat communicative acts as actions in intentional conformity with conventional rules and ultimately motivated by communicative aims. Philosophers such as Wittgenstein, Austin, Grice, Searle, Lewis and Stalnaker have pioneered this type of approach. Speakers aim to influence the beliefs of their audiences and audiences aim to acquire new information. Speakers know that audiences generally respond to utterances in conformity with the rules and audiences know that speakers generally make utterances in conformity with the rules. This knowledge allows speakers and audiences to further their communicative aims by acting in accordance with the rules. There are characteristic rules for each kind of linguistic act (assertion, question, etc.).

Up to this point, most theorists of speech acts are in agreement. But they diverge considerably when it comes to the nature of the rules and the nature of the conventionality involved. I shall briefly sketch two approaches that seem to me to be particularly promising and comment on their suitability for a methodology of radical interpretation. For simplicity I shall discuss only assertion.

The first approach is broadly along the lines of Lewis's game-theoretical view of linguistic conventions and explains communicative acts directly in terms of belief–desire psychology (see Lewis 1969 and 1975). Lewis defines a convention as a certain type of regularity in the behaviour of a population of agents who face a recurring coordination problem. A coordination problem is a game-theoretical situation in which there are several equilibria on one of which the agents need to coincide. A convention is a solution to such a recurring problem:

agents conform to a certain regularity of behaviour because they expect the others to conform to the same regularity and it is in their interest to conform if the others conform. Thus conventional behaviour can be explained directly in terms of a simple belief–desire psychology. In the case of linguistic conventions, in particular conventions regarding assertoric sentences, the relevant regularity might require agents (i) to utter a sentence assertoric of a content $p$ only if $p$ and (ii) to respond to utterances of such a sentence by coming to believe that $p$.

This rule is only a first shot. It wrongly assumes that speakers who conform to linguistic convention are always truthful and sincere, and that audiences always believe what they are told. Clearly, speakers often inadvertently assert a content that $p$ even though it is false that $p$. Moreover, speakers often deliberately assert $p$ even though they don't believe $p$ themselves. Similarly, audiences often fail to believe contents that have been asserted, or even fail to believe that the asserter believes what he or she has asserted. But let us assume that we can solve this problem by modifying Lewis's account in the following way (as I argue in Köl-bel 1998). The appropriate speaker regularity is that of asserting $p$ only if one (i) believes that $p$, or (ii) wants to give the impression that one believes that $p$, or (iii) wants to give the impression that one wants to give the impression that one believes that $p$, or ... . And the corresponding audience regularity is that of responding to assertions of $p$ by (i) coming to believe that the utterer believes that $p$, or (ii) coming to believe that the utterer wants to give the impression that he or she believes that $p$, or (iii) coming to believe that the utterer wants to give the impression that he or she wants to give the impression that he or she believes that $p$, ... . As before, these regularities are conventions in Lewis's game-theoretical sense.

We would then have a way of testing our combined theory against general psychological assumptions. Suppose the theory says that some sentence $s$ is as-sertoric and expresses the proposition that $p$. If the theory is correct, then speakers will expect that audiences of $s$ come to believe that the utterer either believes that $p$ or wants to give the impression that he or she believes that $p$ or ... . If speakers' communicative aims together with these expectations provide a good explanation of utterances of $s$, then the theory is confirmed. The same goes, *ceteris paribus*, for audience behaviour.

The advantage of such an account is that it offers an immediate integration of the combined theory into a general belief–desire psychology. Speakers have mutual knowledge of their conformity to certain regularities, and this, together with their communicative desires, motivates them, via ordinary instrumental rea-soning, to engage in linguistic action.[15] On this model, a methodology of radical interpretation makes no explanatory use of the notion of truth. At least it does not so long as the notions of belief, desire and their contents are independent of the notion of truth. But there is no prima facie reason to believe that these no-tions depend on the notion of truth—except perhaps for Davidson's own reason for the truth doctrine, which I have discredited above.

The second approach I want to discuss might be called a 'conversational approach to communicative action'. It differs from Lewis's approach in two ways. First, instead of Lewis's simple regularities concerning individual utterances of sentences, the conversational account states rules that specify the role of assertions in entire conversations, i.e. in interconnected series of assertions by several agents. Second, the conversational approach makes these rules a matter of social norms, while Lewis's game-theoretical approach denies social norms and sanctions any role in linguistic convention. As an example for a conversational account, I shall here use the account of assertion proposed by Robert Brandom.[16] According to Brandom, there is a system of social norms and rules that governs our linguistic interactions. Within this system, assertion has a central role: an assertion that $p$ counts (i) as an undertaking to justify $p$ if challenged to do so, and (ii) as issuing a licence to use $p$ as a premiss. Quite obviously, these rules rely on the normative vocabulary of social duties and licences, which are ultimately explained in terms of notions such as authority and sanction. Thus a conversational account of assertion does not immediately yield reductive explanations of utterances in terms of the beliefs and desires of the utterer. All the same, the account provides an empirical test for bipartite theories of meaning for particular languages. If a general theory of action together with a candidate theory of meaning—now combined with a theory of communicative acts interpreted as social linguistic acts—can explain speakers' behaviour, then this confirms the candidate theory.

Again, if a conversational account of communicative acts is used in our methodology of empirically testing a combined theory of meaning, there is no reason to believe that the notion of truth plays an explanatory role.[17] Thus two promising theories of the communicative acts are at our disposal for use in a truthless methodology of radical interpretation. Nothing therefore prevents us from viewing the predicate 'is $T$' as contextually defined by the theory in which it occurs. There is no need to assume that the predicate expresses some pre-theoretically familiar notion of truth, or that this pre-theoretical grasp is required to endow the theory with explanatory power.[18] This confirms the conclusion of my earlier argument (in §3 of the present chapter) that the truth doctrine is a dogma.

## 5 'Meaning as truth condition'

I have argued that the ultimate theorems of a theory of meaning do not need to take the extensional form '$s$ is $T$ iff $p$' and that the use of the predicate 'is $T$' can be viewed as merely an expedient in the recursive machinery of the theory. Pursuers of Davidson's programme can coherently believe that the notion of truth has no explanatory significance in semantics. Where does that leave plausible-sounding slogans such as

(S1)   The meaning of a sentence is its truth condition

and

(S2)   To know the meaning of a sentence is to know under what conditions it would be true?

Is the label 'truth-conditional semantics' a misnomer?

The answer is that the terminology of truth conditions is indeed partly misleading. (S1) is informative only on the background of Davidson's biconditional dogma. It is correct in so far as it expresses the underlying Davidsonian insight that one can construct a theory of meaning for a language that explains compositionality by exploiting recursive techniques first devised by Tarski to define truth in a formal language. But often (S1) is misleadingly used to suggest a deeper significance.

(S2) is true only in so far as it expresses the insight that to know the meaning of a sentence is to know how to use it correctly. In some typical cases it is correct to use a sentence only if its content is true, so knowing under what conditions it would be true (whatever that means) will often help one to use it correctly. But this insight is quite independent of Davidson's main idea of 'Truth and Meaning', namely to use a theory of a certain recursive structure as a theory of content for a language. Rather it belongs in a theory of communicative (illocutionary) acts, which might state, for example, that one should assert that $p$ only if $p$ (= that one should assert that $p$ only if it is true that $p$).[19]

But isn't it still too much of a coincidence that it should be possible correctly to use the predicate 'is true' in the intermediate lemmas of the theory, if in fact any uninterpreted predicate would have served just as well?

The answer is that this is not a coincidence. It can be neatly explained by minimal (deflationist) assumptions about the function of the truth predicate without uncovering any deep link between truth and meaning (as done in Williams 1999). Deflationists about truth claim that truth is not a mysterious property. All we need to know about truth is encapsulated in the way the truth predicate solves a simple syntactic problem. The problem arises, for example, when there are sentences (or propositions) that we can mention but cannot use (that we cannot make explicit). For example, many people are unable to state Fermat's theorem. Nevertheless, they can easily make reference to it by just using the expression 'Fermat's theorem'. (They often know that Fermat's theorem has only recently been proven.) Merely making reference to the theorem, however, does not yet allow one, for example, to assert the theorem or to use it as the antecedent of a conditional. This is where the truth predicate is useful. It is governed by the rule that by applying it to the name of any sentence (or proposition), one gets a new sentence that is equivalent to the sentence of which truth was predicated (or that expresses a proposition equivalent to the proposition of which truth was predicated). Some have expressed this by calling the truth predicate a pro-sentence-forming operator (see e.g. Brandom 1994: chapter 5). For example, the sentence 'Fermat's theorem is true.' expresses a proposition equivalent to Fermat's theorem. Another typical example is the sentence 'All of Davidson's doctrines are true.', which is equivalent to the conjunction of Davidson's doctrines but much easier to state.

This simple function of the truth predicate explains why it should be possible to interpret the predicate used in T-theorems as the truth predicate. In generating our meaning-specifying theorems from semantic axioms, we need to pair structural descriptions of object-language sentences with their metalanguage translations. In temporarily 'filling the gap', we ought to use the material biconditional, as that helps our derivations (via a rule of substitution of equivalents, see §4 above). Since a structural description of a sentence cannot flank the biconditional, we need to complete it with some predicate 'is T' to form a sentence. Since the other side of the biconditional is that sentence's translation (if the theory is correct), it is no coincidence that interpreting 'is T' as the truth predicate makes the T-theorems come out true. For as we have seen, the truth predicate forms sentences that are equivalent to the sentence of which it is predicated. The usefulness of Tarski's methods in a compositional theory of meaning does not, therefore, indicate any deep connection between the notion of truth and that of meaning.

I conclude that the role of the truth notion invoked in truth-conditional semantics is not constrained by any pre-theoretical intuitions about the objectivity of truth. There are no obstacles, from this point of view, to viewing truth in semantics as being compatible with lack of objectivity.

# Chapter 6

# Relative Truth and Linguistic Communication

I have argued in previous chapters that a solution to the problem of excess objectivity ought to proceed along the lines of the soft-truth strategy, that is by allowing truth-evaluability to be available independently of objectivity. Contents of speech or thought are generally truth-evaluable, but not all contents are objective in the precise sense of objectivity defined by (CO):

(CO) For any *p*: it is an objective matter whether *p*, just if: for all thinkers *A* and *B*: it is a priori that if *A* believes that *p* and *B* believes that not-*p*, then either *A* has made a mistake or *B* has made a mistake.

I argued in Chapter 2 that the only way to secure the possibility of non-objective contents is to conceive of the relevant notion of truth, i.e. the notion in terms of which all contents are to be evaluable, as relative. If truth were not relative, minimal assumptions about truth would ensure that of any two disagreeing thinkers, at least one must have committed the mistake of believing something not true, so that mere truth-evaluability would entail objectivity (see Chapter 2, §5).

What is truth going to be relative to? I have already given a brief sketch of my framework of relative truth in Chapter 2: the truth value of contents is to vary with standards of evaluation or 'perspectives'. Perspectives are theoretical entities very similar to (but in crucial respects different from) possible worlds. Each perspective will assign a truth value to every content, and contents can accordingly be true in one perspective and not true in another. Even though every (consistent) content will be true in some perspective, this does not mean that every belief is automatically correct. For despite its relativity, the relative truth notion has a normative dimension: thinkers ought to believe only contents that are true in their *own* perspective. The relation of *possession* between thinkers and perspectives therefore plays a key role in the framework. The nature of this relation will be such that thinkers' perspectives can diverge in their evaluation of some contents, while they cannot diverge in their evaluation of others. The latter contents are objective, the former not.

In this chapter, I shall unfold the details of the framework. I shall do so by presenting an independently motivated theory of linguistic communication, in which postulating the relativity of truth to perspectives, and a relation of per-spective possession serve to explain a well-known aspect of our discursive be-haviour, namely the fact that we view some disagreements as faultless and re-gard argument on certain topics as pointless. I shall first outline a commonsensi-cal account of linguistic communication that presupposes that contents are ab-solutely evaluated. I shall then modify the account to make room for faultless disagreements and the associated discursive attitudes. Finally, I will attempt to give my account of perspective possession more substance by embedding it into a more general account of our methods of belief acquisition and our ways of learning these methods. This account, incidentally, explains the notion of a priori used in the definition of objectivity (CO).

## I An absolutist model of linguistic communication

### Background assumptions

For a simple model of linguistic communication, all one needs is a population of thinkers who share a common language. Let us assume that each thinker has be-liefs, and that to have a belief is just to be related in a certain way to a belief content or proposition. Let us further assume, in accordance with the account given in Chapter 1, that knowledge of a language $L$ consists in three parts: first the *syntax* of $L$, which defines the notion of sentential phrase and sentence of $L$. Second, the *semantics* or *theory of content* of $L$: this is a function that assigns a content to each sentential phrase of $L$ (for indexical languages, this will be a function from pairs of sentential phrase and context of utterance to contents).[1] The third part is the *pragmatics* of $L$: this is a function that assigns to each com-plete sentence of $L$ a communicative function, such as assertoric, interrogative or imperative force.[2] Anyone who knows these three elements of $L$ counts as a user of $L$. Knowledge of these three parts of $L$ will enable a user of $L$ to recognize (his or her own and others') utterances of sentences of $L$ as linguistic acts, such as assertions, questions or commands.

For example, if a well-formed sentence $s$ of $L$ is assigned the content that Bir-mingham is in England by the semantics, and the communicative function of assertion by the pragmatics, then an utterance of $s$ counts as an assertion that Birmingham is in England. Any user of $L$ knows that this is so (even though he or she might not know it under the formulation I just used). This knowledge en-ables users to use $s$, either by intentionally uttering it, or by responding to others' utterances of $s$ in a way that is informed by this knowledge.

But how exactly does one's knowledge of the syntax, semantics and prag-matics of $L$ enable one to use the sentences of $L$ in communication? The answer to this question lies in an account of the various different communicative acts referred to by the pragmatics of $L$, in particular an account of assertion.[3] There are various competing views of assertion, but I shall here rely on only two uncontroversial assumptions that should be true on any view of assertion. The first assumption is that sincerity is *some* kind of norm for assertion:

(S)    One ought to assert a proposition only if one believes that proposition to be true.

The 'ought' in (S) is deliberately vague. Its purpose is to indicate that there is a norm of *some* sort. (S) just says that there is *some* norm that prohibits the assertion of propositions one doesn't believe, i.e. some reason for communicators to avoid asserting propositions they don't believe. The kind of reason one has for complying with (S) will be different on different accounts of assertion. (On a Lewis-style game-theoretical account of assertion, the norm expressed by (S) is just instrumental rationality; on a Brandom-style sociological account of assertion (S) holds in virtue of a system of social rules that are enforced by social sanction.)

Second, I shall assume that truth is a norm for thinkers:

(T)    One ought to believe only truths.

(T) just says that there is *some* norm that prohibits believing contents that aren't true, i.e. some reason for thinkers to avoid believing contents that aren't true. (S) and (T) probably express different kinds of norm: the sort of mistake one makes when believing something not true is quite different from the sort of mistake one makes when asserting something one does not believe. One difference between the two kinds of mistake is that the latter can be committed deliberately, while the former can't. We can't knowingly believe something not true, but we can (and sometimes do) knowingly assert propositions we don't believe.

(T) is meant to be compatible with any theory of truth. In particular, it is not incompatible with deflationism or minimalism about truth. For even those who believe (for whatever reason and in whatever sense) that truth is not a genuine property, or that the notion of truth exists only for a certain grammatical purpose, can agree that truth is a norm in the sense of (T). For them, (T) is just a convenient way of subscribing to all instances of the schema

$(T^D)$    One ought to believe that *p* only if *p*.

In fact, (T) is a typical case that illustrates why we need a truth predicate.[4]

### Simple cases of communication

These assumptions suffice to develop my common-sense account of linguistic communication. How, then, given (T) and (S), can we explain that knowledge of the syntax, semantics and pragmatics of *L* enables thinkers to use the sentences of *L* for communication? First, there are straightforward cases of belief-transfer. Suppose Jack believes that the mushroom is a *Boletus badius*. He knows that uttering a certain sentence *s* counts as an assertion that the mushroom is a

*Boletus badius*. He also knows that Jill knows (from (S)) that he has a reason to try to assert that the mushroom is a *Boletus badius* only if he believes that the mushroom is a *Boletus badius*. Thus, he knows that if he were to utter *s*, Jill would have reason to believe that he believes that the mushroom is a *Boletus badius* — unless she had reason to believe that he had some independent, stronger reason which led him to flout (S) (i.e. to lie). Thus, if Jack believes that Jill has no such independent reason, he will expect Jill to conclude that he believes that the mushroom is a *Boletus badius* from his utterance of *s*. Moreover, if Jill doesn't yet believe that the mushroom is a *Boletus badius*, if she thinks Jack to be competent in this matter (i.e. to comply with (T)), and if she regards the matter worth while, then she will come to believe that the mushroom is a *Boletus badius*. Thus Jack might utter *s* in order to achieve that Jill come to believe that the mushroom is a *Boletus badius*. And if Jack was right in his expectations, then Jill will indeed come to believe that the mushroom is a *Boletus badius*.

In this case, both Jack and Jill would have *used s* for communication — Jack as speaker, Jill as hearer. Speakers and hearers do not need to reason explicitly in the way I suggested. Rather, they will often do so implicitly and automatically without being aware (or being able to report) that this is what they are doing.

This case of Jack and Jill is just a very simple case of linguistic communication: a speaker asserts a proposition he or she believes with the aim of getting the audience to believe that proposition, while the audience believes the speaker to comply with (T) and (S) and therefore actually comes to believe that proposition. Let us call such straightforward cases of communication 'simple cases'. Simple cases are not the only cases. There are also cases of insincere assertion (lying), where the speaker knowingly asserts something he or she doesn't believe; or cases of lacking trust, where the audience does not believe the speaker to believe what he or she has asserted. Moreover, there are cases of superfluous assertion, where the speaker asserts a proposition the audience already believes. Finally, and importantly, there are cases where the hearer fails immediately to come to believe what a speaker has asserted *even though* he or she believes the assertion to have been sincere. This can happen for various reasons. Either the hearer already believes some content that is incompatible with the asserted content, or the hearer believes the speaker to be unreliable with regard to the content asserted. Let us call these cases 'cases of incredulity'.

At first sight, cases of incredulity might seem to be cases where communication fails, because no belief, and a fortiori no information, gets transmitted from speaker to hearer. In fact, however, cases of incredulity are as central and as important for linguistic communication as simple cases. Let me explain why.

### Cases of incredulity

Consider the following case of incredulity. Suppose Jack asserts to Jill that there is a mountain 10 miles high. Even if Jill has no reason to doubt Jack's sincerity (i.e. his compliance with (S)), she might still not be moved to believe that there

is a mountain 10 miles high. One reason for her not believing what Jack has asserted might be that she believes that the highest mountain is just over 29,000
feet, and that 29,000 feet is much less than 10 miles. She thus has beliefs that are
incompatible with what Jack asserted, and therefore concludes that while Jack
has respected the sincerity norm (S), he might unwillingly have violated the truth
norm (T).

If Jill were to take Jack seriously, she would be prompted by his assertion to
start a discussion. She might answer something like

> 'Surely there is no mountain that high.'

or

> 'What makes you believe that?'

or

> 'Everest is the highest and Everest is not even 6 miles high. So there is no
> mountain 10 miles high.'

Each of these answers invites Jack to discuss. The first by openly asserting the
negation of what he has asserted, the second by inviting him to justify what he
has asserted, and the third by justifying the negation of what he has asserted. At
the next stage of the discussion, Jack might recite his reasons for believing that
there is a mountain 10 miles high. Or he might try to undermine Jill's reasons for
believing that there isn't.

In any case, the point of such a discussion (if taken seriously) is for Jack and
Jill to exchange the reasons they have for their respective beliefs. They know
that such an exchange of reasons is useful. For both know that the proposition
that there is a mountain 10 miles high and the proposition that there is no such
mountain cannot both be true, because the second is the negation of the first.
One of them must therefore have a belief that isn't true. An exchange of the reasons that they have for their respective belief might therefore enable them to find
out which of the two is in error and how that error arose (perhaps through some
further error, which can be exposed incidentally).

Let me explain the communicative value of cases of incredulity in a generalized way. Cases of incredulity, to repeat, are cases where the hearer fails to
come to believe what the speaker has asserted, even though he or she thinks that
the assertion was sincere. For more precision, let us distinguish two different
kinds of cases of incredulity according to the different reasons a hearer might
have for not believing what has been asserted. First, there are cases of *disagreement*, such as my last example: here the reason for the hearer's incredulity is that
he or she believes the negation of the proposition asserted, or at least has beliefs
that entail the negation of the proposition asserted. Jill disbelieves what Jack has
asserted, that's why she refuses to believe him. Jill *disagrees* with Jack on the
proposition asserted. Second, there are cases of *insufficient grounds for belief*.

These are cases where the hearer, even though he or she doesn't *disbelieve* what has been asserted, nevertheless considers the speaker's believing it insufficient grounds for believing it himself or herself.

Both cases of disagreement and cases of insufficient grounds for belief play crucial roles in linguistic communication. A case of disagreement typically provides both communicators with a reason to conduct a discussion. For in these cases there is a content $p$ such that one communicator believes $p$ and the other believes not-$p$. Since at least one of $p$ and not-$p$ must be false (or so we will assume for the moment), discussion may reveal which of the two communicators believes a false content, and how he or she got to believe it. The discussion will consist in one or both of the communicators revealing to the other the reasons that led him or her to believe his or her part of the contradictory pair. This gives them an opportunity to re-evaluate their reasons. The one may criticize the other's reasons by either denying the propositions cited in evidence or denying that they constitute a reason.[5] Or alternatively, the one may accept the other's reasons as cogent and concede error. They may, when their own reasons are exposed to such criticism, either reject that criticism or accept it (and then perhaps concede error). In any case, the better justified the disagreeing parties are in their beliefs, the more potentially profitable is a discussion in which these justifications are subjected to critical attention.

In cases of insufficient grounds for belief, the potential benefit of discussion is not as obvious as in cases of direct disagreement. In these cases, the content asserted is not one on which the participants disagree, therefore it is not the necessary presence of error about *that* content that motivates discussion. Nevertheless, even in these situations discussion is typically desirable for both parties, because there often is at least one further content on which they disagree. If Jack asserts that $p$, and Jill, even though she doesn't *dis*believe that $p$, refuses to come to believe that $p$ on the evidence of Jack's assertion, then she does so because she doesn't (yet) believe that her own or Jack's reasons for believing $p$ are sufficient. If Jack, on request, spells out his reasons for believing that $p$, Jill will respond in one of two ways: either she will accept Jack's justification as sufficient, in which case she will come to believe that $p$ herself. Or, alternatively, she will regard his justification as insufficient, in which case she will disagree with Jack's belief that his justification is sufficient. (This may be because she disbelieves one of the contents cited by Jack as evidence, or because she does not regard those contents as sufficient evidence.) In other words, just one verbal exchange will typically turn a case of insufficient grounds for belief either into a simple case of belief transfer, or into a situation of direct disagreement. This explains why even cases of insufficient grounds for belief are cases in which discussion is desirable.

Before praising the virtues of a system of communication of this kind, let me expose a few idealizing assumptions I made in my account of discussion. One assumption was already explicit: I was talking only about cases where the sincerity of the speaker is not in doubt (this was part of the definition of cases of incredulity). Second, I assumed that each participant finds the proposition under discussion sufficiently interesting to merit discussion. Third, I assumed that the participants were ideally cooperative, and not driven by other concerns, such as an exaggerated reluctance to concede error or a strong motivation to conceal their reasons. Fourth, I assumed (explicitly) that whenever one communicator believes that $p$ and another communicator believes that not-$p$, one of them must be guilty of error. Eventually, of course, I want to question the generality of this last assumption, for it is my aim to make room for faultless disagreement in certain areas of discourse by relativizing truth.

If my brief idealized sketch is roughly along the right lines, then linguistic communication is a much more sophisticated process than just the simple transfer of belief as it occurs in simple cases. Cases of incredulity are not, as might at first appear, counterproductive, but they are rather the starting point for an essential and valuable part of communication: discussion and argument. Disagreement often indicates that someone has made a mistake; discussion enables us to diagnose and eradicate the mistake. Discussion enables us to profit from the fruits of others' cognitive efforts not only when we can blindly rely on their competence, but also when, as in many cases, we have reasons to be sceptical. Discussion enables us to make a much more informed use of others' judgements in justifying our own beliefs. That this is a crucial part of the function of linguistic communication is evident if one considers how many of the beliefs each of us has are justified indirectly through relying on the word of others, and how much of our knowledge therefore depends for its accuracy on the reliability of others. It is the possibility of discussion that makes this degree of reliance on others sustainable.[6]

I have so far tried to elucidate the purpose of linguistic communication from the point of view of the individual communicator's aims. It is each communicator's individual aim to have only true beliefs (to conform to (T) above). Linguistic communication is a form of cooperation with other communicators that furthers that aim. But, linguistic communication can also be seen as serving the purposes of a community of communicators as a whole. It is the aim of the community to improve its cognitive state. In other words, even though the members of the community will have their individual beliefs, there will be interdependencies between those belief states. This is because the members communicate. In simple cases, they just transmit beliefs from one person to another; in more complicated cases, they mutually influence each other by entering discussion and argument. Very roughly, each time a new true belief is acquired, each time a disagreement is resolved by exposing some mistake, the cognitive state of the community is improved.[7] Communication can be seen as a community's tool for improving its cognitive state.

Huw Price has long emphasized this social advantage of reasoned argument:

> Disagreements thus become socially unstable, and we are led to defend our opinions, to argue and to seek agreement. In the long run, I suggested, such disputes can be expected to have a beneficial effect on the behavioural dis-

positions of individual speakers. They help to ensure that as individuals we hold and act on attitudes that reflect, to some extent, the combined wisdom of our linguistic community. Our behavioural dispositions can thus be tested against those of other speakers, before they are put to use in the world. The guiding principle is that it is better to be criticized for claiming that tigers are harmless than to discover one's mistake in the flesh. (1988: 145)

Price even goes so far as to claim that this behavioural advantage explains the existence of dispute and argument in evolutionary terms (1988: 134). This evolutionary angle may help to give substance to the idea that the improvement of speakers' belief states via belief transmission and argumentative exchange is among the *functions* of linguistic communication.

I believe that this view of linguistic communication is commonsensical and attractive. But what evidence can be offered in favour of it? One line of argument is that communicators do in fact exhibit the sort of behaviour that one would expect on this view of communication: they do sometimes come to believe a content because another communicator has asserted that content (simple cases), they do in fact often request justification for a content that has been asserted, and they do in fact often discuss a content when a disagreement arises (cases of incredulity). My account explains this practice, and it does so in more detail and more adequately than accounts that merely focus on simple cases. I do not believe that this is conclusive evidence, but I expect that the account nevertheless meets with broad agreement given its commonsensical nature, and given that its broad outline could be developed in detail to comply with a number of different views on language and truth.[8]

I shall now raise a problem for the picture of linguistic communication just presented. The problem is that this picture predicts that under certain conditions it is always rational to engage in discussion, but that this prediction is false for non-objective propositions. I shall propose a modification that removes this problem. As advertised, my modification will consist in construing the evaluation of a content as relative, and adjusting the rest of the account to that change.

## 2 Disagreement without error

According to my account in the last section, one would expect every sincere disagreement to lead to discussion, as long as the disputed proposition is of sufficient importance to the two sides and as long as both sides are sincere and cooperative. For, one might argue, whenever one thinker believes the negation of what another believes, one of the two believes something not true, and the prospect of finding out who is the one believing the falsehood would make a discussion worth while—again, *if* the issue is of sufficient importance, and *if* both sides are sincere and cooperative.

This prediction, however, is patently untrue. Even when the matter is important, we do not always regard discussion as valuable. Consider, for example, a disagreement on whether laver bread is delicious.[9] Belief in the content that laver bread is delicious may be of considerable importance, in the sense that whether one believes that proposition can have important practical consequences.[10] Nevertheless, when one communicator sincerely asserts that laver bread is delicious and another communicator disagrees they will usually choose not to discuss the matter, even when they are cooperative. The saying 'De gustibus non disputandum' suggests that quite generally arguing on matters of taste is not appropriate.

Can this be rational? If the proposition that laver bread is delicious is truth-evaluable, then it would seem that one of the two communicators believes something not true. But if this is so, a discussion would appear to be worth while: discussing the matter might reveal which of the two is wrong and why he or she made that mistake. How come most people would regard discussion as pointless? We can hardly suppose that these people are being irrational, or that they just never attach any importance to matters of taste, or that they are never cooperative when it comes to matters of taste.

Unfortunately, I do not have any statistical data on how frequently people argue about matters of taste, but I believe that my readers will agree that a lack of argumentative energy on matters of taste is quite typical, and the saying 'De gustibus non disputandum' widely accepted. Now, some might argue that this lack of argumentative energy is due to the lesser importance of matters of taste. But I think one can easily construct examples that show this to be implausible. Compare for example a disagreement on whether Elvis Presley weighed more that 25 stone when he died. Even communicators for whom this is a fairly unimportant issue will often quite happily argue about that matter, and weigh their reasons for and against.[11] By contrast, communicators will be reluctant to argue about whether laver bread is delicious, even in situations where this issue is of importance, such as a situation where each has to decide what to choose from the menu.

I suggest that our reluctance to argue in these cases is due to non-objectivity in the sense of my above definition (CO) of objectivity: if a content $p$ concerns a matter of taste, then it is possible that one thinker believes that $p$ and another thinker believes that not-$p$, without either of the two making a mistake. There is a difference between those propositions where disagreement is a sure sign of a mistake and those propositions where it isn't. This difference becomes manifest in the different ways in which we respond to disagreements, i.e. in our communicative practices.

In previous chapters, I have rejected alternative responses to the difficulty. One possible response is to claim that some apparent disagreements aren't in fact disagreements, and that our failure to discuss, for example, matters of taste is due to this phenomenon. When I say that laver bread is delicious and you say that it isn't, I am in fact asserting the proposition that I like laver bread and you are asserting that you don't like it. So there is no disagreement. I have called this view 'revisionism' and rejected it in Chapter 3.

Second, one might attempt to make sense of our failure to discuss certain matters by claiming that the contents in question are not evaluable in terms of truth. A disagreement would then no longer guarantee that one party has a belief that is not true. This expressivist strategy was the subject of Chapter 4, where it was shown that viable forms of expressivism lead away from the truth-conditional paradigm.

A third response would be to reject (T), the view that truth is a norm for thinkers, i.e. to embrace global objectivism. On this view, it is sometimes OK to believe something not true, and that's why people fail to discuss matters of taste. There are, however, good reasons to think that (T) holds.[12] On this view, non-objective contents are true or false, but whether they are true has no longer any normative significance. One wonders what it is to be true, if believing non-truths is OK.

My own response is to deny that if two thinkers have contradictory beliefs, one of them must be in error. There are disagreements without error, or in other words, some propositions are not objective. However, minimal constraints on truth show that if it is true that $p$, then it is not true that not-$p$, and if it is true that not-$p$, then it is not true that $p$. So if one thinker believes that $p$ and another thinker believes that not-$p$, one of them makes the mistake of believing a proposition that is not true. The only way to allow faultless disagreement is therefore to relativize truth to perspectives: one disputant's belief is true in his or her own perspective, and the other disputant's contradictory belief is true in his or her own perspective. Thus neither is wrong in his or her own perspective. In the next section, I want to explain how the common-sense account of communication can be adjusted to this framework of relative truth.

## 3 The relativized truth framework

We can refine our conceptual apparatus to allow for non-objective propositions. The key elements of this conceptual framework are (a) the relativization of truth to perspectives, (b) a theory of perspective possession and (c) a refinement of our concept of mistake, i.e. of the normative aspect of truth. In a nutshell, truth is relative to perspectives, each thinker possesses one perspective at any one time, and one makes a mistake if one believes a proposition that is not true in one's own perspective. Let me set out this framework in detail.

Elements (a) and (c) are explained easily enough: a *perspective* is just a function from contents to truth values.[13] Thus a content is true according to a given perspective, if that perspective assigns the value 'true' to that content. The normative significance of truth is characterized thus: a thinker commits a *mistake* (an *error*) if he or she believes a content that is not true according to the perspective he or she possesses (at that time). This leaves the whole explanatory weight of the theory on the notion of perspective possession, as this will determine when exactly a thinker commits a mistake, and consequently when exactly it is possible for two thinkers to disagree[14] without mistake on either side. The outcome should obviously be that this is possible just if the content concerned is a non-objective one. Before I say more about perspective possession, I need to make a few remarks about the notion of a perspective.

Perspectives are very similar to possible worlds in that it is a minimal feature of a perspective that it assign a truth value to each content. Therefore the theory faces some of the same questions regarding conceptual status as does any theory of possible worlds. According to the present theory, contents need not be reduced to sets of perspectives in analogy with Lewis's reduction of propositions (contents) to sets of possible worlds (Lewis 1986: 53–5). Contents are to be theoretical entities in their own right, identifiable independently as objects of belief and assertion. Contents are definitely not to be reduced to sets of possible worlds in the ordinary sense. For ordinary possible worlds are purely objective and contain no evaluative elements. Some of the contents with which I am operating, however, are non-objective. Apart from this, a major difference between possible worlds and perspectives is still to emerge: the analogue of perspective possession, i.e. the relation that connects a thinker to the world he or she 'inhabits' is construed in such a way that any two individuals who are causally related to one another must inhabit the same world. By contrast, two thinkers may be causally related yet possess different perspectives.

What, then, can be said positively about the relation of perspective possession? The disappointing bit first: I will not be able explicitly to define the relation of perspective possession, i.e. to provide a *reductive* analysis. In other words, I will not be putting forward any suggestion as to what should replace $F$ in

> For all times $t$, all thinkers $r$ and all perspectives $s$: $r$ possesses $s$ at $t$ iff $F(t, s)$.

However, I shall propose a constraint on the relation of possession between thinkers and perspectives—a constraint that ensures that the theory of perspectives can explain those observable phenomena of linguistic communication that I have described above. The methodological status of the theory of perspectives and of perspective possession is thus that of a postulate that is justified by its explanatory value in a theory of linguistic communication. That's why a reductive analysis of possession is not necessary.

The constraint ensures that the theory can explain and allow a difference between objective and non-objective contents (in the sense of (CO)). If a proposition $p$ is non-objective, then it is possible that there be two thinkers, such that the first believes that $p$ and the second believes that not-$p$, and neither of them has made a mistake. The perspectives of two such thinkers must be such that the perspective of one assigns the value 'true' to $p$ and the perspective of the other the value 'true' to not-$p$—otherwise one of them would be committing a mistake. Perspective possession must therefore be such that it is possible that the perspectives of two thinkers diverge in their evaluation of non-objective contents. This yields the following constraint:

(C1)    For all $p$: $p$ is non-objective iff it is possible[15] that there be thinkers $A$ and $B$, such that $p$ is true in $A$'s perspective and $p$ is not true in $B$'s perspective.

Objectivity is just absence of non-objectivity: a content is objective just if it is *not* possible for two thinkers to possess perspectives that diverge in their evaluation of that content. As a result, when two thinkers disagree on an objective content, one of them must be committing a mistake in the sense of believing a content that is not true in his or her own perspective. This yields the equivalent constraint:

(C2)    For all $p$: $p$ is objective iff it is not possible that there be thinkers $A$ and $B$, such that $p$ is true in $A$'s perspective and $p$ is not true in $B$'s perspective.

(C2) ensures that by relativizing truth to perspectives, we do not lose objectivity altogether. As far as objective contents are concerned, the situation is as before the relativization: any disagreement must be down to someone's mistake, because the perspectives of everyone necessarily agree in their evaluation of objective contents.[16]

We could even define a notion of absolute truth in terms of the notion of relative truth: a content is *objectively true* just if it is objective and true in everyone's (or equivalently: someone's) perspective. Similarly, we can define objective falsehood: a proposition is *objectively false* just if it is objective and false in everyone's (or equivalently: someone's) perspective. Objective truth and objective falsehood are not bivalent: some contents are neither objectively true nor objectively false. One of the attractions of this account is that this need not worry us, because we can formulate all the theories for which bivalence is convenient (e.g. semantics and logic—see Chapter 2, §1) in terms of simple truth, i.e. in terms of the relative notion. Every content is either true or false (= not true), or explicitly: for every perspective, every content is either true in that perspective or not true (= false) in that perspective.

I believe that the theory is already useful in this bare outline. It allows us to combine the attractive view that all contents are truth-evaluable with the attractive view that not all contents are objective. It explains why communicators' responses to disagreements vary with subject area. They will normally enter a discussion when they disagree on an objective content, because they know that disagreement on such a content is a sure sign of someone being in error, and discussion may help eradicate that error.[17] They will often *not* enter a discussion when they disagree on a non-objective content, because the mere occurrence of a disagreement on such a content is not yet a sign of anyone being in error. A theory of perspective possession that complies with (C1) provides a theoretical model for the knowledge of communicators as to when a disagreement safely indicates error and when it does not.

## 4 The explanatory status of the theory

In its present outline, however, the theory only provides a purely formal and theoretical solution. Its explanatory value would be increased if this theoretical solution could be underpinned by an explanation of how communicators come to possess perspectives in such a way that constraint (C1) is met.

(C1), moreover, does not yet sufficiently constrain the relation of perspective possession. Nothing, as far as (C1) is concerned, prevents people from possessing absurd perspectives, such as a perspective in which it is true that London is in Finland. Presumably, the content that London is in Finland is objective. Thus if *anyone* possesses a perspective in which London is in Finland, *everyone* possesses a perspective in which London is in Finland. Therefore, if most people disbelieve (as they surely do) that London is in Finland, that would (absurdly) show most people to be in error about the location of London.[18] We thus need a constraint that makes sure, for example, that every perspective that is actually possessed by anyone evaluates the proposition that London is in Finland as false.

At this point it is useful to remember the normative role of the relation of perspective possession. It is a mistake to believe something not true in one's own perspective, and thinkers ought to believe only contents true in their own perspective. Thus, if a speaker possesses a perspective, then truth in that perspective is what that speaker aims at. Thus we might further constrain perspective possession as follows:

(C3)   For all thinkers $t$ and all perspectives $s$: $t$ possesses $s$ iff for all contents $p$: $t$ ought to believe $p$ only if $p$ is true in $s$.[19]

But now we seem to be in an odd position. I proposed earlier that we could explain speakers' discursive behaviour (in particular their varying responses to perceived disagreements) by saying that they aim at truth in their own perspective, and that they know which contents are such that their own and others' perspectives cannot diverge with respect to them. But now suppose that (C3) is (part of) the definition of perspective possession. Then the remark that thinkers aim at beliefs that are true according to their own perspectives would amount to the tautological remark that thinkers aim at what they aim at.

What looks like an explanatory deadlock, however, is an entirely healthy situation, analogues of which are generally accepted in many theories. Consider the theory that postulates unobservable theoretical entities called 'electrons' to explain the observable behaviour of macroscopic objects. We say that macroscopic objects behave in a given way *because* of the properties of electrons. When asked what electrons are, we say they are the things that explain why macroscopic objects behave in such and such a way. Thus our earlier explanation begins to look tautologous: macroscopic objects behave in a given way *because* of the properties of those things that explain why macroscopic objects behave in that way.

The way to escape from this apparent explanatory circle is to be realistic about the point and scope of such theories. First, a certain amount of tautology is to be expected of a theory that postulates theoretical entities. After all, these entities are assumed to exist, and to have certain properties, *only* in order to explain (or predict) certain other phenomena. *That* these entities and their properties explain the phenomena in question is therefore in a sense tautologous. Nevertheless, the theory will do more than just say that the phenomena are explained by what explains them. What the theory postulates will usually clarify and organize the observable data in a way that facilitates explanation and prediction. The observable range of phenomena will be variously connected with the theoretical level, and this might in favourable cases allow interconnections with other theories. Electrons might be defined by their role in an explanatory theory, but they nevertheless do substantial explanatory work.

Similarly, perspectives, and the relation of possession between perspectives and thinkers, do valuable explanatory work. For even though thinkers' behaviour is our only evidence for this theory, and even though these notions are defined only through their theoretical role in this theory, they still permit us to describe the behavioural phenomena in a new, systematic way and thereby improve our understanding. Moreover, (C3) doesn't stand alone. Perspective possession is further constrained by (C1) and (C2). If perspective possession conforms to all these constraints, then it can explain thinkers' behavioural variations in response to disagreements in different areas of discourse. Thinkers tend to argue about certain contents and not about others because they recognize a relevant difference between these kinds of contents—they know that these contents differ in some way. The theory of perspective possession provides a model of this knowledge. The claim is that disagreeing parties tend to argue about certain contents because they *know* (implicitly) that the perspectives of both cannot diverge in their evaluation of these contents. And they tend *not* to argue about certain other contents because they know that their perspectives can legitimately diverge on these other contents. Therefore, it should not worry us if (C3) at first appears to render our explanation tautologous. It should be even less worrying if it can be explained how thinkers come to acquire the knowledge this theory attributes to them. Such an explanation is available.

The explanation draws on a general account of how we learn to acquire beliefs and to communicate linguistically. This account forms, in my view, the basic level of explanation. Principles concerning truth, perspectives, contents, etc. are explanatorily posterior and are correct only in so far as they help make sense of our cognitive and communicative methods and the ways in which we acquire them.

## 5 Methods of belief acquisition

We acquire beliefs not randomly, but via various channels of belief acquisition, such as perception, reasoning and communication with others. These channels are governed by certain methods, and if we acquire beliefs in accordance with these methods, they are justified. We learn these methods when we grow up, and we may never stop developing and changing them. But a certain core of these rules is, so to speak, part of the human legacy that gets passed on from generation to generation. Our methods of detecting simple colours and shapes of sensible objects, for example, are hardly ever subject to change. Similarly, certain basic conceptual connections are highly resilient, such as the conceptual truth that a city is in a country if it is within the country's borders. Now, justification is rarely conclusive in the sense that it rules out error. We will often detect error by first detecting that different methods yield conflicting beliefs, and then usually exposing a failure to apply one of these methods correctly.[20] Very occasionally, if it turns out after repeated investigation that two methods continue to yield conflicting results, we will revise our methods. But a certain small core of methods, which belong to the human legacy, will hardly ever be challenged (and if they ever *appear* to be challenged, then this is presumably not because our core methods are changing, but rather because we have come to use some words differently).

Now, our communicative methods for acquiring beliefs consist centrally in the sort of practices I described earlier. We sometimes accept what communicators assert, we sometimes challenge assertions by asking for justification, and we sometimes disagree and engage in discussion. We learn the rules of how to do this properly in the process of acquiring our communication skills. Some of the rules are rules on disagreement. Among other things, these rules specify the topics disagreement on which indicates a mistake and warrants discussion, and other topics disagreement on which does not indicate a mistake and therefore does not necessarily warrant discussion. This is why our knowledge as to whether a disagreement is a sure sign of a mistake is a priori knowledge: communicators know this just in virtue of having learnt the methods of communicative belief acquisition. If we ever change these methods concerning a given concept or word, we thereby also change the concept or the meaning of the word: if one person uses the word 'delicious' in such a way that disagreement on whether something is delicious does indicate a mistake, and another person uses 'delicious' in such a way that there may be faultless disagreement on whether something is delicious, then these two persons are using the word with different meanings. These rules and methods are constitutive for the identity of the concepts we use. This explains how it is that perspective possession does in fact comply with (C1) and (C2).

Our perceptual and conceptual methods of belief acquisition are also part of our repertoire as competent thinkers. We learn how to detect colours and shapes reliably via perception. That we can learn these methods is largely the result of our communicative rules of belief acquisition: we know that if one communicator believes the book is green and another communicator believes that it is not, then at least one of them has made a mistake in acquiring his or her belief. If these two communicators are in a teaching–learning situation, the teacher will be presumed to be more reliable, and thus disagreement will normally be taken to show that the learner has made a mistake and needs to adjust his or her method.

Similar learning processes ensure that we largely concur in our *con*ceptual methods of belief acquisition. Learners will acquire the ability to apply conceptual methods by modelling their methods on teachers who are presumed already to be competent. In this way, a whole community of communicators can be calibrated to apply the same methods of belief acquisition. Let us call this process 'harmonization'. Harmonization isn't always perfect, but it is near perfect for core methods.

Harmonization of the methods used by a community of communicators is crucial for the ultimate practical purposes of communication. It is only because communicators concur in their methods that communication is useful. But the process of harmonization differs from objective to non-objective areas: in an objective area, the aim of the harmonization is that communicators arrive at the same belief when they apply the same methods in the same way. Thus calibration is straightforward: whenever the same method yields conflicting results, some participant needs to improve on his or her application of the method—in a learning situation this will presumably be the learner. In a non-objective area, the aim will not necessarily be that the same method applied by different people yield the same beliefs. In such an area, the methods for acquiring beliefs may be such that two thinkers may arrive at conflicting beliefs (conflicting in the sense that one is the negation of the other) even when they apply the method correctly. But there will be other criteria by which it can be judged whether different thinkers are applying the same method in the same way. The methods may involve thinkers' perceptual responses and conceptual connections in ways that do not require that application of the method by different thinkers must yield the same beliefs.

High time for some concrete examples. When a thinker learns by what method to form beliefs on whether something is delicious, he or she will not normally be required by his or her teacher to adjust his or her methods in such a way that his or her beliefs on deliciousness concur with the teacher's. But he or she will be taught conceptual connections, such as the following: if one believes that something is delicious, then that gives one some reason to desire to eat it. Thus if one believes that something is delicious but nevertheless has no desire to eat it (in the absence of overriding reasons), then one has not applied the method correctly. By contrast, when a learner learns how to form beliefs on an objective matter, such as whether a given visible object is yellow, it will be presumed that the teacher's and the learner's beliefs ought to coincide.[21]

The above account explains how communicators come to know under what conditions argument is appropriate, which contents are objective and which contents aren't. It is tempting to try to exploit the account further, and to use it in constructing a reductive analysis of perspective possession. I have in mind something along the following lines:

(C3*)  For all thinkers $t$ and all perspectives $s$: $t$ possesses $s$ iff for all contents $p$: if $p$ is true in $s$, then $t$ would arrive at $p$ if $t$ employed the methods of belief acquisition correctly.

This, however, is not possible. We cannot say that someone who applies the methods of belief acquisition correctly will never, as a result, come to believe propositions that are not true according to the perspective he or she possesses. First, our methods are rarely completely reliable, so even the correct use of a method may still yield erroneous belief. Second, we occasionally discover that different methods yield conflicting results even when correctly used, which will normally prompt a revision of our methods. We can't know whether the system of methods we are using won't one day turn out to be inconsistent in this way, so we can't know whether correct use of the methods guarantees freedom from error. Perhaps we can weaken (C3*) and say instead that someone who applies the methods correctly will *rarely*, as a result, come to believe propositions that are not true according to the perspective he or she possesses. But this would again fall significantly short of a proper reductive analysis.

## 6 Extension of the framework: shades of objectivity

Even without a reduction of the possession relation, the framework can be further extended and refined. I want to make room for a finer differentiation of *degrees* of objectivity. So far, I have distinguished only objective contents, which are such that disagreement on them is a sure sign of someone having committed a mistake, and non-objective contents, which are such that disagreement without error is conceptually possible. But even within the realm of non-objective contents, thus defined, there might be contents disagreement on which is a sure sign of a mistake *if* the communicators who are in disagreement stand in a certain relation. I believe that this idea can serve to do justice to finer differences of status within the non-objective realm.

Let us consider morally evaluative propositions. There is a meta-ethical dispute as to the metaphysical and epistemological status of these propositions. One possible view on their status renders them less than fully objective but not completely non-objective either. Without arguing that such a view is correct, let me show how some such view might be accommodated within my theoretical framework.

Even though there may not be a constraint on moral propositions that says that disagreement on such a proposition is *always* a sign of error, there may be a constraint that says that a moral disagreement *among friends* is a sign of error and motivates discussion.[22] If we were to observe that friends tend to discuss moral issues, while non-friends often don't, then this would be evidence for such a constraint. Perhaps it is part of our concept of friendship that friends ought to share the same moral principles. On this view, one might say, moral matters are not completely non-objective, as there are at least some groups of people who necessarily have perspectives that coincide on moral contents. I am not arguing that this view on the status of moral matters is correct, but it is surely a respectable view, and the capability to accommodate it is an advantage of the relativistic framework. Moreover, there are many other candidate relations besides friendship that might be exploited in this way. Perhaps it is friends and family who cannot disagree on morals without error, or people who are members of the same community or culture. Perhaps moral discourse isn't even uniform in this respect: perhaps there are some moral propositions that are entirely objective, while there are others that are objective among friends, and yet others that are objective among members of the same family. The framework provides space for a lot of differentiation.

Probability is another example of a discourse where objectivity is controversial. Here again, the framework provides ample opportunity to formulate various different views on the precise sense in which probability is or isn't objective. On the subjectivist (Bayesian) view, for example, two people cannot disagree without error on the probability of an event if they have started out with the same probability assignment and have exactly the same evidence. On a Keynesian view, having the same evidence is sufficient for ruling out the possibility of disagreement without error. On a Popperian (objectivist) view, no two people can disagree on the probability of an event without one of them being in error.

Let me introduce a terminology for all these shades of objectivity. Let us say generally that a proposition is *objective among Xs*, just if any disagreement among Xs on that proposition must be the sign of an error. Thus subjectivists about probability think that probability-ascribing propositions are objective among thinkers who have started with the same probability function and have the same evidence. This terminology allows the expression of very nuanced views on the objectivity of any given area of discourse. We can debate whether moral propositions are objective among friends, or perhaps also among friends and family. We can debate also whether matters of taste are entirely non-objective or perhaps objective among certain very tight-knit social groups.

I began the exposition of my framework with a substantial simplification: I made it seem as if the main achievement of the framework would be the room it makes for a bifurcation between objective and non-objective contents. It now emerges that the framework is much richer. It not only explains a two-way distinction between the objective and the non-objective in accordance with (CO); it also allows us to mark off and explain pockets of local objectivity of various kinds (objectivity among Xs, where not everyone is an X). Thus, in effect, the framework provides an entirely new approach to the question of objectivity. Objectivity *tout court* (according to (CO)) turns out to be a limiting case of an interesting phenomenon of communication: communicators use each other—selectively—as standards for measuring the world around them. The limiting case is one where communicators need no longer be selective. If the matter is objective *tout court*, they can use anyone reliable and sincere as a standard.

## 7  One further application: fiction

I would like to mention one additional application of the relative-truth framework, in order to demonstrate further that the framework is useful. The hypothesis that truth is relative to perspectives yields an appealing solution to a problem with the semantics of fictional utterances.

Consider the following sentence

(F)    In the year 1984, the word 'bad' is illegal in Britain.

If someone utters (F) in the context of talking about George Orwell's *1984*, then the utterance counts as correct. But if someone, even the same person, were to utter (F) in a non-fictional context, then it would count as incorrect, for in fact the word 'bad' was not illegal in Britain in 1984. This much, I think, is intuitively clear.

But how could it be possible that of two utterances of the *same* sentence one should be correct and the other incorrect? Surely, the two utterances must have expressed different contents (propositions). How else could one have been correct, the other incorrect? But how could two utterances of the same sentence express different contents (propositions)? Surely, there are only two possibilities: either (F) is ambiguous, i.e. has several meanings, or (F) is indexical, i.e. the content it expresses depends systematically on features of the context of utterance.

However, the trouble is that (F) does not seem to be either ambiguous or indexical. (F) does not contain any ambiguous words, nor is there syntactic ambiguity. So how could (F) be ambiguous? Nor does (F) contain any indexical elements, so why should (F) express different contents on different occasions of utterance?

We could claim that (F) is implicitly indexical. This move resembles revisionism (Chapter 3). It is an unattractive move, because it involves the ad hoc and implausible claim that (F) is indexical. Moreover, any proposal as to the way in which the indexicality can be made explicit will face the sort of problem revisionism faced.

The hypothesis that truth is relative to perspectives, however, explains everything immediately. Both utterances of (F) express exactly the same content (proposition), a content that is not true in relation to anyone's perspective, but is true in relation to the perspectives associated with Orwell's fiction. So in assessing whether a non-fictional utterance of (F) is correct, we check whether the content in question is true in relation to all our perspectives (since this is an objective matter, all our perspectives will agree on (F)). To judge whether a fictional utterance of (F) is correct, we check whether that content is true in the perspective associated with George Orwell's *1984*.[23]

Thus the hypothesis that truth is relative to perspectives, and that thinkers possess perspectives, is useful in solving this puzzle concerning fictional utterances.

## 8 Alan Gibbard: revisionist, expressivist or relativist?

In Chapter 4, I deferred discussion of Alan Gibbard's norm-expressivism (Gibbard 1990: chapter 5). This was because the interpretation of Gibbard's view is no straightforward matter, and because a discussion and assessment of his view is easier after a full exposition of all three responses to the problem of excess objectivity: revisionism, expressivism and relativism. That's why this section is entirely devoted to the interpretation of Gibbard's view. I shall argue that Gibbard fails to clarify one crucial issue, and that this makes it difficult to decide whether he should be interpreted as a revisionist or a relativist. On neither interpretation, however, does he qualify as an expressivist (in the strict sense in which I introduced the term in Chapter 4). I shall also argue that some of Gibbard's remarks make it seem likely that he would prefer a relativist interpretation.

The core claim of Gibbard's semantics of normative sentences is that 'the meaning of normative terms is given by saying what judgements normative statements express—what states of mind they express' (1990: 84). Gibbard has in mind normative judgements and statements of the sort that attribute rationality. Moral judgements and statements also belong in this category. Thus the meaning of moral sentences should be accounted for in terms of the sorts of rationality judgement they serve to express. But what is a rationality judgement? To judge something rational 'is to accept a system of norms that on balance permits it' (1990: 84). Now, whether something is rational, period, is not a factual matter. By contrast, whether it is rational in relation to a given system of norms N, i.e. N-permitted, is a purely factual matter. These are the basic ingredients on which Gibbard constructs his semantics of normative sentences.

Gibbard provides a formal representation of the contents of normative judgements in order to be able to represent the logical relations among normative statements. This in turn is supposed to allow him to assign to normative sentences the sort of semantic structure that allows a recursive semantics à la Tarski (see Chapter 1, §§2 and 4), and which at the same time solves the unendorsed contexts problem (see Chapter 4, §2 and Gibbard 1990: 94).

In order to represent the mental state of a normative thinker, Gibbard introduces the notion of a 'factual–normative world', i.e. of an ordered pair $<w, n>$ of an 'ordinary' possible world $w$ and a complete system of norms $n$ (where a complete system of norms is one that determines for every possible situation what is permitted and what isn't). Gibbard illustrates this with an imaginary goddess, whose 'completely opinionated credal–normative state' (1990: 95) might be represented as such a factual–normative world, because she is omniscient and possesses a complete system of norms. Ordinary thinkers, however, are not completely opinionated, because they lack sufficient brainpower. So their states of mind can be represented as sets of several factual–normative worlds, namely those that are completions of their incomplete systems of norms and their incomplete views of the world. Moreover, an individual judgement that something X is rational can be represented as the set of all factual–normative worlds $<w, n>$ which fulfil the condition that $n$ permits X in $w$. In other words, the judgement that X is rational *rules out* all combinations of facts and norms that fail to permit X (1990: 96–7). Thus,

> when a speaker makes a normative statement, he expresses a state of mind. … the state of mind he expresses consists in his ruling out various combinations of normative systems with factual possibilities. (1990: 99)

Representing the contents of normative judgements and statements in this way permits a systematic representation of the logical relations among such contents. If we regard the content of a factual judgement or statement $p$ as a set of possible worlds, namely of those worlds in which $p$ holds, then we can regard, for example, the conjunctive content that $p$ and $q$ as the intersection of the contents of $p$ and $q$, i.e. the set of those worlds in which $p$ and $q$ hold. Or we can treat the content that not-$p$ as the complement to the content that $p$. Similarly, suppose we represent contents of judgement generally (including factual and normative) as sets of factual–normative worlds, i.e. in each case the set of factual–normative worlds in which the content holds. Then this immediately allows us to identify the content that $p$ and $q$ with the intersection of the content that $p$ and the content that $q$, and to identify the content that not-$p$ with the complement of the content that $p$.

Now, for a factual content $p$ to hold in a factual–normative world $<w, n>$ is just for $p$ to hold in the factual possibility $w$. But whether a normative content that $p$ holds in $<w, n>$ is also a factual matter: every normative content $p$ has a factual counterpart $p_n$ for each system of norms $n$. For example, the normative content that giving battle is rational has as N-counterpart the content that giving battle is permitted by N. This allows Gibbard to stipulate that generally a content $p$ holds in a factual–normative world $<w, n>$ just if $p$'s $n$-counterpart holds in $w$.

This method of formally representing contents solves the Frege–Geach problem, for it shows how the content expressed by a complex sentence is a function of the contents expressed by its constituent sentences.[24]

There are obvious analogies between Gibbard's factual–normative worlds and my perspectives. Just as a perspective is an evaluation of all contents, objective or not, a factual–normative world is an evaluation of all contents, normative or factual. Just as Gibbard's contents can be construed as sets of factual–normative worlds, mine could be construed as sets of perspectives. In each case the set contains those perspectives or factual–normative worlds that evaluate the content as true. How far does the analogy go? A comparison of the role Gibbard's and my contents play in assertoric communication will be illuminating.

On my view, belief is governed by the norm that one ought to believe only contents that are true relative to one's own perspective. Since perspective possession is constrained by certain intersubjective a priori rules, two communicators can be sure that their perspectives coincide in their evaluation of objective contents (in the extended framework proposed in §6 they can also be sure of a mutual agreement of perspectives when the content is one that is objective among a group to which they both belong). Thus, when Lola asserts that $p$, and hearer David assumes (possibly implicitly) that his and Lola's perspectives agree regarding $p$, and if David regards Lola as sincere and reliable (in the sense that she is likely to believe only what is true in her perspective), then David will come to believe that $p$ as a result of Lola's assertion that $p$. On this view, what Lola has asserted is *not* that $p$-in-her-own-perspective. Rather, the content of her assertion is the content that $p$, a content whose truth value can vary from perspective to perspective. This is what distinguishes my view from revisionism.

Is Gibbard's account of assertoric communication similar? Gibbard says that to assert a normative sentence ('make a normative statement') is to express a state of mind that consists in 'ruling out various combinations of normative systems with factual possibilities' (1990: 99). This is compatible with both revisionism *and* relativism (of a sort I have outlined in this chapter). Let me sketch these two interpretative possibilities in turn.

First, let's suppose a revisionist interpretation of Gibbard is correct.[25] Gibbard's view is that each normative content (in fact every content) is a set of factual–normative worlds, namely the set in which it holds. But for a content $p$ to hold in a factual–normative world $<w, n>$ just is for $p$'s factual $n$-counterpart, i.e. $p_n$, to hold in $w$. (As mentioned earlier, a normative content that X is rational has an $n$-counterpart for any system of norms $n$, namely the content that X is $n$-permitted.)

On the revisionist interpretation of Gibbard, each time a speaker utters an assertoric normative sentence $s$ that expresses the normative content that $p$, he or she in effect ultimately asserts some factual content. Which factual content? There are at least two variants. On the first variant, there is one contextually determined system of norms $n$, and A asserts the $n$-counterpart of $p$, i.e. $p_n$. Thus, on this view, if Lola utters 'X is rational', then she is in effect asserting the factual content that X is permitted by the contextually salient system of norms. Some of Gibbard's remarks suggest—and this is a plausible suggestion—that it is the speaker's own system of norms that is determined by the context. Thus the content asserted by uttering 'X is rational' is the same as the content asserted by uttering 'X is permitted by my system of norms'. Assertoric communication via normative sentences thus works on the model of communication via indexical sentences (a set of factual–normative worlds = a Kaplanian character, as Dreier (1999) proposes).

On this first revisionist variant, the content of a normative sentence is, as it were, represented as a propositional function (a function from a context to a proposition) which gets completed on an occasion of utterance by one particular system of norms inserted as argument. On the second variant, the propositional function is completed instead by a quantifier. That is, just as in the first variant, the propositional function $F(x)$, completed by an individual constant $a$, yields a proposition $F(a)$, in the second variant, the propositional function $F(x)$, completed by a quantifier, yields the proposition $\exists x(F(x))$ or $\forall x(F(x))$. For example, Gibbard's view might be that when Lola utters 'X is rational' she asserts the factual content (proposition) that

> for all complete systems of norms $n$, such that $n$ is a completion of Lola's own incomplete system, X is $n$-permitted.

Again, on this variant of the revisionist interpretation, Gibbard's view would assimilate normative sentences to indexical ones (1990: 88).

Clearly, Gibbard does not qualify as an expressivist on either variant of the revisionist interpretation. For even though he might claim that, in a sense, normative sentences have a non-truth-evaluable content (namely a Kaplanian character), this is only superficial. For ultimately to make a normative statement is to assert a factual content.

The reader can extrapolate from Chapter 3 why I regard these forms of revisionism as inadequate: 'Giving battle is rational.' just does not mean the same as 'My system of norms permits giving battle.' or 'All completions of my system of norms permit giving battle.'. The last two indexically refer to the system of norms of the speaker. The first does not.

There is some weak indication in Gibbard's text that discourages the revisionist interpretation. Gibbard emphasizes (1990: 84) the difference between expressing some state of mind and saying that one has that state of mind (= expressing one's belief that one has that state). This suggests that Gibbard would equally distinguish expressing the acceptance of norms that permit X from saying that one accepts norms that accept X. Let us therefore now consider the alternative, relativist interpretation of Gibbard's theory.

Consider again Lola who utters 'X is rational'. This sentence expresses the set of factual–normative worlds in which it holds that X is rational, i.e. the set of factual–normative worlds $<w, n>$ such that X is $n$-permitted in $w$. What is the ultimate object of assertion? On the relativist interpretation, it is not some factual content constructed via context from the propositional function that X is $n$-permitted. Rather, it is the genuinely normative content that X is rational, whose truth value is relative to systems of norms.

How does assertoric communication work if we allow that genuinely normative contents can be the ultimate objects of assertion? The story goes much like my own (see §5, above). If the hearer of a normative utterance thinks that his or her own and the speaker's norms coincide (and if he or she thinks the speaker is sincere and reliable), then he or she can come to adopt the normative content that has been asserted:

> Suppose Cleopatra thinks that Caesar accepts the same basic norms that she accepts ... Suppose also that she takes him to be an excellent judge ... She can therefore take his normative judgement for her own. (Gibbard 1990: 86)

The reader may think that this passage establishes the relativist interpretation as correct. However, the passage is consistent with the revisionist reading too. Suppose Caesar said 'dividing the command is rational', and thereby asserted that his own norms permit dividing the command. In order for Cleopatra to arrive at a judgement that has motivational force for herself, she needs to come to believe that *on her own norms* dividing the command is rational. But all she can come to believe as an *immediate* result of Caesar's assertion is, on the revisionist reading, that Caesar's norms permit dividing the command. Thus she needs to consider whether Caesar's and her own norms coincide before she can draw her own motivationally relevant conclusion.

Despite this similarity between the revisionist and the relativist interpretation, they are nevertheless clearly distinct. For on the revisionist view, a speaker performing a normative utterance *refers* to his or her own norms, the utterance is *about* them, while on the relativist view it is not. On the former view, all ultimate objects of assertion are factual, on the latter not.

Gibbard does not qualify as an expressivist (in my sense) on either interpretation. I introduced expressivism about a class of sentences $X$ as the view that (i) the sentences in $X$ aren't truth-evaluable and (ii) the meaning of sentences in $X$ should therefore be accounted for in terms of a special kind of illocutionary force (or communicative function). On both readings, Gibbard's semantics and pragmatics (i.e. theory of illocutionary force) is uniform across normative and factual sentences. So neither reading meets condition (ii). Moreover, Gibbard's account does not unqualifiedly comply with condition (i) on either reading.

Finally, let me highlight two differences between the relativist version of Gibbard's view and my own. First, Gibbard's view presupposes a sharp border between the factual and the normative. There is no directly analogous division in my own view. True, some contents have the same truth value in everyone's perspective, i.e. are objective, and some do not. But I left it open which contents belong to this category—this will simply be a matter of our a priori discursive rules. Moreover, my view leaves room for finer distinctions of objectivity status. For example, some contents may be objective only among thinkers who are related in a certain way (see §6, above). Second, my view links these differences in objectivity status to a priori discursive rules, while Gibbard's distinction between the factual and the normative rests on an independently motivated metaphysics.

These differences may not amount to much. Thus my view may well be very close to a certain relativist version, or elaboration, of Gibbard's view. I regard that as a desirable outcome.

# Chapter 7

# Defence of Relativism

There is a widespread view among philosophers that relativism, quite generally, is hopeless. Such a view is about as undiscerning and unjustified as the view that eating fat, quite generally, is unhealthy. There are many different kinds of fat and whether eating a particular kind of fat is unhealthy depends on the quantity one eats, on the other things one eats with it, and on one's style of life generally. The same goes for relativism. There are many different forms of relativism, and whether a particular form of relativism is a healthy view to take might depend on one's other views.

In this book, I have argued for a particular form of relativism. I have urged that the notion of truth invoked in semantics ought to be construed as relative to perspectives. The aim of this chapter is to defend this particular form of relativism against the sorts of objection that are widely held to refute relativism in general. To this end, I shall first introduce a system of classification that allows a clear differentiation between different forms of relativism, but which also clarifies what all these forms have in common (§§1–2). I shall then put these terminological tools to work by examining whether some well-known and less well-known objections refute the relativisms they are directed against (§§3–5). It turns out that it is extremely difficult to make any of these objections stick. This shows not only *a fortiori* that my particular form of relativism escapes the objections but also that relativism generally ought to get a much fairer hearing.

## I The essence of relativism

What is relativism? What makes a view a form of relativism? Let us consider four sample forms of relativism and try to discover what they have in common. First, Protagoras (as portrayed by Plato in the *Theaetetus*) claims that it is relative to judges whether any judgement is true. Second, Hartry Field (1982) claims that it is relative to the choice of an evidential system whether a belief is justified. Third, according to Einstein's special theory of relativity, whether two events are simultaneous is relative to a frame of reference. Fourth, Harman (1975) claims that it is relative to certain considerations and motivating attitudes whether a person ought to perform an act.

These four relativisms all involve the claim that it is relative to some parameter whether items of a certain sort have a certain feature. Thus, any relativism seems to involve a claim which can be represented as an instance of the following schema:

(R1)   For any $x$ that is an $I$, it is relative to $P$ whether $x$ is $F$.

We can then represent our sample relativisms by the following instances of (R1):

(Prot.)   For any $x$ that is a judgement, it is relative to judges whether $x$ is true.

(Field)   For any $x$ that is a belief, it is relative to evidential systems whether $x$ is justified.

(Ein.)   For any $x$ that is a pair of events, it is relative to frames of reference whether the events in $x$ are simultaneous.

(Har.)   For any $x$ that is a pair of an agent and an act, it is relative to certain considerations and motivating attitudes whether $x$ is such that the agent ought to perform the act.

An instance of (R1) alone does not yet constitute a form of relativism, as we shall see shortly. But any form of relativism will involve some instance of (R1) as a central element.

It is important to emphasize that among my sample relativisms, only (Prot.) is explicitly about truth. All the other formulations are neutral as to whether the relativism in question is a thesis about truth. Field's relativism about justification, for example, may not concern truth at all.

One might object that any thesis to the effect that it is relative to some parameter whether some $x$ is $F$ must immediately infect truth as well. If it is relative whether $x$ is $F$, then it must also be relative whether it is true that $x$ is $F$. This, however, does not follow. For it may not be a matter of truth whether $x$ is $F$. The judgement that $x$ is $F$ may not be truth-evaluable. A philosopher such as Field, for example, may claim that it is not a matter of truth or falsehood whether a belief is justified, thus combining the relativism about justification captured in (Field) with absolutism about truth. And his reason for excluding judgements as to whether some belief is justified from evaluation as true or false might be just his relativism about justification.

But if truth is independent, how is the key phrase in (R1), 'is relative to', to be understood? What is relativity to a parameter? It is very difficult to explain this in a way acceptable to all relativists. But here is what little I think all relativists will agree on. There is a fundamental norm, governing belief, which says whether one may believe that some $x$ is $F$, or whether one ought not to believe it.[1] In other words, the norm in question determines whether or not it is correct to believe something. Now, to say that it is relative to a parameter whether some $x$ is $F$ is to say that whether one may or may not believe that $x$ is $F$ depends on how the parameter is fixed. It may be that for some ways of fixing the parameter, the norm permits that one believe that $x$ is $F$, while for other ways it does not. But as long as the parameter is not fixed, the norm is silent. Different relativists can differ in their views on which norm it is that depends on the fixing of the parameter, and on what it is to 'fix the parameter'.

Why is an instance of (R1) not enough to guarantee a form of relativism? Consider an instance of (R1) combined with the view that there is only one correct way of fixing the parameter, or that the norm always gives the same verdict for all the ways of fixing the parameter. The resulting view would not be a genuine form of relativism. So, in addition to an instance of (R1), any genuine form of relativism involves the claim that there is no unique way of fixing the parameter, and that different ways of fixing it may at least sometimes yield different verdicts. Any genuine form of relativism can therefore be represented as an instance of the following trio of schemata:

(R1)   For any $x$ that is an $I$, it is relative to $P$ whether $x$ is $F$.
(R2)   There is no uniquely relevant way $P_i$ of fixing $P$.
(R3)   For some $x$ that are $I$, and for some $P_i$, $P_j$, $x$ is $F$ in relation to $P_i$ but not $F$ in relation to $P_j$.

## 2  Classifying relativisms

We are now in a position to recognize and characterize forms of relativism. This also allows us to generalize in an informed way over relativisms in general or over just a certain range of relativisms. To this end, some further distinctions will be useful, namely between fairly tame forms of relativism and not-so-tame forms of two different kinds.

Tame forms of relativism are not at all affected by the usual objections to relativism. Harman's moral relativism is a good example. Harman (1975) claims that for any agent and any act, it is relative to certain considerations and motivating attitudes whether that agent ought to perform that act. According to Harman, this is so because of the logical form of the predicate 'ought', which is a four-place predicate, with argument places not only for an agent and an act, but also for considerations and motivating attitudes. Saying, for example, that Peter ought to lie, one leaves two of the argument places empty and therefore fails to specify a complete proposition.[2] It is like saying that Peter gives: what is missing is information about what he gives and to whom he gives it. Since all that is specified is a propositional function with two empty argument places, the question whether Peter ought to lie (or whether he gives) can receive a different answer for different ways of turning the propositional function into a complete proposition.

For Harman, the norm that comes into play only once the parameter is fixed, i.e. once the empty argument places are filled, is simply the norm that one ought to believe only true propositions. Since to believe that Peter ought to lie is not to believe any determinate proposition, the norm is silent on whether or not the belief is permitted. But as soon as considerations and attitudes are specified, the belief's content is described as a complete proposition, and the norm grips.

Harman's tame logical-form-relativism contrasts with forms of relativism that are not so tame in one of two ways. First, a relativism is not tame, if it involves the claim that the *truth* of *propositions* (or *contents*) of some kind can be relative, i.e. has the form:

(RP)   For any $x$ that is a proposition of a certain kind $K$, it is relative to $P$ whether $x$ is true.

Second, a relativism might not be tame in the sense that it is a *global* form of relativism, i.e. has the form:

(GR)   For all $x$ and for all $F$: it is relative to $P$ whether $x$ is $F$.

It can be shown that no global relativist can accept Harman's view that relativity is always a matter of logical form and empty argument places. For if he accepted that, any predicate would have an indefinite number of argument places. Consider some object A and some feature F. According to (GR), it is relative whether A is F, and according to Harman's logical form view this would be due to an empty argument place in the predicate 'is F'. But if we fill that argument place, saying that A is F in relation to G, then the relevant instance of (GR) would force us to say that it is again relative whether A is F in relation to G. So there would again have to be an empty argument place in the predicate 'is F in relation to G'. This reasoning could be repeated indefinitely. So, global relativists must have a different view of what is involved in it being relative to some parameter whether some $x$ is $F$. [3]

Some philosophers think that it is relativisms about truth that should be marked off as particularly radical (see e.g. Meiland 1980). I disagree. To hold that it is relative to some parameter whether entities of a certain sort are true is not in itself contentious. It is, for example, widely agreed that the truth of indexical sentence-types is relative (consider the sentence-type 'I am hungry.'). The view that truth is relative only becomes contentious when, as in (RP), particular kinds of truth-bearers are concerned (compare Kirkham 1992: 59–63). However, both (RP) and (GR) do involve relativism about truth, for relativism about whether anything is true is entailed as a special case by (GR).

I shall now discuss four different kinds of objection that concern different forms of relativism.

## 3 Newton-Smith and the traditional conception of proposition

W. Newton-Smith has argued against any relativism about the truth of propositions, i.e. against any relativism that is not so tame in the first way (see (RP) above). He says that holding such a view 'is to take the short road to incoherence', because 'propositions are individuated in terms of truth-conditions' (1982: 107–8). This, he seems to think, excludes the possibility that one and the same proposition be true in relation to one way of fixing a parameter and not true in relation to another way. He adds a consideration to do with the interpretation of the utterances of some foreign group, the Herns. It cannot be the case that the Herns express, in their utterances of a sentence *s*, a proposition *p*, which is such that *p* is true for them but false for us. For if they hold *s* to be true, and we hold *p* to be false, but nevertheless think that *p* is what *s* expresses, then we would be 'committed to saying that they are just plain mistaken' (1982: 108).

Let's take one point after the other. The first point does not seem to have a direct bearing on relativisms about the truth of propositions. Take someone who claims, like Prior (1962), that there are propositions whose truth is relative to times. This relativist can agree with Newton-Smith that propositions are individuated in terms of truth conditions. But unlike Newton-Smith, he or she will think that the truth condition corresponding to a proposition can be satisfied at one time, and not at another. This might be because he or she thinks either that truth is a property that some propositions can possess temporarily, or that it is a relation between propositions and times. In the former case, the biconditionals that 'give' the truth condition of a proposition *p* will have the usual form:

(BC)   The proposition that *p* is true iff *q*

where it is relative to times whether *q*. In the latter case, where truth is thought to be a relation, the biconditionals will take a different form, namely something like:

(BC*) For all times *t*: the proposition *p* bears the relation of truth to *t*, iff *q* at *t*.

Admittedly, Newton-Smith's understanding of what a truth condition is is quite different from that of a relativist who thinks that truth is a relation. But still, both forms of relativism about the truth of propositions of a certain kind are compatible with Newton-Smith's claim that propositions are individuated in terms of truth conditions.

To be fair, however, one must concede that Newton-Smith has the mainstream conception of proposition on his side, namely that conception according to which a proposition is *essentially* something absolutely true or false. Frege had such a conception of a proposition (thought). He argued in 'The Thought' that indexical sentences do not express a complete proposition (thought) precisely because their truth value varies with the context of utterance.

But a relativist about the truth of some range of propositions will have a different conception of proposition. His conception of a proposition might involve that a proposition is essentially true or false, but not both, in relation to a time, even though it might be true in relation to one time and false in relation to another. Even though different in this respect from the traditional conception, this relativist's conception of a proposition might share other features with the traditional one: propositions might continue to be the objects of belief and assertion, for example. In this way, the relativist conception could still recognizably be the conception of a proposition. For the opponent to insist on the Fregean conception of a proposition is just to beg the question against the relativist.

Now Newton-Smith's second point. The relativist can also make sense of a situation of radical interpretation where the Herns are attributed a belief in a proposition $p$ such that $p$ is true for the Herns and false for the interpreter. A plausible example of such a proposition might be the proposition that large earlobes with large holes in them are beautiful. There is nothing incoherent about an interpreter taking the stance that this proposition is true for the Herns and false for him. To insist that there cannot be such a proposition is again to beg the question.

Perhaps there is more behind Newton-Smith's radical interpretation example. Perhaps the point of the example is that any relativism about the truth of propositions makes radical interpretation impossible. For in comparing different hypotheses as to what propositions foreign utterances express, we need to employ some kind of principle of charity, according to which, say, the propositions asserted by foreigners are by and large true. But if it is relative to, for example, cultures (to take a form of relativism that matches the case) whether a proposition is true, how are we to apply such a principle of charity?

Relativists can answer the challenge. They will have to provide a suitably modified version of the charitable assumption, one that does justice to the relativity. If we stick to the example of a cultural relativism, one proposal for such an assumption would be the principle that propositions asserted by foreigners are by and large true according to their culture. Now, if truth according to the foreign culture and truth according to the interpreter's culture were to diverge radically, then it would be hard to see what the interpreter could go by in interpreting.[4] In such a case interpretation based on any charitable principle would be impossible. But if the divergence between truth according to the interpreter and truth according to the foreigners is restricted to some areas, then I don't see why the relativistic charitable principle could not guide interpretation effectively. Moreover, in addition to a comparison between his or her own and the interpretee's judgements of truth, the radical interpreter can also compare conceptual connections among propositions. In Chapter 5, §4, I sketched a methodology of radical interpretation that does not rely on any notion of truth, but only on general psychological principles.

So, there are two lessons from Newton-Smith's objection. First, relativists about the truth of propositions of some sort must reject the traditional conception of proposition and provide a different one. Such relativists may need to justify their departure from the traditional conception, and explain their own conception. But if they do so, nothing need be wrong with their position. The second lesson is that in explaining how we can interpret speakers of an unknown language, they must give a modified account of what it is to be charitable. Moreover, if such relativists claim that interpretation is possible, they cannot claim that truth according to the foreigners diverges radically from truth according to themselves.

## 4 The dilemma/self-refutation

There is an important kind of objection against relativism that often takes the form of a dilemma.[5] As I understand it, it is directed against any *global* relativism (see (GR) above).

The objection, in its dilemma form, says that the proponent of (GR) holds either that

(i)    it is *not* relative to P whether (GR) is true,

or that

(ii)    it *is* relative to P whether (GR) is true.

Horn (i) is clearly unacceptable, because it entails something that contradicts (GR): if it is not relative to P whether (GR) is true, then there is an x, namely (GR), and a feature F, namely truth, such that it is not relative to any P whether x is F, which contradicts (GR). Horn (ii) is alleged to be unacceptable too, but for various different reasons, which I shall consider one by one.

### Horn (ii) contradicts (GR)

First, it is sometimes thought that horn (ii) straightforwardly contradicts (GR). Mackie (1964: 200) claims that the operator 'it is absolutely true that ...' is what he calls 'strictly prefixable', i.e. is governed by the rule that from 'q' one can infer 'it is absolutely true that q'. In turn, 'it is absolutely true that q' presumably entails 'it is not relative to any P whether q is true'. Thus what the global relativist asserts, namely (GR), entails 'it is not relative to P whether (GR) is true', which is the negation of horn (ii).

I think there are two ways for the global relativist to respond, which correspond to two ways of understanding the operator 'it is absolutely true that ...'. First, the relativist might agree with Mackie that if it is absolutely true that q, then it is not relative to P whether q is true. On this reading of the operator, no global relativist in his or her right mind would accept that it is strictly prefixable.

On the second reading of the operator, absolute truth is defined in terms of relative truth (in the way I proposed in §3 of Chapter 6): to be absolutely true is just to be true in relation to every way of fixing the parameter in question. On this reading, 'it is absolutely true that p' does not entail 'it is not relative to any parameter whether p is true'. A global relativist might think that while some propositions receive different truth values on different ways of fixing the parameter, other propositions receive the same truth value on all ways of fixing the parameter. Propositions of the latter kind are absolutely true, or absolutely false, in the sense that they are true, or false, in relation to all ways of fixing the parameter. Thus, on the second reading of the operator 'it is absolutely true that ...', Mackie's objection fails whether or not the relativist accepts that the operator is prefixable in Mackie's sense.

## Horn (ii) is pragmatically self-refuting

Second, it is sometimes thought that by asserting (GR), relativists pragmatically commit themselves to it not being relative to $P$ whether (GR) is true, because by asserting something, one generally commits oneself to the absolute truth of what one asserts. We might call this the 'pragmatic self-refutation argument against global relativism', because it relies on a certain view of the pragmatics of assertion.[6] Unlike Mackie's objection, this objection does not involve the claim that (GR) is strictly self-contradictory. According to this objection, (GR) might well be true, but even if it is, it should not be asserted. It should not be asserted, because by asserting (GR) one pragmatically commits oneself to the negation of (ii).[7]

Again, the objection only works if absolute truth is taken in such a way that it being absolutely true that $q$ is incompatible with it being relative to $P$ whether $q$. Suppose we grant this understanding of absolute truth. Then this objection relies on a certain account of the pragmatics of assertion. And it is in this that the global relativist ought to part company with the objector. The relativist might concede that asserting something does constitute certain commitments, such as the obligation to state reasons for what one has asserted if asked to do so, to defend what one has asserted if challenged, and to retract one's assertion if one is unable to defend it against challenge. But he or she will deny that commitment to the absolute truth of what has been asserted is among the commitments constituted by an assertion. Now, the objector might pursue the matter further and claim that (GR) is incompatible with these other commitments. I'll treat this further objection below, in §5.

## Given horn (ii), it is pointless to assert (GR)

Third, it might be objected that it is pointless for global relativists to put forward their view if they take horn (ii). The idea is that in asserting (GR), global relativists must have the aim of convincing their audience, but if they take even (GR) itself to be true only relative to something, then how could they reasonably aim to do so? Note that this third objection to horn (ii) is the weakest so far, for even if it succeeded, the most it could show is that the relativist's *assertion* of (GR) is *unmotivated*.

However, even this weak objection falls short of its modest goal. It presupposes that one can convince others only if one takes what one wants to convince them of to be absolutely true in a sense in which absolute truth is incompatible with (GR). Relativists might either (rather incredibly) deny that they want to convince (perhaps they just want to express their views, as suggested in Meiland 1980), or insist that convincing is possible even on the assumption of global relativity. Now, if relativists want to show that convincing is possible, they will have to show that their position does not prevent them from giving reasons for their view—reasons that others could reasonably take into account. Again, I shall defer a discussion of this to the next section, where the global relativist's account of linguistic communication is discussed.

## 5  The possibility of communication

A third kind of objection concerns the core of any relativism, and therefore affects any form of relativism, even though it doesn't affect all forms in the same way. Any relativism in my scheme has the form 'For any $x$ that is an $I$, it is relative to $P$ whether $x$ is $F$'. Moreover, any relativism that is at all interesting involves two further claims: first, that no way of fixing the parameter $P$ is the only correct or relevant one; and second, that sometimes an $I$ will be $F$ in relation to one way of fixing the parameter, but not $F$ in relation to another way of fixing the parameter (see (R1)–(R3) in §1 of this chapter). For example, an interesting global relativist about the truth of propositions, which takes persons as the parameter, will deny that there is only one relevant person, and insist that there are propositions that are true in relation to some persons but not true in relation to others. Now, the objection from the possibility of communication says that it is hard to see what communicative point there could be in asserting that some $x$ is $F$ if it is relative to something whether $x$ is $F$ (compare Evans 1979).

The point is intimately connected with the normative aspect of any relativism: to say that it is relative to a parameter whether $p$, is to say that the norm that says whether it is correct to believe $p$ only grips once the parameter is fixed. Now, this norm governing beliefs has a key role in assertoric communication. An episode of assertoric communication typically goes something like this:

Suppose someone A asserts that $q$. A's audience might then reason as follows: 'A has asserted that $q$ sincerely, thus A believes $q$. A is reliable in the sense that what A believes is normally correct, so $q$ is probably correct.' Now if the audience were to take it to be relative to some parameter $P$ whether $q$, then it could no longer reason in this way. If $P_1$, $P_2$, etc. are the different ways of fixing the parameter $P$, then $q$ might be correct in relation to $P_1$, but incorrect in relation to $P_2$, and no $P_i$ is privileged. So what would it mean to say that A's beliefs are normally correct? Correct in relation to which $P_i$? The norm remains silent until the parameter is fixed.

In general, no relativist can solve this problem unless he or she allows communicators to differentiate in some way among the ways $P_i$ in which the parameter in question can be fixed. The way in which he or she ought to allow this will vary from one form of relativism to another.

The solution is straightforward in the case of Harman's tame form of relativism. When someone asserts that Peter ought to lie, Harman would say, then the *context* will normally determine certain considerations and motivating attitudes that are relevant. The audience will know what to conclude if it takes the speaker to be sincere and reliable: that Peter ought to lie in relation to the relevant considerations and motivating attitudes. It is as if the sentence 'Peter ought to lie.' were indexical, as if it meant the same as 'Peter ought to lie in relation to the currently relevant considerations and the currently relevant motivating attitudes'. The context of utterance determines in which way the empty argument places are to be filled.[8] Similarly, on Field's relativism about justification, the relevant evidential system will be the one the speaker uses; on Feyerabend's cultural relativism (see Feyerabend 1978), it will be the speaker's culture that is relevant.

On my own view, elaborated in Chapter 6, above, it is each speaker's own perspective that is relevant to the correctness of an assertion, or rather the belief expressed by an assertion. Thus, if Alfred asserts that $q$, addressing Barbara, she can reason as follows: 'Alfred is sincere, his belief is probably correct, i.e. true in his own perspective, his perspective agrees with mine on $q$, so I won't go wrong if I come to believe that $q$'. My account, of course, went further and explained those cases where Barbara, even though she believes Alfred's belief that $q$ to be correct, fails to come to believe that $q$ herself, because she does not believe that her perspective and Alfred's perspective agree on $q$.

It is worth pointing out that there is no conflict between saying that an audience can recognize which way of fixing a parameter is relevant to a given assertion and a relativist's claim that no way of fixing the parameter is privileged. I may recognize, for example, that a speaker is using one particular evidential system without holding that this evidential system is the only correct or good one. I may even recognize that a speaker who addresses me is employing an evidential system that is different from the one I use, and I may consider my own superior. Nevertheless, I'll need to take into account that the speaker is using his or her own evidential system if I want to take advantage of the consideration that the assertion was sincere and reliable.

Now, there might seem to be a special difficulty for global relativisms. Consider the view that for any $x$ and for any $F$, it is relative to persons whether $x$ is $F$ (i.e. an instance of (GR) above). First, any relativist with such a view will have to specify which person is relevant to the correctness of a given assertion. Suppose that it is always the speaker who is relevant. When a speaker, Alfred, asserts that some $x$ is $F$, his audience, Barbara, will be able to reason: 'The speaker is sincere and reliable, so $x$ is indeed $F$ in relation to the speaker.' Now, since the relativism in question is global, it will also be relative to persons whether $x$ is $F$ in relation to the speaker. Which person is relevant to the conclusion our hearer has drawn? I want to suggest that it is the hearer herself. So the hearer's conclusion will be that it is in relation to herself that $x$ is $F$ in relation to the speaker.

But aren't we now threatened by a regress? Which person is again relevant to *this* conclusion; in relation *to whom* is it to be taken to be correct?

I think there is a regress here, but the hearer need not go through the regress in order to draw her conclusions from the speaker's utterance. She will relativize at the first stage, concluding from the assertion's being sincere, and the speaker's being reliable that $x$ is $F$ in relation to the speaker. But she'll normally stop relativizing here. She'll not now reason that this conclusion is correct in relation to herself, and that this itself is correct in relation to herself, and so on. Rather, she will think about the more interesting issue of whether $x$'s being $F$ in relation to the speaker warrants that she herself believe that $x$ is $F$. Of course, anyone may enter the regress, if he or she likes, and continue as long as he or she likes. But no one needs to do this in order to communicate successfully.

Compare the analogous situation of a fan who considers whether Frank Sinatra is dead. Is it true that he is dead? And, moreover, is it true that it is true that he is dead? And, moreover, is it true that it is true that it is true that he is dead? And so on. Here too we have a regress that isn't threatening at all. The fan need not decide whether it is true that Frank Sinatra is dead in order to decide whether he is dead. Rather, when he or she finally decides that Frank Sinatra really is dead, he or she decides the whole infinite series at once.[9]

We have now seen how communication can proceed if relativism, even global relativism, is true. But what about arguing, giving reasons and convincing (under global relativism)? Once we know how assertoric communication works, the situation is straightforward. Suppose Alfred asserts $q$ (and that it is relative to persons whether $q$). The hearer, Barbara, believes Alfred to be sincere, but even though she believes that $q$ is correct in relation to Alfred just if it is in relation to herself, she has her doubts about Alfred's reliability in this matter. So she says: 'But why $q$?'—and Alfred might answer '$r$' and '$r$ is a reason for $q$'. A has made two assertions, and the hearer can treat them as she treats any other assertion. If she comes to believe, like Alfred, that $r$ and, moreover, that $r$ is a reason for $q$, then she has been convinced by the reasons A has given in defence of his views.

I conclude that global and non-global relativists can make sense of assertoric communication. Moreover, they can make sense of giving reasons and convincing, which removes any doubt left from the pragmatic self-refutation objection and from the objection that on horn (ii), asserting (GR) is pointless (§4 of this chapter).


## 6 Problems for Protagorean relativism

Finally, I want to discuss two objections that affect *only* Protagorean relativism. Protagorean relativism involves the claim that for any $x$ that is a judgement, it is relative to judges whether $x$ is true, as I pointed out in the very beginning of this chapter. However, Protagorean relativism is not completely characterized by this instance of my schema (R1). For Plato's Protagoras has a very specific view on the *way* in which the truth of judgements is relative to persons. First, he believes that the person relevant for evaluating a judgement as true is the person who is making the judgement. But that isn't all. He also believes that a proposition is true in relation to a person if and only if that person believes that proposition:

(PR)  For all $p, s$: $B(s, p)$ iff $T(p, s)$.[10]

It is a consequence of (PR) that whenever someone $s$ judges that $p$, $p$ will be true in relation to $s$. Now, on a plausible view, one is in error just if one believes something that is not true. Reformulating this for a Protagorean relativist context, one is in error just if one believes something that is not true in relation to oneself. It is easy to see that error in this sense is impossible according to Protagorean relativism. Since $s$'s believing $p$ is sufficient for $p$'s being true in relation to $s$, error can never occur (at least not the error of believing something untrue for oneself). The first argument against Protagorean relativism is then: according to Protagorean relativism error is impossible. But evidently, error is possible and actually occurs. So Protagorean relativism must be wrong.

Now, most of us (including myself) probably believe that error is possible, and therefore reject Protagorean relativism. But the Protagoreans will turn the argument on its head: since (PR) entails the impossibility of error, and (PR) is true, the appearance that error is possible must simply be deceptive. Protagoreans thereby put themselves into a dialectically difficult position, not only because they deny the obvious, but also because they cannot say that their opponents, who reject Protagorean relativism, are in error.

This objection from the possibility of error quite specifically concerns *only* Protagorean relativism. Other relativisms, even global relativisms, are not affected at all. It is very important to keep this in mind, because relativism is often illegitimately dismissed in general on the grounds of this objection against a very specific form of relativism.[11] Thus, it is often said that according to relativism, every judgement is equally correct. This *is* true of Protagorean relativism, but there are many different forms of relativism, even not-so-tame ones, of which it is *not* true.

The second objection against Protagorean Relativism is one that Myles Burnyeat (1976) claims to find in Plato's *Theaetetus* (171a–b): Protagoras makes the claim (= (PR)) that, for all persons $s$ and for all propositions $p$, $p$ is true for $s$ just if $s$ believes that $p$. Now, this claim is meant as 'a theory of truth' (Burnyeat 1976: 181), and therefore Protagoras claims that everyone 'lives in a world in which his mere belief in a proposition is [both] a sufficient [and] a necessary condition for its truth in that world' (1976: 182). If, however, Protagoras admits that his opponents do not believe (PR), then he has to admit that (PR) is not true for them. But in admitting that, he admits that belief is neither sufficient nor necessary for truth in *their* world. Thus, *not everyone* lives in a world in which belief is sufficient and necessary for truth in that world, which contradicts the original claim. Thus, if Protagoras merely grants his opponents that they disagree with him on (PR), then he thereby refutes his own theory of truth.

What is this 'theory of truth' that Plato attributes to Protagoras according to Burnyeat? What exactly is meant by the phrase '$s$ lives in a world in which $p$'? This phrase is just a paraphrase of '$p$ is true for $s$'.[12] Thus the theory of truth Plato is said to attribute to Protagoras is the theory that it is true for everyone that his or her believing any $p$ is sufficient and necessary for $p$ being true for him or her:

(P1)   For all $r$: T([for all $p$: B($r, p$) iff T($p, r$)]; $r$).[13]

Now suppose, the argument continues, that Protagoras admits that he has opponents, people who do not believe (PR):

(P2)   For some $s$: not B($s$, (PR)).

From this it follows, via (PR), that there are people for whom (PR) is not true:

(P3)   For some $s$: not T((PR), $s$).

Burnyeat now claims that 'such persons do not, as Protagoras alleges we all do, live in a world in which their mere belief in a proposition is a sufficient and necessary condition for its truth (in that world)' (1976: 183). It seems, thus, that Burnyeat perceives (P3) to be incompatible with (P1).

Luckily we don't need to settle the question as to whether (P3) is incompatible with (P1). For surely, Protagoras would have to admit not only that there are people who don't believe (PR), but also that there are some people who don't believe that whatever they believe is true for themselves, and vice versa:

(P4)   For some $r$: not B([for all $p$: B($r, p$) iff T($p, r$)]; $r$)

Now (P4) clearly contradicts (P1), so Burnyeat is right in his judgement that (P1) is fatal for Protagoras, at least if he wants to admit opponents.

But why should Protagoras commit himself to (P1)? I believe that it is just the suggestive paraphrasal of (P1) in terms of 'living in a world in which ...' that created the false impression that Protagoras was committed to it. Thus, if Burnyeat's interpretation is correct, then Plato's famous self-refutation objection against Protagoras fails.[14]

So, even against the most extreme form of relativism, Protagorean relativism, there is only the argument from the possibility of error, which is, as I said, inconclusive.

Showing that some objections against relativism fail is not yet to say anything in favour of any form of relativism. But it may undermine the widespread prejudice that relativism is incoherent, and thereby ensure that any case for a specific form of relativism gets a fair hearing. I have presented such a case in the first six chapters of this book.

# Notes

## Introduction

1 Thus the slogan seems to tie in with Wittgenstein's claim in the *Tractatus* 4.024 that to understand a sentence is to know what is the case if it is true.

2 This book is concerned *only* with this kind of reason. I do not consider, e.g., verificationist reasons for denying truth-evaluability, or reasons to do with vagueness.

## I Truth-Conditional Semantics

1 In the context of this book, I frequently need to mention complete sentences, the punctuation being part of what is mentioned. In order to be able to do this with precision, I sometimes contravene certain stylistic rules. In the sentence to which this footnote is appended, for example, I mention a sentence, including its full stop. I am *using* the final full stop (after the closing quotation mark), while I am *mentioning* the full stop that occurs within the quotation marks.

2 Arabic is traditionally described in that way: its syntax provides for each root a whole battery of nouns and verbs which would be well-formed syntactically. However, many of these well-formed expressions are not (yet) meaningful, and if they have meaning, it rarely depends on the meaning of the root and the syntactic operation by which the compound was derived from the root.

3 A similar way of arriving at the same conclusion is to notice that natural languages contain a potential infinity of expressions. It is therefore impossible to come to understand, in a finite lifetime, all the expressions of a natural language by learning what they mean one by one. But people do learn languages. So they cannot be doing it one by one. Compare Davidson 1965 and 1967a, p. 17.

Schiffer (1987, chapter 7) has argued that the fact speakers understand novel sentences does not show natural languages to be compositional. But even Schiffer does not deny compositionality (see chapter 8, p. 206). Lahav (1989) presents a different case against compositionality; see Fodor 1998, chapter 5, and Siebel 2000 for critical discussion of this case.

4 It can, however, be used in an elliptical manner to assert something. I count such a use as not 'proper'. There is nothing wrong with improper uses. But the sort of meaning theory I have in mind begins by first describing the proper functions of

expressions (or their 'literal uses'), leaving other, more difficult cases for later. See §6 below.

5  Some theorists (e.g. Edgington 1995) argue that force indicators can be qualified with conditional sub-clauses. For example, the sentence 'If he isn't at home, is he in college?' could be viewed not as having a conditional content with interrogative force, but rather as having a categorical content and conditional interrogative force. On this view, which is motivated by special problems with 'if', this sentence can be properly used to ask whether he is in college conditionally upon him not being at home, rather than to ask whether he is in college if he isn't at home. On one view, the 'if'-clause is part of a complex force indicator, on the other, it is part of the content indicator.

6  This project is often called 'Davidson's programme', as it was formulated in Davidson 1967a.

7  Greek letters are metalanguage variables over object-language expressions. In my use of corner quotes, I follow Quine 1951, §6: $\ulcorner \alpha\Pi \urcorner$' should be read as 'the expression formed by concatenating $\alpha$ and $\Pi$ in that order'; $\ulcorner \neg\theta \urcorner$' as 'the expression formed by concatenating $\neg$ and $\theta$ in that order'.

8  This is Martin Davies' solution to the problem, see Davies 1981: 33. For more detailed discussion of the problem of uninterpretive T-sentences see Chapter 5, §3, below.

9  This way of, in effect, deriving intensional meaning-stating theorems of the form '$s$ has the content that $p$' or '$s$ means that $p$' runs against Davidsonian orthodoxy. For a detailed defence of this view see Chapter 5, §3, below.

10  Refer to, e.g., Mates 1972, chapters 3 and 4 or Guttenplan 1986, chapter 17 for standard expositions.

11  Not every truth-conditional semanticist would share my exact terminology, nor would everyone approve of the way in which I have set out the theory of force for L1. All truth-conditional semanticists, however, share the view that in a theory of meaning, sentences' contents should be specified via a definition of truth of the kind I outlined. This feature of a truth-conditional theory of meaning clearly requires that all sentential phrases (or sentence contents, if you prefer) are evaluable as true or false. This presupposition of global truth-evaluability is, of course, the source of the main problem I tackle in this book.

12  The hearer might reason, and be expected by the speaker to reason, that it cannot be the speaker's only communicative aim to ask whether fish ride bicycles, because he or she obviously knows that fish don't ride bicycles, and that therefore the speaker's communicative aim might have been to draw attention to the fact that the answer to the question originally asked by the hearer is obviously 'no', by asking a question to which the answer is obviously 'no'.

13  He or she would also need to be able to parse these utterances correctly, i.e. to recognize them as instances of the sentence types of the language. This is by no means trivial, as anyone who has ever learnt a foreign language will be able to testify.

14  See for example Lewis 1975, Peacocke 1976, Davies 1981, Schiffer 1993 and Kölbel 1998.

15  I have been using a pre-theoretically understood notion of assertion, question, etc. in my description of theories of meaning, and these theories yield descriptions of ut-

terances as assertions that (questions whether) *p*. Thus, if there were a *true* theory of this sort, it would in fact be a description of a language that is actually used. So the picture of languages as abstract objects not necessarily used by a population doesn't fit my exposition very well. The issue is purely terminological, however. Modify my account by thinking of a theory of meaning for a language *L* as a theory that defines a predicate 'true in *L*' and as yielding meaning specification of the form 'By uttering *s* one asserts in *L* that (asks in *L* whether) *p*'. Then there are many such theories, each defining a language as a purely abstract system of meaning assignments. Then one can ask the question familiar from the literature: what makes it the case that one of these languages is the language of a given population of language users? I shall, however, stick to my terminology and use an absolute notion of assertion (question, etc.) instead of relativized notions of assertion in *L*, question in *L*, etc.

## 2 Excess Objectivity

1 It might seem that this is not a great loss because we could easily make up for the loss with phrases such as 'I agree with Wolfgang.'. The truth predicate is, however, not so easily replaced. Consider, for instance, 'If what the weatherman says is true, then the weather will be fine tomorrow.'—a replacement of the antecedent by 'If I agree with the weatherman, ...' does not preserve the meaning of the sentence.

2 'Aesthetic' in a wide sense, which includes matters of taste in general.

3 A denial of global truth-evaluability does not, of course, make abandoning truth-conditional semantics immediately necessary. Expressivists like Blackburn (1984, 1988) have argued in favour of a split semantics: standard truth-conditional semantics for unproblematic sentences, and non-truth-conditional expressivist semantics for problematic sentences. I argue in Chapter 4 that a split semantics is not a viable option.

4 I am here using Castañeda's quasi-indicator 'he himself' to identify the egocentric indexical content in question.

5 Even though Wright severs the tie between realism about a discourse and the admission that its sentences are truth-apt, he does not deny the connection between truth and the facts. To be true, according to him, is indeed to correspond to the facts, but the notion of fact here is as minimal and metaphysically lightweight as is the notion of truth (1992: 34). Thus in attempting to draw a contrast between objective and non-objective areas of discourse, recourse to the notion of fact will not help within Wright's framework.

6 Wright's other criteria mark out different aspects that are associated with realism: mind-independence (Euthyphro contrast) and ontological or epistemological basicness (wide cosmological role).

7 A criterion for *X* is often just a sufficient condition for *X*. Cognitive command is presumably sufficient and necessary for objectivity, thus it is not only a criterion for objectivity, but lack of it is also a criterion for lack of objectivity.

8 Even though they cannot agree on this criterion if it is read in Wright's way, as I shall argue in §6 of this chapter.

9 My derivation of (NE) from (ES) follows (*ceteris paribus*) Wright's derivation of an analogous schema from the disquotational schema. See Wright 1992: 20.

10  Similar difficulties are raised by Wright himself (1992: 149), by Williamson 1994: 140, and by Shapiro and Taschek 1996: 84.

11  Wright will admit this much, because he himself argues the point at length in his confrontation with deflationism (1992: 15–18).

12  Shapiro and Taschek (1996) raise an additional difficulty for Wright. They argue that untrue belief cannot fail to constitute cognitive failure in those discourses where truth is evidentially constrained, i.e. where there is no truth that could not be known. For if someone believes that $p$ and it is false, then it is true that not-$p$. But if truth is evidentially unconstrained then one *could* know that not-$p$. But someone who falsely believes that $p$ when he or she could know that not-$p$ is guilty of cognitive shortcoming.

Wright has recently (in Wright 2001) responded to this objection by giving up his original response (that of insisting that untrue belief may not amount to *cognitive* shortcoming). However, Wright does so at the price of slipping back into the verificationist view of realism debates—something he had originally hoped to avoid (see 1992: 9). I discuss Wright's new position in detail in Kölbel unpublished.

13  'Contradictory' is to be understood in a purely syntactical way here: a pair of contents is contradictory iff one is the negation of the other.

14  One way of refining (CO) would be to restrict the range of people whose disagreement indicates error to people who are related in a specified way:

(CO*)  For all thinkers $A$ and $B$ who are $R$-related: it is a priori that if $A$ believes that $p$ and $B$ believes that not-$p$, then either $A$ has made a mistake or $B$ has made a mistake.

Different substitutions for $R$ in (CO*) will yield criteria for different degrees of objectivity.

15  David Lewis (1988) thinks that some temporary features are intrinsic and not relational, and therefore prefers to resolve the problem by relativizing the individuals that can have those features.

16  But not even Protagorean relativism is easily refuted.

## 3 Revisionism

1  Proponents of a view of this kind concerning moral sentences include Harman (1975) and Dreier (1990), and, according to Dreier 1999 possibly also Gibbard (1990). Harman and Dreier call themselves moral relativists, and this relativism consists in the claim that 'the content of a sentence containing a moral term varies with the context in which it is used' (Dreier 1990: 6). This kind of relativism is very different from the kind of relativism I wish ultimately to defend, which involves not a variation of content with context (i.e. indexicality familiar from Kaplan 1989) but *contents* whose evaluation is relative. Thus on Harman's and Dreier's view, in uttering a moral sentence such as 'X is good.', one asserts a factual content about certain contextually selected norms, namely that according to these norms, X is good. Which factual content that is may vary from utterance to utterance. On the view I shall be defending, such an assertion is not *about* any norms, and the object of assertion, i.e. the sentence's content for a given context, can vary in truth value from perspective to perspective.

2 This possibility of two different negations of (1*) highlights another difficulty for the suggestion that (1) is elliptical, or an abbreviation, for (1*). For there are two distinct ways of attaching any sentential operator to (1*), depending on the scope that operator is to take. For example, we can attach the operator 'surprisingly—' in two different ways: either

(S1*) Surprisingly, I find licorice tasty.

or

(S1*') I find licorice surprisingly tasty.

If (1) were elliptical or an abbreviation for (1*), one would therefore expect the results of attaching sentential operators to (1) to exhibit scope ambiguities corresponding to the difference between (S1*) and (S1*'). But 'Surprisingly licorice is tasty.' does not seem to exhibit any such scope ambiguity. (But see Grice's (1989: 269–82) ingenious attempt to explain away the apparent lack of ambiguity—in the case of definite descriptions—by appeal to his notion of implicature.)

3 Admittedly, there are some special contexts where a *reply* to an indexical utterance can change the reference of the indexical element. Consider the following exchange:

(D3)   A: 'I broke my ankle yesterday.'
       B: 'I didn't.'.
       (≈ 'I didn't break my ankle yesterday.')

Here B would under normal circumstances be interpreted as saying that he didn't break *his* ankle the previous day. But this is not a case where B *denies* what A has said. Thanks to Denis Walsh for discussion here.

## 4 Expressivism

1 Ayer's expressivism is also often called 'emotivism'. An even earlier statement of expressivism can be found in Ogden and Richards 1923. See also Stevenson 1937.

2 A single-case probability (SP) sentence is one that permits paraphrase in 'the syntactic form $Pq$, where $P$ is a sentential operator, containing the probabilistic reference, and $q$ is a non-probabilistic sentence' (Price 1983: 396). For example, 'There's a good chance of snow tonight.' is an SP sentence, while 'Green snakes are probably harmless.' is not.

3 Price cites the non-objectivity of probabilistic matters (in a sense close to the one developed in Chapter 2, above) as the motivation for his view (1983: 403).

4 I say 'can be used to present oneself as approving' and not 'can be used to express one's approval', because I want to leave room for insincere utterances of sentences like (1).

5 This claim alone commits Searle to the systematic ambiguity of 'not', since, as he claims, it normally functions as a modifier of contents, and only in certain contexts involving performatives functions as a modifier of the illocutionary force indicated.

6 Searle is silent on transformations such as 'If I promise to come, I'll come.

7 Susan Hurley (1984) discusses a different version of Geach's objection, which is based on a more literal reading of Geach's source in Frege 1919. Her version differs in that it requires not only that (4)–(6) be valid in a way that requires the coincidence

in meaning of the occurrences of 'gambling is bad', but also that (4)–(6) be an instance of modus ponens.

8 Hurley's version (see previous note) imposes the further constraint that this alternative explanation ought to render arguments like (4)–(6) instances of modus ponens.

9 At least in his *Spreading the Word* (1984). In his later article 'Attitudes and Contents' (1988), Blackburn revises his semantics of evaluative discourse. The new approach seems to me to be a content indicator approach. Blackburn there attempts to legitimize his claim to a genuine expressivist logic by making use of Hintikka's (1970) model set semantics for deontic operators. However, the syntactic status of 'B!' and 'H!' is highly obscure in that paper. (Do they operate on sentences, nominal expressions? Do they iterate?) Moreover it is unclear what work Hintikka's semantics for deontic sentential operators is doing for the expressivist's explanation of the validity of Geach's modus ponens argument, since the validity of *that* argument already falls out of Hintikka's semantics before the deontic operators are added. See Hale 1993 for a detailed discussion of the 1988 version of Blackburn's expressivist semantics. Blackburn 1998 omits detailed discussion of the semantics of evaluative language.

10 Alternatively, one could read a deep structure into the surface denoting expression 'stealing money', and view it as expressing a content, perhaps as the content that stealing of money occurs. The attitude expressible by the whole sentence would then be that of disapproval of *there being* thefts of money. Going into more detail here would lead too far afield.

11 Wright (1987: 33 and note 19) has objected that a 'clash of attitudes' à la Blackburn need not constitute *logical* inconsistency. Wright seems to make two points. First, he says that not doing something of which one approves may constitute some form of failure, perhaps a moral failure, but not a logical one. But this is simply to beg the question: the expressivist, since he or she denies the truth-evaluability of moral premisses in valid arguments, claims that there is logical validity and inconsistency beyond those areas where the traditional conception of validity and consistency (in terms of truth) applies. The expressivist can, moreover, cite independent cases of logical validity, where the traditional conception fails, e.g. arguments with imperative premisses and conclusions. The second point Wright makes is that on Blackburn's construal of valid moral modus ponens arguments, there is no corresponding tautology (consisting in a conditional formed by the conjunction of the premisses as antecedent and the conclusion as consequent) which commands assent (on pain of irrationality) independently of acceptance of the premisses. This is not true, for Blackburn could easily formulate corresponding tautologies, dissent from which constitutes irrationality. Compare also Hale 1993, Blackburn 1998: 72 and Kölbel forthcoming.

12 See Evans 1976 on the relativity of formal validity to choice of logical constants. Evans's attempt at developing a non-relative notion of a logical constant leads to an unfamiliar new notion.

13 In Blackburn 1998: 72 the irrationality involved is characterized as a violation of normative constraints that constitutively govern the mental states involved. For the significance of this to Blackburn's project, see Kölbel forthcoming.

14 See notes 7 and 8 above.

15 My account of assertion in Chapter 1 may leave room for the assertion of non-truth-evaluable contents, since to assert, on that view, is to undertake certain justificatory

obligations as well as to issue a permission to use what has been asserted as a premiss in further justifications. However, the notion of justification used may rely on the truth-evaluability of assertable contents. So the expressivist would need to elaborate by supplying a theory of justificatory relations among contents that doesn't presuppose contents are truth-evaluable. The sketch of a conceptual role account of 'opinion', below, proceeds along these lines.

16　The content-indicator approach makes expressivism look quite unlike the familiar forms of expressivism. The reason I explore it under the heading of expressivism is threefold. First, it shares the essential expressivist contention that the contents of certain sentences are not truth-evaluable. Second, the global considerations of the next section will drive the force-indicator approach towards something structurally very similar to the content-indicator approach. Third, global considerations favour the content-indicator approach over the force-indicator approach.

17　Compare Matthews 1994, who explores this analogy in some detail.

18　To be clear, a quasi-predicate 'is tasty' is something quite different from the force indicator 'is tasty' in §3 of this chapter. Unlike the force indicator, it can be applied to a noun-phrase without thereby yielding a complete sentence. The result is merely a sentential phrase, which needs further complementation to be usable as a complete sentence.

19　There is an issue here, as to whether (7) ought to be treated as making reference to a dish—probably a type of food, i.e. an abstract object, or whether it should be viewed as introducing implicit universal quantification, along the lines of: $(\forall x)$ if $x$ is an instance of the type haggis, then $x$ is tasty. Issues of this sort are not a special problem of expressivist semantics.

20　The same can be said about other connectives that are standardly treated truth-functionally, i.e. Geach's objection can be equally made for, say, disjunctive embeddings.

21　Compare Hale's suggestion for a moral nominal conjunctive ';', made in Hale 1986.

22　Blackburn's view has developed and—I think—radically changed. In Blackburn 1988, he seems to me to have switched to the content indicator approach.

23　In Hale 1986, a critical discussion of Blackburn 1984.

24　Strictly speaking, the trilemma is not yet exhaustive. There might be solutions intermediate between (ii) and (iii), where $d$ receives a constant interpretation $M_M$ in all mixtures beyond a certain order of complexity. Such a solution would be liable to a difficulty analogous to that arising in (ii). For as $d$ can be attached to any kind of sentence when interpreted by $M_M$, $M_M$ should have been the uniform meaning of $d$ in the first place.

25　We could go on to introduce general question- and command-indicating force indicators 'Q!( )' and 'C!( )' as well.

26　The escape-hole I left for expressivisms not affected by globalizers is not just an empty possibility. Expressivism about conditionals, as defended by Dorothy Edgington (1986, 1995) is interesting in this respect. Edgington makes a plausible case that there are no globalizers for the class of if-sentences—the class of if-sentences is not syntactically irrelevant. In Kölbel 2000, however, I argue that her account nevertheless faces some difficulty with conditionals that are embedded within quantifiers.

27 Hence the appeal of a programme like Crispin Wright's in Wright 1987 and 1992.

## 5 Soft Truth

1 The notion of a priori used in (CO) has already been briefly explained in Chapter 2, where I claimed that there are a priori differences in the status of disagreements, differences which stem from functional constraints on belief formation and communication and which are manifested in our communicative practices. I shall elaborate the framework theory of linguistic communication in the next chapter.

2 Note that this also shows that pragmatists and coherentists must either deny that all instances of the schema '*p* is true iff *p*' are true or concede that truth is relative. (For proof, see again the discussion on the problem of a priori error in Chapter 2.) A denial of the validity of the schema is, however, not an option for those pragmatists and coherentists who wish to invoke their notion in truth-conditional semantics.

3 Twice casually polling students with a questionnaire, I found that they varied widely in their use of the truth predicate, that the truth predicate was used in both the selective and the global way and that sometimes even the same student used 'true' in both (incompatible) ways.

   A remark on other languages: it was once suggested to me that in German the phrase 'es stimmt' has unambiguously the meaning of a deflationary truth predicate, while 'es ist wahr' has either only the restrictive meaning or is ambiguous in the way I am describing.

4 It is important to realize that Davidson never argued that this is the *only* way of constructing such a theory. All he says is that so far 'we have no other idea how to turn the trick' (1967a: 23).

5 This difficulty was originally raised in Foster 1976. See Segal 1999 for an excellent discussion of Davidson's way around the difficulty. Segal thinks that (T3) could be ruled out on the grounds that it is not part of a maximally *simple* theory (1999: 50).

6 Davies spells out such a canonical proof procedure (1981: 33). See also Peacocke 1976 and Larson and Segal 1995.

7 Thanks to Gabriel Segal for discussion of these issues.

8 See the previous section.

9 Some theorists might require that all inference rules be encapsulated in the formal definition of a derivability notion. Adding a rule of inference, on this view, must take the form of adding a clause to the definition of 'derivable' or 'theorem'. This requirement is unproblematic, at least for my proposed modification of Larson and Segal's theory. Since it is already the case that only interpretive T-theorems are derivable in their theory, and since the definition of 'T-theorem' (as well as the corresponding metatheoretical instruction in (R**)) is in purely syntactic terms, (R**)'s work can be done by a clause like the following:

(R***)   If ⌜s is T iff p⌝ is a T-theorem, then ⌜s means that p⌝ is also a theorem.

Things are less straightforward in the case of the proposal, made above, to add (R) to the T-theories of more standard Davidsonians (i.e. those who operate with the notion of a canonical theorem). Unlike Larson and Segal, these theorists apply general deductive rules to their axioms, which then generate non-interpretive T-theorems. In order to do (R)'s work in a formal definition of derivability it may be necessary to start from scratch with a notion of derivability that doesn't allow the derivation of non-interpretive T-theorems in the first place (i.e. basically Larson and Segal's strategy).

10 This conclusion does not affect Davidson's reasons for rejecting theorems of the form '*s* means *p*' where '*p*' *refers* to a meaning (i.e. his slingshot argument).

11 This quote may seem to permit the following reading: we need to grasp the concept of truth because we need to assess whether the theory, its theorems, are correct, i.e. whether they are true. This, however, seems to me to be the wrong reading; for one of the most important lessons drawn in Tarski 1956 is that we must distinguish 'true' as a predicate of the object-language and 'true' as a predicate of the metalanguage. The concept of truth whose grasp is required according to the current reading would correspond to a predicate in the meta-metalanguage, as it gets applied to metalanguage sentences. Thus it would be distinct from the truth notion allegedly required to understand the T-theory itself and its theorems. Moreover, if this were the sense in which an understanding of truth was required, then this requirement wouldn't be a special feature of meaning theories, but rather a requirement of *any* theory.

12 Davidson 1973: 134. This isn't in fact an accurate description of what Tarski does in his article, as Tarski did not define truth, but only defined truth in a particular formal language, as Davidson never gets tired to point out in later works (e.g. in Davidson 1990, 1996).

13 And in any case, if *that* were required, then it wouldn't be *the* notion of truth that is presupposed, but the notion of truth in the language under discussion.

14 Even though I follow McDowell in his assessment of the role of the concept of truth in these theories, I depart from him in the details of my account of radical interpretation, in particular in my treatment of illocutionary force (communicative function).

15 A disadvantage of such an account is that the knowledge it attributes to speakers is at best implicit knowledge. Speakers do not go explicitly through the kind of instrumental reasoning this account suggests. The status of a combined meaning theory as a psychological hypothesis would therefore be unclear. Compare Laurence 1995.

16 Brandom 1983 and 1994. Another example would have been Robert Stalnaker's pragmatic theory (e.g. in Stalnaker 1978), which has been further developed by David Lewis (Lewis 1979). However, since Stalnaker always speaks of contents as truth conditions (which in turn he takes to be sets of possibilities) I prefer to use, for current purposes, an account that does not in any way appear to make explanatory use of the notion of truth.

17 The Brandom account fares slightly better than Lewis's as far as the needed independent account of the contents of belief and desire is concerned. There is no danger that the use of the notion of content of belief and desire reimports reference to the notion of truth, for Brandom already provides an independent account of this notion: the content of an assertion is constituted by its (material) inferential relations with others, i.e. by what would count as a justification of the assertion and for what it would count as justification. To count as justification, of course, is another notion within the theory of social action, to be explicated, ultimately, in terms of authority and sanction.

18 There are reasons to believe that 'is *T*' as contextually defined by a theory of meaning for a language *L* will be coextensive with 'is true' in those areas where both can be applied. See McDowell 1980: 121; Wiggins 1980: 203–4; Wiggins 1992: 73–4. But this does not show that 'is *T*' and 'is true' express the same concepts. As

McDowell emphasizes, the coextensiveness of the two predicates, where the ranges over which they are defined overlap, should come as a *discovery*.

19 See the discussion in the previous section for more accurate thoughts on assertion.

## 6 Relative Truth and Linguistic Communication

1 The assignment of contents to sentences (or pairs of contexts and sentences) is of course to be effected *via* a Davidsonian T-theory. In Chapters 1 and 5, I have already discussed the fact that such a theory does not by itself assign contents to sentences. It needs to be supplemented in some way to yield content ascriptions from interpretive T-sentences. I understand *semantics* here in such a way that it includes the relevant supplement, but shall not dwell on the exact form of the supplement, as I want to keep the account compatible with many different views. See Chapter 5, §3, above, for my own view.

2 I am aware that the term 'pragmatics' has been used in many different ways. I am here using it in the sense of an assignment of communicative function in the sense of Chapter 1. If a reader wants to reserve that term for something else (such as a theory studying among other things Gricean implicatures), then he or she should replace my 'pragmatics' by 'theory of communicative function'.

3 Such as accounts by Lewis 1975, Davidson 1979, Brandom 1983, or Rumfitt 1995.

4 See Horwich 1998: 2–6; Kölbel 1997: 44. (T) is also supposed to be neutral with respect to Strawson's 'Gigantomachia', i.e. neutral on the issue as to whether the notion of truth is somehow prior to the notion of meaning or content (Strawson 1970).

5 This distinction corresponds to Huw Price's distinction between evidential and inferential disagreement; see Price 1988: 158.

6 Recently, testimony as a source of knowledge has deservedly received renewed attention, see for example Coady 1992, Fricker 1995 and Goldman 1999.
  The point that the possibility of challenging assertions and conducting discussions is part of the function of linguistic communication can be taken to support—independently of my purposes here—accounts of assertion that stress this aspect, such as Brandom 1983 and Searle 1969.

7 I say 'very roughly', because (a) some beliefs are more important than others, and (b) it is conceivable that temporary false belief may sometimes be a necessary step on the path to new knowledge.

8 For example, it is compatible with different views on how it is that particular sentences express the propositions they do express, have the illocutionary force they have and what it is for communicators to know this (e.g. Searle 1969, Lewis 1975, McDowell 1980, Brandom 1983, Grice 1989, Larson and Segal 1995, Laurence 1995, Rumfitt 1995, Horwich 1998). Moreover, it is compatible with various competing views of truth, in particular with those views that assign to truth an explanatory role in the theory of meaning (e.g. Davidson 1990, Wright 1992) as well as those that don't (e.g. Strawson 1970, McDowell 1980, Horwich 1998, Williams 1999).

9 Laver bread is a Welsh culinary speciality made from seaweed.

10 If I believe this proposition this might, for example, bring me to buy laver bread, or disbelieving it may bring me to leave the main course untouched at an official dinner with the vice-chancellor of my university.

11 *The Guinness Book of Records* is not only a good source for examples of unimportant propositions people argue about, its very existence is also proof that people do argue about them. See Matthews and McWhirter (eds) 1994.

12 See Chapter 2, §4, above. Crispin Wright also presents a convincing case that truth must be a norm in Wright 1992: chapter I.

13 Alternatively, we can define a perspective in Adams's style as a maximally consistent set of propositions (contents) or as a Carnapian 'state-description', even though it is perhaps not a 'state' that is described. See Adams 1974: 225 and Carnap 1956: 9.

14 'Disagree' in the sense of one believing a proposition and the other believing its negation. In other words, two people disagree just if they have contradictory beliefs, where 'contradictory' is understood syntactically. A semantic notion of contradiction can also be defined within this framework: two propositions are contradictory just if it is impossible for both of them to be true in the same perspective.

15 The notion of possibility here employed is conceptual. It is related to the aprioricity mentioned in (CO). Roughly, 'possible' here means 'not ruled out by a priori constraints on language use'. The next section will give more substance to this.

16 Objective contents thus have what Huw Price calls the 'Same Boat Property': they are true for everyone if true for anyone. See Price 1988: 152.

17 By 'normally' I mean 'when the disputed proposition is of some importance to them and there are no overriding reasons (such as being in a hurry, loathing the other communicator, etc.) to avoid discussion'.

18 Of course, the constraints shouldn't *rule out* massive error a priori either, for that would amount to construing objective truth as a matter of consensus. Massive error should be rare but possible.

19 For simplicity, I have ignored that standard possession can change over time, so that it is a three-place relation among times, thinkers and perspectives.

20 We will, of course, also have to employ some methods when detecting such conflicts. Compare Wright 1984.

21 I ignore problems arising from vagueness, as they seem to me to be independent.

22 Compare Gibbard's notion of a 'community of judgement'; see Gibbard 1990: chapter 13.

23 It may be argued that Orwell's *1984* does not determine one complete perspective. So perhaps we ought to say that it determines a set of perspectives—those that are compatible with what is said in *1984*. A fictional utterance is then correct just if it is true in all the perspectives in the set. The same problem might befall individual communicators: perhaps (C3) does not determine a unique perspective possessed by each communicator. This problem can be solved in the same way.

24 This will not only work for sentential modes of composition, as illustrated, but also for compounds constructed with quantifiers.

25 In an excellent article (1999), Dreier considers one version of this interpretation in detail. He calls my revisionist an 'indexical theorist'.

## 7 Defence of Relativism

1  I use a wide notion of belief here, according to which beliefs need not be truth-evaluable.

2  How these argument places are to be filled is usually determined by the context of utterance, so that Harman's thesis is in effect the thesis that sentences such as 'Peter ought to steal.' are implicitly indexical. Thus Harman is a proponent of revisionism, discussed above in Chapter 3.

3  In Nicholas Denyer's terminology, this argument shows that if relativity is a matter of missing qualifiers, then it cannot be global—independently of whether the qualifiers are thought to be 'repeatable' or 'unrepeatable' (Denyer 1991: 90–4).

4  Compare Davidson 1974.

5  See e.g. Meiland 1980, Preston 1992, Hales 1997, Moser *et al.* 1998.

6  Mackie (1964) called it 'operational self-refutation', because Passmore (1961) had used the label 'pragmatic self-refutation' for something else.

7  Moreover, if absolute truth is understood to be incompatible with relativity, then one would, on this view, commit oneself to the negation of (GR) by making *any* assertion.

8  I am not saying that it is a straightforward matter for Harman to say how exactly the context determines the relevant considerations and attitudes. On the contrary, I regard this as a problematic aspect of Harman's position. Rather, what is straightforward is how Harman will tackle the current problem—namely, in exactly the way in which he tackles it in the case of other indexical sentences.

9  Any resemblance with Frege's regress argument for the indefinability of truth (Frege 1918: 60) is intended. Frege's regress fails to be vicious for the same reasons.

10  Whether this is what Protagoras really *meant* by his famous doctrine that man is the measure of all things, I don't know. But see Burnyeat 1976: 178 for a defence of the view that (PR) is the view attributed to Protagoras in Plato's *Theaetetus*.

11  e.g. by Harvey Siegel, who in the first chapter of his book *Relativism Refuted* (1987), never seems to discuss anything but Protagorean relativism, but nevertheless takes himself to be refuting relativism in general.

12  This can be gathered from the remarks by which Burnyeat introduces the idiom (1976: 181 and from his claim that S3 (1976: 182) paraphrases S2 (1976: 180).

13  I am uneasy about quantifying into the position marked by the square brackets, but I think this is the best way to make sense of what Burnyeat calls 'Protagoras' theory of truth'. Another way to make sense of it would be as the view that (PR) is true for everyone:

(P1*)  For all $r$: T((PR), $r$)
       (read: (PR) is true for all subjects $r$.)

Evidently, someone who holds (P1*) and (PR) contradicts himself or herself as soon as he or she admits that his or her opponent does not believe (PR), i.e. ¬B(opponent, (PR)). For by (PR) this entails that ¬T((PR), opponent), and by existential generalization, this entails that for some $r$: ¬T((PR), $r$), which contradicts (P1*). Again, why should Protagoras be committed to (P1*)?

14 In fact, the argument Burnyeat attributes to Plato is slightly more complicated—it has the form of a dilemma, of which this is one horn.

# Bibliography

Adams, Robert (1974) 'Theories of Actuality'. *Nous* 5: 211–31.

Ayer, Alfred J. (1946) *Language, Truth and Logic*, 2nd edn, London: Victor Gollancz.

Blackburn, Simon (1984) *Spreading the Word*, Oxford: Clarendon Press.

Blackburn, Simon (1988) 'Attitudes and Contents'. *Ethics* 98: 501–17. Reprinted in Blackburn 1992.

Blackburn, Simon (1992) *Essays in Quasi-Realism*, Oxford: Oxford University Press.

Blackburn, Simon (1998) *Ruling Passions*, Oxford: Oxford University Press.

Brandom, Robert (1983) 'Asserting'. *Nous* 17: 637–50.

Brandom, Robert (1994) *Making it Explicit*, Cambridge, Mass.: Harvard University Press.

Burnyeat, Myles (1976) 'Protagoras and Self-Refutation in Plato's *Theaetetus*'. *The Philosophical Review* 85: 172–95.

Burnyeat, Myles (1990) *The Theaetetus of Plato*, Indianapolis: Hackett.

Carnap, Rudolf (1956) *Meaning and Necessity*, Chicago: University of Chicago Press.

Coady, C. A. J. (1992) *Testimony*, Oxford: Oxford University Press.

Davidson, Donald (1965) 'Theories of Meaning and Learnable Languages', in his *Inquiries into Truth and Interpretation* (1984), pp. 3-15, Oxford: Oxford University Press.

Davidson, Donald (1967a) 'Truth and Meaning', in his *Inquiries into Truth and Interpretation* (1984), pp. 17–36, Oxford: Oxford University Press.

Davidson, Donald (1967b) 'The Logical Form of Action Sentences', in *Essays on Actions and Events* (1980), pp. 105–48, Oxford: Oxford University Press 1980.

Davidson, Donald (1973) 'Radical Interpretation', *Dialectica* 27: 313–28. Reprinted in his 1984: 125–39. Page references are to the reprinted version.

Davidson, Donald (1974) 'Belief and the Basis of Meaning', *Synthese* 27: 309–23. Reprinted in his 1984: 141–54. Page references are to the reprinted version.

Davidson, Donald (1976) 'Reply to Foster', in Evans and McDowell (eds) 1976. Reprinted in his 1984: 171–9. Page references are to the reprinted version.

Davidson, Donald (1979) 'Moods and Performances', in his *Inquiries into Truth and Interpretation* (1984), pp. 109–21, Oxford: Oxford University Press.

Davidson, Donald (1984) *Inquiries into Truth and Interpretation*, Oxford: Oxford University Press.

Davidson, Donald (1990) 'The Structure and Content of Truth'. *Journal of Philosophy* 87: 279–328.

Davidson, Donald (1996) 'The Folly of Trying to Define Truth'. *Dialogue and Universalism* 1–2/1996: 39–53. Also in *Journal of Philosophy* 93 (1996): 263–78.

Davies, Martin (1981) *Meaning, Quantification, Necessity*, London: Routledge and Kegan Paul.

Denyer, Nicholas (1991) *Language, Thought and Falsehood in Ancient Greek Philosophy*. London: Routledge.

Dreier, James (1990) 'Internalism and Speaker Relativism'. *Ethics* 101: 6–26.

Dreier, James (1999) 'Transforming Expressivism'. *Nous* 33: 558–72.

Edgington, Dorothy (1986) 'Do Conditionals Have Truth Conditions?'. *Crítica* 18: 3–30.

Edgington, Dorothy (1995) 'On Conditionals'. *Mind* 104: 235–329.

Evans, Gareth (1976) 'Semantic Structure and Logical Form', in G. Evans and J. McDowell (eds), *Truth and Meaning*, pp. 199–222, Oxford: Clarendon Press.

Evans, Gareth (1979) 'Does Tense Logic Rest on a Mistake?', in his *Collected Papers* (1985), pp. 341–63, Oxford: Clarendon Press.

Evans, Gareth and McDowell, John (eds) (1976) *Truth and Meaning*, Oxford: Oxford University Press.

Feyerabend, Paul (1978) *Science in a Free Society*, London: New Left Books.

Field, Hartry (1982) 'Realism and Relativism'. *Journal of Philosophy* 79: 553–67.

Fodor, Jerry (1998) *Concepts: Where Cognitive Science Went Wrong*, Oxford: Clarendon Press.

Foster, John (1976) 'Meaning and Truth Theory', in Evans and McDowell (eds) 1976, pp. 1–32.

Frege, Gottlob (1892) 'Über Sinn und Bedeutung'. *Zeitschrift für Philosophie und philosophische Kritik* NF 100: 25–50. Reprinted in Günther Patzig (ed.), *Function, Begriff, Bedeutung* (1986), pp. 40–65, Göttingen: Vandenhoeck & Ruprecht.

Frege, Gottlob (1918) 'Der Gedanke. Eine logische Untersuchung'. *Beiträge zur Philosophie des deutschen Idealismus* 1, 2: 58–77. Reprinted in Günther Patzig (ed.), *Logische Untersuchungen* (1986), pp. 30–53, Göttingen: Vandenhoeck & Ruprecht.

Frege, Gottlob (1919) 'Die Verneinung. Eine logische Untersuchung', *Beiträge zur Philosophie des deutschen Idealismus* 1, 3/4: 143–57. Reprinted in Günther Patzig (ed.), *Logische Untersuchungen* (1986), pp. 54–71, Göttingen: Vandenhoeck & Ruprecht.

Fricker, Elizabeth (1995) 'Telling and Trusting: Reductionism and Anti-Reductionism in the Epistemology of Testimony'. *Mind* 104: 393–411.

Geach, Peter (1960) 'Ascriptivism'. *Philosophical Review* 69: 221. Reprinted in his *Logic Matters* (1972), pp. 250–54, Oxford: Blackwell.

Geach, Peter (1965) 'Assertion'. *Philosophical Review* 74: 449. Reprinted in his *Logic Matters* (1972), pp. 254–69, Oxford: Blackwell.

Gibbard, Allan (1990) *Wise Choices, Apt Feelings*, Oxford: Clarendon Press.

Goldman, Alvin I. (1999) *Knowledge in a Social World*, Oxford: Clarendon Press.

Grice, Paul (1968) 'Utterer's Meaning, Sentence Meaning and Word Meaning'. *Foundations of Language* 4: 1–18. Reprinted in John Searle (ed.), *The Philosophy of*

*Language* (1971), Oxford: Oxford University Press. Page references are to the reprinted version.

Grice, Paul (1989) *Studies in the Ways of Words*. Cambridge, Mass.: Harvard University Press.

Guttenplan, Sam (1986) *Languages of Logic*, Oxford: Blackwell.

Hale, Bob (1986) 'The Compleat Projectivist' (critical study of Blackburn 1984). *Philosophical Quarterly* 36: 65-84.

Hale, Bob (1993) 'Can There Be a Logic of Attitudes', in Crispin Wright and John Haldane (eds), *Reality, Representation and Projection*, pp. 337–63, Oxford: Oxford University Press.

Hales, Steven D. (1997) 'A Consistent Relativism?'. *Mind* 106: 33–52.

Hare, Richard M. (1970) 'Meaning and Speech Acts'. *Philosophical Review* 79: 3–24.

Harman, Gilbert (1975) 'Moral Relativism Defended'. *Philosophical Review* 84: 3–22. Reprinted in M. Krausz and J. Meiland (eds) 1982.

Hintikka, Jaakko (1970) 'Some Main Problems of Deontic Logic', in R. Hilpinen (ed.), *Deontic Logic: Introductory and Systematic Readings*, pp. 59–88, Dordrecht: D. Reidel.

Hodges, Wilfred (1983) 'Elementary Predicate Logic', in D. Gabbay and F. Guenthner (eds), *Handbook of Philosophical Logic*, vol. I, pp. 1–131, Dordrecht: D. Reidel.

Horwich, Paul (1998) *Truth*, 2nd edn, Oxford: Clarendon Press.

Hurley, Susan (1984) 'Frege, the Proliferation of Force, and Non-Cognitivism'. *Mind* 93: 570–6.

Kaplan, David (1977) 'Demonstratives', in J. Almog, J. Perry and H. Wettstein (eds), *Themes from Kaplan* (1989), pp. 481–563, Oxford: Oxford University Press.

Kirkham, Richard L. (1992) *Theories of Truth*, Cambridge, Mass.: MIT Press.

Kölbel, Max (1997) 'Wright's Argument from Neutrality'. *Ratio* 10: 35–47.

Kölbel, Max (1998) 'Lewis, Language, Lust and Lies'. *Inquiry* 41: 301–15.

Kölbel, Max (2000) 'Edgington on Compounds of Conditionals'. *Mind* 109: 97–108.

Kölbel, Max (forthcoming) Review of Blackburn 1998. *Mind* 111.

Kölbel, Max (unpublished) 'The Possibility of Blameless Disagreement'.

Krausz, Michael and Meiland, Jack (eds) (1982) *Relativism: Cognitive and Moral*, Notre Dame: University of Notre Dame Press.

Lahav, Ran (1989) 'Against Compositionality: The Case of Adjectives'. *Philosophical Studies* 57: 261–79.

Larson, Richard and Segal, Gabriel (1995) *Knowledge of Meaning*, Cambridge, Mass.: MIT Press.

Laurence, Stephen (1995) 'A Chomskian Alternative to Convention-Based Semantics'. *Mind* 105: 269–301.

Lewis, David (1969) *Convention*, Oxford: Basil Blackwell.

Lewis, David (1975) 'Languages and Language', in Keith Gunderson (ed.), *Minnesota Studies in the Philosophy of Science*, vol. VII, pp. 3–35, Minneapolis: University of Minnesota Press. Reprinted in David Lewis, *Philosophical Papers*, vol. I (1983), pp. 163–88, Oxford: Oxford University Press.

Lewis, David (1979) 'Scorekeeping in a Language Game'. *Journal of Philosophical Logic* 8, 339–59. Reprinted in David Lewis, *Philosophical Papers*, vol. I (1983), pp. 233–49, Oxford: Oxford University Press.

Lewis, David (1986) *On the Plurality of Worlds*, Oxford: Blackwell.

Lewis, David (1988) 'Rearrangement of Particles: Reply to Lowe'. *Analysis* 48: 65–72.

Mackie, John L. (1964) 'Self-Refutation—A Formal Analysis'. *Philosophical Quarterly* 14: 193–203.

Mates, Benson (1972) *Elementary Logic*, Oxford: Oxford University Press.

Matthews, Peter and McWhirter, Norris D. (eds) (1994) *The New Guinness Book of Records*, Enfield: Guinness Publishing.

Matthews, Robert J. (1994) 'The Measure of Mind'. *Mind* 103: 131–46.

McDowell, John (1976) 'Truth Conditions, Bivalence and Verificationism', in Evans and McDowell (eds) 1976, pp. 42–66.

McDowell, John (1980) 'Meaning, Communication and Knowledge', in Van Straaten (ed.) 1980, pp. 117–39.

Meiland, Jack (1980) 'On the Paradox of Cognitive Relativism'. *Metaphilosophy* 11: 115–26.

Moser, P. K., Mulder, D. H. and Trout, J. D. (1998) *The Theory of Knowledge*, Oxford: Oxford University Press.

Newton-Smith, W. (1982) 'Relativism and the Possibility of Interpretation', in Martin Hollis (ed.), *Rationality and Relativism*, pp. 106–22, Cambridge, Mass.: MIT Press.

Ogden, C. K. and I. A. Richards (1923) *The Meaning of Meaning*, London: Kegan Paul.

Passmore, John (1961) *Philosophical Reasoning*, London: Duckworth.

Peacocke, Christopher (1976) 'Truth Definitions and Actual Languages', in Evans, G. and McDowell, J. (eds), *Truth and Meaning*, pp. 162–88, Oxford: Oxford University Press.

Plato: *Theaetetus*, in John Burnet (ed.), *Platonis Opera*, vol. 1, Oxford: Oxford University Press 1900. English translation by M. J. Levett in Burnyeat 1990, pp. 251–351.

Preston, John (1992) 'On Some Objections to Relativism'. *Ratio* 5 (New Series): 57–73.

Price, Huw (1983) 'Does "probably" modify Sense?'. *Australasian Journal of Philosophy* 61: 396–408.

Price, Huw (1988) *Facts and the Function of Truth*, Oxford: Basil Blackwell.

Prior, Arthur N. (1962) 'Changes in Events and Changes in Things', Lindley Lecture, University of Kansas. Reprinted in A. N. Prior, *Papers on Time and Tense* (1968), Oxford: Clarendon Press.

Quine, W. V. (1951) *Mathematical Logic*, Cambridge, Mass.: Harvard University Press.

Quine, W. V. (1970) *Philosophy of Logic*, Englewood Cliffs, NJ: Prentice-Hall.

Rumfitt, Ian (1995) 'Truth Conditions and Communication'. *Mind* 104: 827–62.

Schiffer, Stephen (1987) *Remnants of Meaning*, Cambridge, Mass.: MIT Press.

Schiffer, Stephen (1993) 'Actual Language Relations'. *Philosophical Perspectives* 7: 231–58.

Searle, John R. (1969) *Speech Acts: an Essay in the Philosophy of Language*, Cambridge: Cambridge University Press.

Segal, Gabriel (1999) 'How a truth theory can do duty for a theory of meaning', in Zeglen 1999, pp. 48–58.

Shapiro, Stewart and Taschek, William W. (1996) 'Intuitionism, Pluralism, and Cognitive Command'. *Journal of Philosophy* 93: 74–88.

Siebel, Mark (2000) 'Red Watermelons and Large Elephants: A Case against Compositionality?'. *Theoria: Revista de Teoría, Historia y Fundamentos de la Ciencia* 15: 263–80.

Siegel, Harvey (1987) *Relativism Refuted*, Dordrecht: D. Reidel.

Stalnaker, Robert (1978) 'Assertion'. *Syntax and Semantics* 9. Reprinted in Stalnaker 1999, pp. 78–95.

Stalnaker, Robert (1984) *Inquiry*, Cambridge, Mass.: MIT Press.

Stalnaker, Robert (1999) *Context and Content*, Oxford: Oxford University Press.

Stevenson, C. L. (1937) 'The Emotive Meaning of Ethical Terms'. *Mind* 46: 14–31.

Strawson, Peter F. (1970) *Meaning and Truth* (Inaugural Lecture), Oxford: Oxford University Press. Reprinted in his *Logico-Linguistic Papers* (1971), pp. 170–89, London: Methuen. Page references are to the reprinted version.

Tarski, Alfred (1956) 'The Concept of Truth in Formalized Languages', in his *Logic, Semantics, Metamathematics*, J. H. Woodger (trans.), pp. 152–278, Oxford: Clarendon Press.

Thagard, Paul (1978) 'The Best Explanation: Criteria for Theory Choice'. *Journal of Philosophy* 75: 76–92.

Van Straaten, Zak (ed.) (1980) *Philosophical Subjects: Essays Presented to P. F. Strawson*, Oxford: Clarendon Press.

Wiggins, David (1980) 'What would be a Substantial Theory of Truth?', in Van Straaten 1980, pp. 189–221.

Wiggins, David (1992) 'Meaning, Truth-Conditions, Proposition: Frege's Doctrine of Sense Retrieved, Resumed and Redeployed in the Light of Certain Recent Criticism'. *Dialectica* 46: 61–90.

Williams, Michael (1999) 'Meaning and Deflationary Truth'. *Journal of Philosophy* 96: 545–64.

Williamson, Timothy (1994) Critical study of Wright 1992. *International Journal of Philosophical Studies* 2: 130–44.

Wittgenstein, Ludwig (1922) *Tractatus Logico-Philosophicus*, C. K. Ogden (trans.), London: Routledge and Kegan Paul.

Wright, Crispin (1984) 'Inventing Logical Necessity', in J. Butterfield (ed.), *Mind, Language and Logic*, pp. 187–209, Cambridge: Cambridge University Press.

Wright, Crispin (1987) 'Realism, Antirealism, Irrealism, Quasi-Realism' (Gareth Evans Memorial Lecture), in *Midwest Studies in Philosophy* 12: 25-49.

Wright, Crispin (1992) *Truth and Objectivity*, Cambridge, Mass.: Harvard University Press.

Wright, Crispin (2001) 'On Being in a Quandary'. *Mind* 110: 45–98.

Zeglen, U. (ed.) (1999) *Donald Davidson: Truth, Meaning and Knowledge*, London: Routledge.

# Index